The War on Drugs and the Global Colour Line

The War on Drugs and the Global Colour Line

Edited by
Kojo Koram

PLUTO  PRESS

First published 2019 by Pluto Press
345 Archway Road, London N6 5AA

www.plutobooks.com

Copyright © Kojo Koram 2019

The right of the individual contributors to be identified as the authors of
this work has been asserted by them in accordance with the Copyright,
Designs and Patents Act 1988.

British Library Cataloguing in Publication Data
A catalogue record for this book is available from the British Library

ISBN 978 0 7453 3882 8 Hardback
ISBN 978 0 7453 3880 4 Paperback
ISBN 978 1 7868 0408 2 PDF eBook
ISBN 978 1 7868 0410 5 Kindle eBook
ISBN 978 1 7868 0409 9 EPUB eBook

Typeset by Swales & Willis

Simultaneously printed in the United Kingdom and United States of America

For Yaara

Contents

Acknowledgements

This book is the product of a series of workshops focused on critical approaches to drug policy held at the University of Essex between 2017–2018. The first workshop was sponsored by the Open Society Foundation and the International Centre on Human Rights and Drug Policy, who both deserve my unending gratitude for supporting this project in its fledging stages. I am deeply indebted to Dr Nayeli Urquiza Haas, my co-conspirator in organising the first conference and a source of endless inspiration for the project as a whole. Also, my heartfelt thanks is extended to Julie Hannah, the Co-Director of the International Centre on Human Rights and Drug Policy, who has been a constant champion of the project and supported us at every turn.

From that initial meeting, I was fortunate to assemble an exciting collection of authors to collaborate on further workshops, including one focusing specifically on race and drug policy. These workshops resulted in the writing of this book. I owe a deep thanks to all of my contributors for being willing to lend their insights to my project in such fascinating ways. It was a real privilege to have curated such an exciting group of authors.

In guiding the book to publication, I was lucky to receive the support of David Shulman and everyone at Pluto Press. Finally, this book would not be possible without the support of my partner, Kim Simpson and the inspiration of my daughter Yaara whose impromptu arrival coincided with my submission deadline, meaning the final drafts of this book were written with one hand whilst carrying a sleeping baby with the other. It is to you, Yaara, that this book is dedicated and hopefully by the time you are old enough to read it, the world will be a different world from the one we describe here.

Introduction

Kojo Koram

In 1903, canonical African-American sociologist W. E. B. Du Bois famously declared that 'the problem of the twentieth century is the problem of the colour-line.'[1] In the nineteenth century, the 'age of empires' reached its apex as European colonial powers competed with each other to control more and more of the globe's resources and territory. A racial logic underpinned the European empires' behaviour to a greater or lesser extent, with 'scientific' racism giving rise to an idea of a fixed hierarchy between peoples of different skin colour, which could subsequently be used to justify White Europeans claiming dominion over the earth. However, with the twentieth century bringing with it increasing internal crisis within this imperial world order, the 'age of empires' would collapse into global warfare shortly after the turn of the century. In anticipation of this decline of the world of empires, Du Bois correctly recognized that any vision of a new, more universal international order would have to address the question of the colour line that had been drawn across the globe by European imperialism and that in many countries – South Africa, Australia and of course Du Bois's own United States of America, for example – was explicitly enshrined in law. And yet, despite Du Bois's haunting premonition, by the mid-twentieth century, with the victories of civil rights and decolonization as well as the wider cultural shift away from the accepted norms of scientific racism, the problem of the colour line appeared to have been solved, or at least be set upon a historical trajectory that would lead to it to being solved by the turn of the new millennium.

Now writing from within that new millennium, the idea that the problem of 'the colour line' was effectively concluded with the end of formal colonialism and segregation holds little water. While both the letter of the law and wider cultural discourse disavow racial categorizations, empirical research continues to reveal deep divisions in terms of the treatment of people persisting to operate along racial lines.[2] This provokes the question of where are the arenas in which racial division is produced if now discredited by formal law? This book responds to this question by focusing on the late twentieth-century War on Drugs – by which we refer to the internationally and domestically enforced prohibition of illegal intoxicants – as a contemporary arena in which difference in racialized subjectivity and experiences continue to be produced.

The argument that the drug laws aid in the production and persistence of a colour line challenges the objective ground upon which these laws draw their authority. The laws that prohibit the production, sale and possession of particular drugs are presumed as being politically neutral and grounded in an objective assessment of harm. The United Nations Single Convention on Narcotic Drugs, 1961 (hereafter referred to as the Single Convention), the UN treaty that serves as the bedrock for the current system of international drug prohibition, claims that the prohibition of drugs will prevent 'social and economic danger for mankind' as a whole.[3] However, in the decades of international drug prohibition that have followed, the result of prohibition is primarily untold millions of people being left dead, displaced and/or incarcerated across the world, without producing the targeted drop in the trade of drugs. Furthermore, this suffering has not been endured universally, but instead has been disproportionally borne by specific groups of people, often groups that were already historically oppressed through the preceding racial and colonial organization of the globe. However, while there has been much scholarship and public debate over the past decade that has analysed how the War on Drugs has fuelled a racist system of mass incarceration and state violence in the US, work that shows that this dynamic has also been reproduced right across the world remains underdeveloped. This collection of essays brings together the work of various scholars and policy experts concerned with drugs and race in order to offer an innovative interrogation of the racist impact of the War on Drugs across multiple continents.

The War on Drugs

What was the twentieth-century invention that is commonly referred to as 'the War on Drugs'? Global drug prohibition originated in the twentieth century as a fringe concern of a few religious missionaries and anti-vice moralists and ended the century as an established international legal norm, backed by a global system of militarized enforcement, at the centre of a worldwide network of police power and prison systems. How was such a transformation produced? In a world in which global consensus often appears impossible, drug prohibition could initially appear as a rare example of a recognized universal legal project. Despite the plethora of different traditional and ritualistic uses of what we now term 'drugs' that have long existed across the globe, the Single Convention commands an unusually high level of compliance amongst the nations of the world: 184 of the 193 members of the United Nations became signatories, while the few non-signatories still tend to follow the demands of the convention.[4] Drug prohibition has generally overridden the protections offered to cultural or customary practices by international human rights law that could be claimed in relation to coca-leaf chewing in the indigenous communities of the Andes or the traditional consumption of khat by Arab and North African societies.[5] In order for the Single Convention to protect this imagined global 'mankind', what was legislated was 'co-ordinated and universal action' which would allow the law to enforce the prohibition of these substances across borders and eventually produce the eradication of their illegitimate use.[6] However the material consequences of international drug prohibition betray some major discontinuities between the humanism and universalism projected by international law and the unequal impact of drug prohibition across the world. The laws prohibiting drugs are supposed to be politically neutral and objective, laws that serve the function of improving the conditions of life for all peoples of the world. This has not been the legacy of drug prohibition, however. For instance, in the familiar example of the United States, the consequence of the War on Drugs has been an estimation that more than half of all federal prisoners are imprisoned because of drug offences.[7] In Mexico, another prominent arena for the drug war, murders between 2006 and 2012 were calculated to total up to 60,000, a number widely accredited to an escalation of the drug war.[8] Even with this catalogue of devastation, the institutions of international law that should be invested in proclaiming drug prohibition to have been a success – such as the United Nations Office on Drugs and Crime (UNODC) – have had to recognize that drug use and drug trading perseveres in the face of draconian international prohibition, with UNODC estimating that between 162 million and 324 million people used illicit drugs recreationally in 2012.[9] Over $100 billion per annum is currently being spent globally on enforcing the War on Drugs and yet the laws continue to fail to make any progress on their stated aim of eliminating illicit drug use.[10] Moreover, in addition to explaining this failure to eradicate the drugs trade, those who champion the War on Drugs must also account for the stark racial and geographic asymmetry in terms of who has felt the consequences of prohibition.

As will be illustrated over the subsequent chapters of this book, the contemporary orthodoxy that we live in a post-colonial/post-racial world is contradicted by the discrepancy in the way the violence of the drug war has been apportioned amongst the peoples of the world. Despite adopting a liberal posture, articulated in terms of the impartiality of law, the twentieth-century project of global drugs prohibition has consistently reinforced racial or ethnic divisions within and between the nations of the world. Differences in the application of over-policing tactics, draconian sentences of imprisonment, modes of displacement and crop eradication or limited rights for cultural rituals and practices, place drug prohibition, in practice, within histories of racialized and colonial violence that contemporary international law argues should be opposed.

Drugs and race: a great American story?

As already mentioned, a current failing of much of the literature that has sought to focus on drug prohibition and race has been its centring on the drug war in the US. Of course, the historical and empirical research that has identified drug prohibition as being a key driver of a racially discriminatory system of mass incarceration in the US has been an essential contribution to wider discussions on both drugs and race and serves as a key foundation upon which the arguments of this collection stand. Michelle Alexander has offered probably the most famous contribution to the field of study with her 2012 bestseller, *The New Jim Crow*, where she highlights that in the US 'Black men have been admitted to prison on drugs charges at rates of 20 to 50 times that of White men', despite the fact there is in fact no discernible discrepancy between the use, supply, or production of prohibited substances between Black and White American communities.[11] This practice of legal discrimination within the execution of the drug war has resulted in a criminal justice system in the US that supports the argument presented by Craig Reinarman and Harry G. Levine, who see the ultimate consequence of the drug war as only the production of a 'bulging prison population ... disproportionately comprised of poor people of color, most of whom had not committed violent crimes'.[12] With each further contribution to this body of literature, it has become harder and harder to see the drug laws in America as anything other than the latest instantiation of the country's particular history of legalized, racialized violence. Doris Marie Provine offers an extensive review of the history of race as it has functioned within anti-drug campaigns, from the moralist temperance movements of the early twentieth century to the panic of the crack epidemic in the 1980s.[13] David A. Sklansky has also written on how the stark discrepancy between the mandatory federal sentences for trafficking in powder cocaine and crack cocaine reflect the different racialized associations of the drugs, with powder cocaine being perceived as a White person's drug while crack cocaine is presumed to be a drug taken only by African Americans and therefore punished far more harshly.[14] For Sklansky, the discrepancy in the sentencing of the two drugs, despite the fact that one is chemically only a derivative of the other, highlights a lie at the foundation of the US's legal order: the belief that all men are created equal. He argues that 'it is hard to find contemporary laws that fail this prophylactic requirement [for equality before the law] more blatantly than the federal crack penalties'; with the different penalties for crack and powder cocaine, the legacy persists of a legal system that promised equality before the law but founded itself on slavery and segregation.[15]

That the US has occupied the focus of scholars concerned with the racialized history of the drug war is, to a certain extent, understandable. The War on Drugs has resulted in the US having the world's largest prison population by some distance and one that is not only marked by a stark over-representation of racial minorities but also connects directly to the US's previous forms of legalized racial segregation. Furthermore, due to the US's position as the hegemonic power in the contemporary global order, its own history of racial oppression can often be taken to function as a stand-in for a global narrative of the history of race. The prominence within the conversation on race of plantation slavery, the civil rights movement, or Barack Obama's presidency, in comparison to land appropriation in Australia, the Haitian revolution, or Kwame Nkrumah's presidency, remains a consequence of the US's own disproportionate power and prominence within world affairs. Yet when analysing the relationship between the War on Drugs and race, despite the important, ground-breaking work undertaken by the scholars above, a failure to push the conversation beyond the American context not only leads to limited understanding of the global picture but also overlooks the inherently transnational nature of race as a global construct, drugs as a global commodity and the laws prohibiting the drugs trade as operating at the global, as well as national, level. While Michelle Alexander and other scholars provide crucial insight into the connections that persist between America's drug-war fuelled model of mass incarceration, and the histories of plantation slavery, Jim Crow segregation and legal White supremacy that underwrote the US's development, it is important to remember when discussing race, drugs and transatlantic slavery, that Alexander is addressing topics that cannot be analysed in full from within the strict confines of any one nation-state. The racial dynamics that have been identified within the War on Drugs in the US are not only mirrored in other countries across the globe, but in fact have their genesis in global, not only American, histories and discourses of racial formation. So overall, this collection will offer a picture of the relationship between drug prohibition and race at an international level, in contrast to the current literature's overly American focus. As was recognized by the lawyers who first advocated drug prohibition at the start of the twentieth century, since the traffic of drugs is an inherently globalized industry, any attempt to analyse this problem must itself function at the level of the global.[16]

A global view of drugs and race

The problem of race exceeds any one national narrative of racial divisions; it spans the globe encapsulating the legacies of apartheid and land appropriation in settler colonies, the hierarchy of populations produced through scientific racism and the notions of sub-humanity, as well as gendered ideas of stronger (masculine) and weaker (feminine) peoples, that continue to haunt the contemporary, ostensibly post-racial world. Once this more global perspective is taken into consideration, we can better understand why the racialized dynamics of the drug war that have been identified in the US are not limited to that country but instead can be seen to reoccur in a number of other nation-states. For instance, one immediate parallel is the United Kingdom, where empirical studies have also illustrated how crucial the race of the defendant is in terms of the punishments that tend to follow a drug arrest. In the UK, Black people are disproportionately imprisoned when found guilty of drug offences, whereas White counterparts are far more likely to escape with a simple informal caution.[17] The discrepancy in the application of drug laws has helped create a situation in which, in opposition to the common conception that the UK is not burdened by the US's racial problems, the proportion of Black people imprisoned, in relation to their proportion of total population of the country as a whole, is in fact larger in the UK than in the US.[18] As Tanzil Chowdhury's chapter in this collection shows, the racialized undercurrent of drug policing in the

UK has resulted in contrasting levels of surveillance and control being imposed on festivals and celebrations associated with the country's Black community as opposed to the White majority. This trend in the racially discriminatory application of drug laws continues in other countries that we have focused on, for example, in Brazil, where drug prohibition has propelled an expansion in a carceral state which is disproportionately populated by bodies racialized as Black, as unpacked at length by Evandro Piza Duarte and Felipe da Silva Freitas in their insightful chapter. In addition to an unequal application of criminal punishments and prison sentences for drug crimes, racial disproportionality in Brazil is also revealed by the piles of Black and Brown bodies that make up many of the fatalities that have resulted from the draconian attempts by police to enforce drug control across the country.[19] The parallels continue across Latin America, including countries such as Colombia, where Oscar Guardiola-Rivera extends the work done by others (such as renowned anthropologist Michael Taussig) to connect the violence of the contemporary cocaine trade to the racialized history of slavery and gold production in Colombia.[20] As the chapter in this collection written by Guardiola-Rivera and myself illustrates, the forced crop eradication and aerial fumigation policies that were extended under the US-backed counter-narcotics strategy known as 'Plan Colombia' have particularly affected Afro-Colombian and indigenous communities, reinforcing the 'historic marginalisation' of these communities.[21] This can occur even in countries that pride themselves on overcoming their history of race, such as Canada. In their chapter, Dawn Moore and Elise Wohlbold show how Canadian drug laws are intimately interwoven with that country's own history of settler colonialism. Similarly, in the 'rainbow nation' of today's South Africa, Shaun Shelly and Simon Howell analyse the way in which apartheid-era security structures and policing tactics have been repurposed in the drug war. Ashley Bohrer and Andrés Fabián Henao Castro's chapter offers a global analysis of policing tactics and shows that how the drug war was fuelled not only militarized policing in the US, but also how this new form of policing has been exported across the globe to help maintain contemporary settler colonialism, particularly in Israel. This collection of essays also contains Ariadna Estévez's unpacking of the gendered and racial aspects that underpin the mass of violence released in the War on Drugs in Mexico since the turn of the millennium, and Asmin Fransiska tying drug prohibition in Indonesia to a suppressed colonial past and a contemporary rise in xenophobia within that country. Finally, Katherine Pettus concludes the collection by arguing for understanding the geographic inequalities in access to internationally controlled essential medicines for the treatment of pain and palliative care today as part of the long legacy of European colonialism and the privileging of pain relief for particular populations instead of others.

It is because of the consistent racial asymmetry in the application of drug laws, across a variety of different jurisdictions and social contexts, that the authors who have contributed to this collection are able to draw together theoretical traditions that have extensively considered the problem of race in the modern world, including post-colonial/decolonial studies, critical race theory and whiteness studies, and apply them to the concrete political problem of the War on Drugs. A shared perception that coheres the disparate arguments and approaches of this collection is the understanding that race is not a natural, a priori, objective phenomenon, but is a social relation that must be maintained and reconstituted on a daily basis through institutions such as the law. Following on from this understanding, the essays in this book illustrate how the racial and geographical discrepancies that have been produced in the application of the international laws on drugs across a variety of jurisdictions are not an aberration but, when looked at collectively, offer a telling account of how racial, ethnic and geographical differences continue to be produced in the contemporary, ostensibly post-colonial/post-racial modern world. The War on Drugs serves as a particularly interesting topic for reading manifestations of race in a 'post-racial' world, as drug prohibition emerges as a historical contemporary of the victories of civil rights and decolonization in the mid-twentieth century that were supposed to erase the global colour line of the preceding centuries. Therefore, when thinking about which arenas and institutions produce and maintain racial disparities in the contemporary era, the co-currency of the emergence of international drug prohibition legislation and the legislation that, formally at least, dismantled the colonized/racialized global order provides an insight into how the problem of the colour line persists within the ostensibly post-racial/post-colonial world.

What is race?

In order to understand the relationship between the War on Drugs and racial divisions/discrimination across a variety of societies, a deeper understanding of race and racism than the one offered by liberal political theory is needed. It cannot be denied that significant progress was made in the fight against racism over the twentieth century. When discussing what it might take to help erase a colour line that appeared interminably fixed at the start of the twentieth century, Du Bois felt that subjugated races had 'to ask three things: 1, The right to vote; 2, Civic equality; 3, The education of youth according to ability'.[22] The successes of the campaigns against racial segregation and formal colonialism that blossomed in the post-Second World War era meant that these three demands were concretized into law across much of the world by the century's end. Consequently, explicit articulations of racial discrimination and prejudice were discredited in conventional political discourse. However, race is not merely a social phenomenon based on prejudice, but instead is invested in material interests, supports particular structures of expropriation and confinement, and serves deep symbolic function in defining what it means to be human. As leading theorists on race such as Lewis Gordon and Frank Wilderson have noted, there is no ontology of the racial other.[23] As opposed to the conflict in class relations or gender relations, the racial other does not have a relation of conflict with the dominant incarnation (whiteness) because it is taken as not having entered into a condition of relationality. The racial other is not a thing in and of itself, but the failure of a thing, a flawed version of what should be. It is not the opposite of a human, but a sub-human. The project of racism was the attempt to push specific human bodies outside of the realm of human relations, to turn being into non-being. One could better understand race by realizing how it is 'constructed by metaphor and metonymy; it stands in, metonymically, for the Other', and therefore could never be what is.[24] Race as it functioned on this material and metaphysical level, was an accepted prism through which to view the world at the start of the twentieth century. The development and establishment of racial discourse was the result of a historical process; race is not the preordained, natural social phenomenon it is often mistaken for. While there is nothing particularly modern about divisions having been drawn between groups, whether that be along cultural, linguistic, or ethnic lines, imbuing this difference with the weight of race was the result of the specific context and historical process of European colonialism following the encounter with the New World at the end of the fifteenth century. Ideas around classification became a central component within the rationality of European Enlightenment thinking and this was applied to humans in order to justify material extraction. However, by the early twentieth century, the order of European empires descended into a cycle of ever-escalating crises, which eventually reached its apotheosis with the World Wars. Once the tragedy of the Holocaust was uncovered at the end of the Second World War, race was slowly discredited as an organizing political principle. Yet in dismissing it, what race had been, on both a philosophical and social level, was reduced in scope to ease the burden of being able to confine it to the past. Not ignoring the historical specificity of the Jewish Holocaust, any effort to fully understand this tragedy should take care to emphasize that it did not emerge free of historical precedents.[25] Instead it gives us an indication of how race was conceived under modernity – not as difference as the liberal tradition tended to imagine it, but rather race was, in Du Bois's words, a 'problem', a problem that would eventually invite a 'final solution'.[26] The figure of the racial other was not a figure that was different to the idealized standard of European 'man', but one that was the negation of 'man', a sub-human who served as a failed version of the ideal. The process of trying to create the ideal social order necessarily precipitated the erasure of the failed forms of 'man', with the 'solution' to the problem of race being found in the project of genocide, the extermination of the defective genes from the collective whole. This process reached its apogee with the Jewish Holocaust enacted by the German Nazi Party, but it can be read as being previewed by the German colonization of South West Africa or the British colonization of Australia amongst others.[27] The discourse of race was a discourse that imagined the replacement of inferior racial groups by superior ones as a natural evolutionary process. In addition to producing the image of the idealized human who should by right span the globe, as Patrick Wolfe describes, race thereby renders 'certain people as being out of place' in the world.[28] The process for being turned into people 'out of place' had long been applied to 'the natives' encountered by European imperial expansion before it was adopted by German national socialists. Fanon perhaps best describes the colonial echoes of European fascism when he stated that 'Nazism transformed the whole of Europe into a veritable colony.'[29]

With the tragedies of the Second World War illustrating the inability to assume any limits on the violence of racialization, international law was faced with the task of reconceptualizing the political sphere. The newly formed United Nations responded by institutionalizing universal human rights and then ratifying legislation committed to eliminating all forms of racial discrimination.[30] However, in seeking to act as a midwife for the birth of a post-racial world, international law approached the issue of race as a moral failure of recognizing 'the dignity and equality inherent in all human beings'.[31] Race became an issue to be resolved by state and international legislation, underpinned by a belief that once open discrimination was delegitimized, the attraction of race as a prism for understanding society would also disappear. Yet once an understanding is gained of race being more than a distorted recognition of difference – that race serves both material interests and a symbolic role – then the inability for hierarchically imposed legislation to address the problem becomes apparent. To reject racism on the basis that it fails to recognize the 'equality inherent in all human beings' overlooks the role that race plays in constituting the very notion of what it means to be a human being under European modernity. While race was explicitly discredited by the late twentieth-century liberal order, the historical project that produced race – European imperialism – was not; therefore it is not seen as contradictory to proclaim that you are both fervently against racism and that you hold the British or French empires had been, on the whole, a positive moment for human progress. Race cannot be extracted from the material and metaphysical process of colonialism; race is, as Patrick Wolfe describes, 'colonialism speaking'.[32] Over the past few centuries of European imperialism, race had become such an integral part of what it meant to be a proper human being that it could not just be commanded out of existence. Instead, what the second half of the twentieth century shows is that the colour line would mutate and be reproduced in new forms. As this collection of essays shows, the universal prohibition of drugs would offer one such new axis along which the old colour line could be redrawn and ideas of racial difference given renewed significance. The UN legislation that established drug prohibition as a global norm was produced in the same era as the UN legislation that claimed to eliminate racial discrimination. This gives an indication of how drugs laws can be read as a key arena in which the discourse of race could transfer from one era to another.

What are drugs?

An immediate question that arises when tracing the twin histories of anti-drug and anti-racist international legislation is the question of what is the specific relationship between the concepts of race and drugs that might allow for any correlation. Similar to race, the concept of 'drugs' is also a social construction that often masquerades as a scientific category. What politicians and moralists will present in their anti-drug campaigns as the inherent biological and social danger presented by prohibited drugs has come to be understood as an objective, scientific fact. The danger of drugs such as cocaine or heroin is read as lying within the very substances themselves, that these drugs are different from other intoxicants in their being, requiring them to be forbidden for human consumption. However, the very idea of 'drugs', of particular substances that offer an inherent threat of depravity for the consumer, is not an inalienable scientific fact but is rather only a historical recent construction, as Roy Porter reminds us:

> If you'd talked about the 'drugs problem' two hundred years ago, no one would have known what you meant. There was no notion then of 'drugs', in the sense of a small group of substances scientifically believed to be harmful because they are addictive or personality destroying, the availability of which is restricted by law. The term 'drugs' as a shorthand for a bunch of assorted narcotics is in fact a twentieth-century coinage.[33]

The concept of 'drugs' as we commonly use the term is inseparable from the historical process of drug prohibition. When international law prohibits the use and trade of different drugs, it should not be seen as a moment of the law legislating over an object that is external to itself; for drugs and drug laws are co-constituted in the moment of prohibition. Jacques Derrida provides one resource for illuminating the discursive field in which drug prohibition is situated, understanding the social and historical contingencies that are required to constitute the very concept of 'drugs' that the law acclaims legislation over. For Derrida:

> There are no drugs 'in nature.' There may be natural poisons and indeed naturally lethal poisons, but they are not as such 'drugs.' As with addiction, the concept of drugs supposes an instituted and institutional definition: a history is required and a culture, conventions, evaluations, norms, an entire network of intertwined discourses.[34]

Derrida's reading of prohibition commences from an understanding that 'the concept of drugs is not a scientific concept, but is rather instituted on the basis of moral or political evaluation.'[35] Within the drug laws, we find a prime example of the law discursively creating a distinction that does not objectively exist. Prior to prohibition, the substances now referred to as 'drugs' were not immediately differentiated from other goods and resources that were being commercially exploited in the world market produced by European imperialism. As the historian

David Courtwright identifies, 'European expansion in the sixteenth, seventeenth, and eighteenth centuries turned psychoactive drugs, including spirituous alcohol and tobacco, into global products.'[36] As will be discussed in a number of the essays in this collection, substances such as opium and coca were sources of great wealth for the British, Dutch and French empires, amongst others. European imperial wealth was built on the profits of psychoactive substances encountered in the colonies; alongside the coffee, sugar and tobacco produced for trade were substances, such as opium, that we now deride as 'drugs'. Furthermore, states of intoxication and the psychoactive substances that could induce such states were glamorized within certain European artistic and literary circles in the age of empire, as seen in the works of Samuel Coleridge, Thomas De Quincey and Charles Baudelaire.[37] However, the historical process that would give rise to the idea of 'drugs' being a collection of substances that posed an existential threat to 'humanity' began at the end of the nineteenth century, which saw a wave of international anti-vice activism of which the birth of global drug prohibition would prove to be perhaps the most dramatic initiative.[38] Thereafter, the course of the twentieth century would see drugs and drug use overtake other popularly held signifiers for 'denigrated' humanity, such as homosexuality or vagrancy, to serve as arguably the prevailing example of depravity and moral failing in societies across the West.[39] Gaining increasing impetus in the latter half of the century, especially following the successful ratification of the Single Convention after the stunted attempts at drug prohibition in the League of Nations era, the previously profitable commodities of cannabis, coca, opium and others would transition from being tradable, naturally growing plants/psychoactive substances into dangerous 'drugs' to be banned across the world. Anthropologist Michael Taussig's work provides a key resource for understanding how objects – naturally occurring plants and chemicals – became discursively infused with such demonic social power. Through his scholarship, Taussig has stressed how the social histories of commodities are interwoven within the symbolic potency that they wield once crystallized in material form. As opposed to the orthodox understanding of 'man' creating commodities through extractive labour and capital, before economically exploiting them for commercial gain, Taussig emphasizes how in practice this relationship is not as unilateral as often envisioned, for once created it can be that, in fact, 'commodities rule their creators.'[40] Writing with a fidelity to the full significance of the idea of fetishization, Taussig recognizes the power for humans to transform objects into totems, and for those totems to then consequently transform the human upon connection. This theoretical perspective, combined with his geographical focus on Latin America, has aided Taussig in developing an innovative understanding of the social life of 'drugs'. Speaking to the discursive production of cocaine as a 'drug', Taussig provides us with the insightful concept of drugs as 'transgressive substances'.[41] Through the term 'transgressive substances', Taussig illustrates how drugs are fetishized to become totems for the disruption of the order of the given world – drugs such as coca making 'a mockery of the notions of "laws" of supply and demand. They decidedly sabotage the notion of "demand" riddling it with phantasmic properties unknown to conventional economics.'[42] Within the conceptualization of prohibitionist law, drugs are not taken as the standard commodity but instead are recognized as commodities that have the power to rule their creators. If race is seen as the negation of humanity, then the fear of drugs held by prohibitionists is that 'drugs' can facilitate the denigration of the human into sub-humanity, with all the racial connotations of the word 'de-nigrate' implied.[43] In the twentieth century, the concept of drugs was created and the 'transgressive substances' were imbued with the phantasmal powers to able to use and consume the human subject as opposed to allowing humanity to use and consume it.

To appreciate the social function of the concept of drugs helps us to understand the moral panic that they engender and why their prohibition often takes the form of reinforcing the old colour line now ostensibly discredited within liberal political discourse. Drugs are not seen as mere plant life in the manner that they appear in nature, nor are they seen as commodities, as natural resources to be exploited for capitalist gain. Drugs are instead discursively produced as 'transgressive substances', elements of the natural world that can call upon the negation of the characteristics that define 'humanity'. As Desmond Manderson argues, the fear of drugs is not merely the fear of the substances themselves; rather, 'what lies beneath is undoubtedly a fear of contamination', a fear of the failed state of humanity they are commonly read as bringing about.[44] Drugs are taken to facilitate movement between different states of being, transferring consumers from the realm of the human to the non-human. The contemporary conceptualization of drugs takes much from the classical notion of *pharmakon*, which Derrida recovers to describe the discursive process for how difference is produced. The *pharmakon* facilitates 'the movement and the play ... (soul/body, good/evil, inside/outside, memory/forgetfulness, speech/writing, etc.)'

threatening any notion of 'internal purity and security' within a social order.[45] Furthermore, unlike the nineteenth-century notion of scientific racism, drugs are not presumed to impact only those who are afflicted; a key element to grasp in order to appreciate the fear that underwrites drug prohibition is to understand that prohibitionists see a mimetic or contagious power within drugs. The fear that drugs might consume the subject who themselves sought to consume the drug is not only a fear of the damage drugs might cause to that specific consumer but that this damage will spread amongst the other members of the community. The fear of these drugs is that they threaten the stability of the social order as a whole, functioning as what Stanley Cohen termed as the societal folk-devil, spreading the addiction amongst the whole community.[46] David Courtwright states that 'absent the idea of addiction, the whole system of controlling drug supply that has developed over the last two centuries would make little moral or practical sense.'[47] I would add to this that an understanding of the fear that drug addiction causes, and importantly spreads, the denigration of an idealized figure of the human is necessary to understand why the drug laws have persisted despite the devastation they have brought upon already oppressed peoples. Early drug prohibition campaigns in the US at the start of twentieth century found much of their success through equating particular drugs with particular groups of racial others – opium with Chinese labourers, marijuana with Mexican migrants, etc. The US's earliest recorded drug law, the 1875 City Ordinance Against Opium Dens passed in San Francisco, was a law produced on 'strictly ethnic grounds', aimed against 'Chinese immigrants' practice of smoking opium' and fuelled by a popular media obsessed with 'images of "yellow fiends" debauching white women and the youth of the nation'.[48] Particularly relevant is the way in which the threat of these drugs was seen as not merely contained to the communities of the racial others, the real danger was how they could spill out into White communities. In short, drugs as 'transgressive substances' are read as having the power to transform even the most rational, autonomous, enlightened and sovereign European 'man' into the lazy, violent, depraved figure of the sub-human. The correlative response to this fear is the aim of expelling these 'drugs' from the collective social order, along with those who might be addicted or particularly susceptible to an addiction to these substances. The metaphysical quality read into drugs is easily transferred into the very material bodies of those already traditionally constructed as being a threat to the boundaries of humanity: racially othered populations.

Sociologist and cultural theorist Jean Baudrillard adds a further element to this argument with his own reading of how indebted the fear of 'drugs' is to a Weberian conception of the economic and social good in western society.[49] For Baudrillard, the West arrogates onto itself a specific capacity for delayed gratification and it is this capacity taken to underlie presumptions of civilization. The condemnation of drugs therefore functions as a stand-in for the fear of the threat of the loss of that capacity for delayed gratification, the defeat of reason and the will, at the hand of the appetite in Aristotelian terms. Baudrillard argues that 'traces of this long-standing condemnation linger on in our own vision of modern drugs and of the occult power they derive from their ancient symbolic virtues.' As opposed to the 'evil' of drug addiction residing in the drug itself and infecting western modernity from the outside, Baudrillard shows us how the 'evil' is instead

> a consequence of the very logic of the system, of the excessive logic and rationality of a system – in this case society in the Industrialized countries – which, having reached a certain level of saturation, secretes antibodies which express its internal diseases, its strange malfunctions, its unforeseeable and incurable breakdowns.[50]

Within the discourse of European modernity, where the social relations between subjects is presumed to be fully secularized and consequently solely mediated through mutual recognition of each other's humanity, the fear has been that 'drug use threatens the social bond' and summons up the spectre of the sub-human that persists within.[51]

Reading race and drugs together

The value of understanding the symbolic threat to human subjectivity that underpins the fear of drugs is what it betrays about the paranoia that always already was operative within the discourse of race. Nineteenth-century scientific racism presented racial hierarchies as fixed, different evolutionary paths, having guaranteed the absolute superiority of the European to be as permanent as the inferiority of the 'negro', the 'oriental' or the 'American Indian'. Yet the policies of brutal racial oppression that were implemented in this era give suggestion to an underlying knowledge of the fiction of race, that the presumed 'fixed' distinctions between these groups were social constructions, not scientific facts and without the violent policing of the boundaries between races, the discourse would inevitably collapse. Race is a fiction, that requires force to give it social form and this is something that the most ardent proponents of race will have, on some level, known and feared. Frantz Fanon most immediately captured the lie of race when he stated 'the Negro is not. Any more than the white man.'[52] To appreciate that racial classifications of difference are porous is to begin to understand better the violence that accompanies the instance of race's certainty; the sub-humanity, the animalism and the deviancy projected onto the racial subaltern subject as a betrayal of what already exists in-potential within the idealized (European) human. James Baldwin poetically described this misrecognition that grounds the discourse of racism when he challenged White America to really question who is the 'nigger' they are afraid of: 'We have invented the nigger, I didn't invent it, white people invented him … I've always known I am not a nigger, but if I am not the nigger and if it's true that your invention reveals you, then who is the nigger?'[53]

This fear of a sub-humanity which will rise unless the boundaries are policed persists in the contemporary moment, though it is no longer articulated in racial terms. The insights of post-structuralism have helped illuminate how the law's forceful insistence upon given norms is a manifestation of this same fear of the ever-present potential for the resurrection of the abnormal within the social order.[54] The normal, proper, sovereign, autonomous and rational human is constituted through the invention and then casting out of the abnormal. The panic about the 'transgressive' power of drugs illustrates the creeping fear that lived underneath ideas of race, that race was always feared to not be fixed but to be porous, the realization that no race was inherently superior or inferior to another, and that the categories ascribed to the racial other were merely characteristics that the dominant racial subject feared from within themselves. In containing these negative characteristics within the category of 'drugs' and by seeking to launch a war upon them, the War on Drugs not only has effects that are racially 'disproportionate' but in fact helps to *produce* race itself, giving material form to old ideas about humanity and sub-humanity in this supposedly post-racial era. When the War on Drugs gives rise to new tropes such as Black mothers in the US being labelled 'crack fiends', Colombian rural workers being 'Narco-Trafficantes' or when Filipino drug users are described as 'vermin' and 'social pests' by President Rodrigo Duterte, new forms of racialized sub-humanity are being actively produced. By unpacking ideas around 'drugs' across multiple jurisdictions, the authors of this collection will show how indebted the fear of the 'transgressive' nature of drugs is to racialized conceptions of 'non-humanity', with drugs feared as being the conduit between ideal and denigrated states of human beings.

Conclusion

Drawing on the collective expertise of its contributors, this book will help to provide some answers for readers looking to understand why, after being used by many cultures over the centuries, a set of intoxicants became illegal across the world in the twentieth century and furthermore, why the impact of this prohibition has consistently fallen hardest upon the poorest and most vulnerable populations of the world, especially groups already social constructed as racially other. The racial asymmetry of the War on Drugs provides a telling insight into the contemporary global political order and its claim to a post-colonial/post-racial universal humanism. The collective weight of the contributions of this book should illustrate how the War on Drugs is not a peripheral, idiosyncratic project of international law but instead betrays the central functions of liberal political order over the twentieth and into the twenty-first century, an acclaimed universalism that remains tied to a Euro-centric conception of humanity in both its history and structure before visiting the force of law on those who fail to meet this predetermined standard of civilization. It gives support to Jean-Paul Sartre's famous claim that in the latter half of the twentieth century 'there is nothing more consistent than a racist humanism.'[55] There is a stark contradiction between the neutral, objective language of the drug prohibition treaties, which echo the universal humanism of contemporaneous post-war human rights/race relations legislation, and the geographical and racial asymmetry in the violence that has been endured in the project of drug prohibition. The failure of the mid-twentieth-century legislative turn away from racial discrimination is that it was limited in trying to include previously excluded subjectivities into a concept of humanity that was founded upon their exclusion, whilst also trying to ensure that this concept of humanity remained the same as before. This notion of humanity continued to be underwritten by a spectre of sub-humanity, with which the characteristics that had come to be associated with drugs – indolence, debauchery, profligacy and depravity – could be easily synthesized. Reading race and drugs together at the level of the global also provides further insight into the concept of 'drugs', which struggles to remain coherent without the haunting spectre of the 'non-human' as its foundation. The distinctions applied by society to different types of plant-life is a product of legal determination; it is the law that cleaves the difference between, for example, the sugar-cane plant that is cultivated and commoditized and the coca-leaf plant that is prohibited and subject to eradication through aerial fumigation. However, as the system of prohibition built over the twentieth century continues to receive greater criticism over the coming decades, it is essential to appreciate how it has been interwoven with the discourse of race in order to reform the laws in a way that do not reproduce the harm already caused.

The authors of this collection employ theoretical approaches to critically unpack the drug laws in Mexico, Colombia, the UK, South Africa and other countries, showing that they do not function as inanimate, impartial instruments of justice, but rather mechanisms through which the global racial divisions are renewed in the 'post-racial' societies of today. Furthermore, the current debates about drug policy reform are still to develop a wider appreciation of this aspect of drug prohibition and have tended to limit the scope of drug policy reform to marijuana legalization, while basing its argument on economic grounds. It is essential for this racial aspect of the War on Drugs to be understood in order to ensure that when reform arrives, it seeks, through clemency for drug sentences or reinvestment for areas damaged by the drug war, to repair the damage that has been disproportionally borne by racially oppressed peoples over past few decades of prohibition.

Notes

1 W. E. B. Du Bois, *The Souls of Black Folk* (New York: Simon and Schuster 2005), p. 3.
2 See Stephen Castles, 'Racism: a global analysis', *Centre for Multicultural Studies, University of Wollongong, Occasional Paper 28* (1993), http://ro.uow.edu.au/cmsocpapers/2; or, for a UK perspective, see The Runnymede Trust, *Submission to the UN Committee on the Elimination of All Forms of Racial Discrimination*, July 2016, www.runnymedetrust.org/projects-and-publications/europe/cerd.html.
3 Preamble of the United Nations Single Convention on Narcotic Drugs, 1961.
4 Christopher Hobson, 'Challenging "evil": Continuity and change in the drug prohibition regime', *International Politics* 51.4 (2014): 525–542 (p. 526).
5 For further on the tension between international drug prohibition and international rights to traditional culture see Sven Pfeiffer, 'Rights of Indigenous peoples and the international drug control regime: The case of traditional coca leaf chewing', *Goettingen Journal of International Law* 5.1 (2013): 287–324.
6 Pfeiffer, 'Rights of Indigenous peoples'.

7 Heather C. West and William J. Sabol, *Prisoners in 2007*, Bureau of Justice Statistics Bulletin NCJ 224280, 2008. See Appendix, Table 12. 'Number of sentenced prisoners in federal prison, by most serious offense, 2000, 2006, and 2007'.

8 See Human Rights Watch, *Mexico's Disappeared: The Enduring Cost of a Crisis Ignored*, 20 February 2013, https://www.hrw.org/report/2013/02/20/mexicos-disappeared/enduring-cost-crisis-ignored [accessed 7 September 2015], or Nick Miroff and William Booth, 'Mexico's drug war at a stalemate as Calderon's presidency ends', *Washington Post*, 27 November 2012, www.washingtonpost.com/world/the_americas/calderon-finishes-his-six-year-drug-war-at-stalemate/2012/11/26/82c90a94-31eb-11e2-92f0-496af208bf23_story.html [accessed 5 October 2015].

9 The UNODC World Drug Report 2014, p. 1.

10 Transform Drug Policy Foundation estimate. See briefing 'Estimating global spending on drug enforcement', Transform Drug Policy Foundation, 2011.

11 Michelle Alexander, *The New Jim Crow: Mass Incarceration in the Age of Colorblindness* (New York: The New Press, reprint edn, 2012), p. 7.

12 Craig Reinarman and Harry G. Levine, 'Crack in the rearview mirror: Deconstructing drug war mythology', *Social Justice* 31.1–2 (2004): 62.

13 Doris Marie Provine, *Unequal under Law: Race in the War on Drugs* (Chicago, IL: University of Chicago Press, 2008).

14 David A. Sklansky, 'Cocaine, race, and equal protection', *Stanford Law Review* 47 (1994): 1284–1355.

15 Sklansky, 'Cocaine, race, and equal protection', p. 1301.

16 Editorial comment, *American Journal of International Law* 19.2 (1925): 327–361 (p. 354).

17 Niamh Eastwood, Michael Shiner and Daniel Bear, *The Numbers in Black and White: Ethnic Disparities in the Policing and Prosecution of Drug Offences in England and Wales* (London: Release, 2013): this report showed that Black people in the UK are far more likely to be charged and sentenced for the same drug offence, with 56 per cent of White people caught in possession of cocaine receiving cautions, while the remaining 44 per cent were charged. In contrast, when Black people were caught in possession of cocaine, 22 per cent received cautions, while 78 per cent were charged for the offence. This disparity continues with regard to sentencing, with Black people being imprisoned for drug offences at almost six times the rate of White people.

18 Randeep Ramesh 'More black people jailed in England and Wales proportionally than in US', *Guardian*, 11 October 2010: 'the proportion of black people in jail in the UK was almost seven times their share of the population, whereas in the US the proportion of black prisoners is four times greater than their population share.' Available at www.theguardian.com/society/2010/oct/11/black-prison-population-increase-england [accessed 21 October 2015]; The Equality and Human Rights Commission, *How Fair Is Britain?* (London: EHRC, 2010): 'there is now greater disproportionality in the number of Black people in prisons in the UK than in the United States', p. 172, www.equalityhumanrights.com/key-projects/how-fair-is-britain/ [accessed 21 October 2015].

19 Jamie Amparo Alvez and Dina Alvez, 'Drugs and drug control in Brazil', in Anita Kalunta-Crumpton (ed.), *Pan-African Issues in Drugs and Drug Control: An International Perspective* (Farnham: Ashgate, 2015), pp. 248–292.

20 Michael Taussig, *My Cocaine Museum* (Chicago, IL: University of Chicago Press, 2004).

21 See Washington Office on Latin America, *Peace, Drug Policy, and an Inclusive Society Eleven Ways Colombian and FARC Negotiators Can Reform Drug Policy and Build a Lasting Peace* (Washington, DC: Washington Office on Latin America, 2013), p. 4.

22 Du Bois, 'Of Mr. Booker T. Washington and others', *The Souls of Black Folk*, p. 53.

23 See Lewis R. Gordon, *Existentia Africana: Understanding Africana Existential Thought* (London: Routledge, 2000), or Frank B. Wilderson, *Red, White and Black: Cinema and the Structure of U.S. Antagonisms* (Durham, NC: Duke University Press, 2010).

24 Anthony Appiah, 'The uncompleted argument: Du Bois and the illusion of race', *Critical Inquiry* 12.1 (1985): 21–37 (p. 35).

25 For scholarship that links colonialism and genocide in a systematic way, see Dirk Moses and Dan Stone (eds), *Colonialism and Genocide* (London: Routledge, 2007) and Enzo Traverso, *The Origins of Nazi Violence* (New York: The New Press, 2003).

26 Du Bois, *Souls of Black Folk*, p. 6. Du Bois asked Blacks to consider 'How does it feel to be a problem?'

27 Mike Davis, *Late Victorian Holocausts: El Niño Famines and the Making of the Third World* (London: Verso, 2000).

28 Patrick Wolfe, *Traces of History: Elementary Structures of Race* (London: Verso, 2015), p. 17.

29 Frantz Fanon, *The Wretched of the Earth* (London: Penguin, 2001), p. 100.

30 See the International Convention on the Elimination of All Forms of Racial Discrimination (1965).

31 International Convention on the Elimination of All Forms of Racial Discrimination, Preamble.

32 Patrick Wolfe, *Traces of History: Elementary Structures of Race* (London: Verso, 2015), p. 7.

33 Roy Porter, 'The history of the "drugs problem"', *Criminal Justice Matters* 24.3 (1996): 3.

34 Jacques Derrida, 'The rhetoric of drugs: an interview', 5 *differences: A Journal of Feminist Cultural Studies* 5.1 (1993): 1–25.

35 Derrida, 'The rhetoric of drugs', p. 1.

36 David T. Courtwright, 'A short history of drug policy or why we make war on some drugs but not on others', *LSE IDEAS!, Governing the Global Drug Wars*, (October 2012): 17–24 (p. 17).

37 For artistic engagements with opium use, see Thomas De Quincey, *Confessions of an English Opium-Eater* (London: Penguin Classics, rev. edn, 2003), Samuel Taylor Coleridge, 'Kubla Khan; or, a vision in a dream: A fragment', in *The Complete Poems of Samuel Taylor Coleridge* (London: Penguin Classics, 1997), pp. 249–252, and Charles Baudelaire, *Artificial Paradises* (*Les Paradis Artificiels*) (London: Kensington Publishing Corp., 1998); For further reading on this trend, see Alethea Hayter, *Opium and the Romantic Imagination* (London: Faber and Faber, 2009).

38 Courtwright, 'A short history of drug policy'.

39 See Erich Goode and Nachman Ben-Yehuda, *Moral Panics: The Social Construction of Deviance* (Hoboken, NJ: Wiley-Blackwell, 1994), Chapter 11 'Drug abuse panics'.

40 Michael Taussig, *The Devil and Commodity Fetishism in South America* (Chapel Hill, NC: University of North Carolina Press, 1980), p. xvi.

41 Taussig, *My Cocaine Museum*, p. xiii.

42 Taussig, *My Cocaine Museum*, pp. 118–119.

43 'To denigrate' derives from the Latin for 'black' – *niger*, translating directly as 'to blacken completely'. For more on the racial implications of the word 'denigrate', see 'On language: Dark words of disapproval', *New York Times*, 28 January 1990, www.nytimes.com/1990/01/28/magazine/on-language-dark-words-of-disapproval.html [accessed 2 April 2016].

44 Desmond Manderson, 'Possessed: Drug policy, witchcraft and belief', *Cultural Studies* 19 (2005): 38.

45 Jacques Derrida, 'Plato's pharmacy', in *Dissemination* (Chicago, IL: University of Chicago Press, 1983), pp. 61–72, pp. 127–128.

46 Stanley Cohen, *Folk Devils and Moral Panics* (London: Routledge, 2011).

47 Courtwright, 'A short history of drug policy', p. 18.

48 David Bewley-Taylor, *The United States and International Drug Control 1909–1997* (London: Continuum, 2001), p. 17.

49 Jean Baudrillard, 'A perverse logic', *UNESCO Courier* (July 1987): 7–9.

50 Baudrillard, 'A perverse logic', p. 9.

51 Derrida, 'The rhetoric of drugs: An interview'.

52 Frantz Fanon, *Black Skins, White Masks* (New York: Pluto Press, 2008), p.180

53 James Baldwin, 'Who is the nigger?' Clip taken from film *Take This Hammer*, www.youtube.com/watch?v=LoL5fciA6AU [accessed 20 April 2018].

54 Michel Foucault, *Abnormal: Lectures at the College de France 1974–1975* (London: Verso, 2003, first English edn).

55 Jean-Paul Sartre, Preface to Frantz Fanon's *Wretched of the Earth* (London: Penguin, 2001), p. x.

1

Benevolent whiteness in Canadian drug regulation

Elise Wohlbold and Dawn Moore

Xenophobia and racism are inscribed in the origins of laws interdicting certain (racialized) substances.[1] Canada is in no way an outlier in using criminal law to target and control certain populations. Contra its popular self-image as a tolerant and open society, Canada is one of the most carceral nations in the world and Canadian prisons are fuelled by a mass over-incarceration of Indigenous peoples and a considerable overuse of criminal justice for other racialized groups. Typically, race is targeted as the 'problem' here, an argument with contestable terms. We begin with the premise that 'race' is deployed as a stand-in for non-White. Whiteness by default is unmarked, natural – invisible to many – and without race.[2] Whiteness, as David Roediger points out, does not need to declare its own name; it is defined by what it is not.[3] As a result, in this chapter we present the possibility that whiteness – as the negation of the notion of 'race' – itself is the problem of the War on Drugs (WOD) in Canada. By naming whiteness, we aim to reveal its invisible yet central position around drug regulation in Canada.[4] This argument is likely more intuitive than innovative, but it does offer an alternate correction to the prevailing narrative of drug control in Canada as well as the important perspective of a nation built largely on a *benevolent whiteness* – the focus of our interrogation.

We offer here a survey of the historical relationships between people, intoxicating substances (IS) and law in Canada. We argue that the problems drug laws have sought to address are routinely underpinned by the desire to shape whiteness in particular ways by regulating threats to the imagined and ongoing colonial project. DiAngelo describes whiteness as 'a constellation of processes and practices rather than as a discrete entity'.[5] Thus, whiteness must continuously be defined, reproduced and protected; it is in constant operation, it is fragile.[6]

Yet, as DiAngelo points out, 'white fragility is not weakness per se. In fact, it is a powerful means of white racial control and the protection of white advantage.'[7] For example, criminal justice systems continue to perpetuate settler violence over Indigenous and colonized, racialized bodies with drug laws as the primary technology.[8] In an evolving state-sponsored colonial system, preserving and protecting the fragility of whiteness serves as a justification for colonial violence.[9] As a result, we shift the focus of drug prohibition in Canada to whiteness, a claim heretofore not concisely made, claiming that the WOD is a response to particular and repeated crises of whiteness – benevolent whiteness – thus re-reading the extant histories as narratives of perilous, ongoing colonial projects.

The problem of benevolent whiteness

I see these souls undressed and from the back and side. I see the working of their entrails. I know their thoughts and they know that I know. This knowledge makes them now embarrassed, now furious! They deny my right to live and be and call me misbirth! My word is to them mere bitterness and my soul, pessimism. And yet as they preach and strut and shout and threaten, crouching as they clutch at rags of facts and fancies to hide their nakedness, they go twisting, flying by my tired eyes and I see them ever stripped-ugly, human.[10]

The undressed souls of the White oppressors reveal for Du Bois a vulnerable truth about the White folk he so subversively makes subject to his own gaze. White folk must maintain a careful veneer to marshal their claims to racial superiority. This observation gives Du Bois cause for question: 'But what on earth is whiteness that one should so desire it? Then always, somehow, some way, silently but clearly, I am given to understand that whiteness is the ownership of the earth forever and ever, Amen!'[11]

Whiteness is a problem of capitalism and domination, and its maintenance is vital to the protection of capital colonial control of land and people. Whiteness, as Ahmed reminds us, 'could be described as an ongoing and unfinished history, which orientates bodies in specific directions, affecting how they "take up" space'.[12]

So too is the WOD an ongoing and unfinished history tied in perpetuity to unfolding histories of whiteness. And though we see a generalizable global theory of colonial whiteness, no colony's story is exactly like another's. Observationally (not comparatively), we offer an understanding of Canada's nationalistic whiteness, a whiteness easily and routinely erased because it is seen as impossibly better than the empire of White supremacy to which it is always compared: the United States. After all, Canada – unlike the US melting pot – is a cultural mosaic where cultural and racial differences are thought to be celebrated.[13]

To describe benevolent whiteness: the term 'benevolent' here is descriptive, not value laden. Our thesis is simple: Canada continues to look pretty good from a global perspective. Canada looks good by appearing to do good. Doing good is a smart trope of nationalism because to do good is to intervene and interventions cue scripts and those scripts are scripts of whiteness and they are scripts of colonialism, patriarchy and control. We argue that Canada's 'good guy' reputation is best described as a benevolent whiteness, by which we mean a whiteness that appears progressive and 'post-racial' even as it re-inscribes racialized, gendered and sexualized bodies with the same tropes of domination and supremacy.

We are not the first to arrive at this conceptualization. Eva Mackey writes about Canada's nationalistic self-image of benevolence in the context of governing Indigenous peoples.[14] The convenient national forgetting of obvious acts of racism and xenophobia on the part of the state is well documented by Lozanski, who makes the explicit link between this national need to forget the aspects of the past that offer a counter-narrative to this benevolent statehood by recognizing the threats remembering poses to bourgeois liberalism.[15]

'I anticipate nothing more intimate than history', writes Dionne Brand in Poem 1 of *Thirsty*.[16] Benevolent whiteness is a whiteness of intimacy; it is a whiteness defined by its ability to gently penetrate and manipulate bodies as a screen for smashing others, often in seemingly non-violent ways. Thus, as we describe the Canadian legal dance around drug regulation as one between three partners: the drugs/users, public health and criminalization. This is not to suggest that public health and criminalization are necessarily different and certainly carry comparable capacity to do violence. On the contrary, maintaining this false binary between health and criminality is the most telling feature of benevolent whiteness in the Canadian WOD.

Taking a cue from Bruno Latour's actor-network theory, substances themselves are also subject to tropes of whiteness.[17] Crises as each substance is added to criminal legislation and again as substances, later, experience movement through the different degrees of schedule, are recognized as transporting embedded meanings of colonialism through both their pharmacodynamics as well as their cultural meaning. Substances are signifiers and their cultural personas (drugalities) dictate their relative level of danger based not on pharmacological knowledge but rather on the populations with whom they are affiliated, as well as the manner in which they are ingested. Smoking, for example, with the exception of tobacco (despite its explicit roots in colonialism), is a distinctly non-White form of consumption, especially when compared with, for example, the hypodermic syringe or the elixir, both consumption formats with the medicalized stamp of White acceptability.

Regulating drugs in Canada

The Constitution of Canada makes the regulation of drugs complicated. After Confederation (1867), legislative responsibilities were divided between the provinces and the federal government. Criminal law falls under federal jurisdiction, while health is a provincial matter. In practice, this means that there is a clear, albeit false, cleavage in Canadian responses to drug use, resulting in diverse use of law. Chiefly this constitutional division sets the terms of drug debate in Canada as a battle over provincial autonomy manifested through arguments of whether IS and their use are matters of health or criminality.

In practice, this divide creates faulty poles between responding to drug use as a health or criminal problem. Typically, discourses of health, rooted in the British model of harm reduction, are seen as necessarily more progressive and benevolent than criminal responses. We want to disrupt this dichotomy by showing that the health/criminal divide is false, making the point clear that health interventions regarding drug use are often tightly bound to criminal justice responses.

Unlike other jurisdictions in which the theme of heavy-handed criminalization remains a constant and ever-amplifying thread, since the enactment of the federal Opiate Act in 1908, Canada oscillates between these false binaries of health and crime, selectively and strategically deploying narratives best suited to the targeted population. The first country in the West to introduce anti-drug legislation, Canada's foray into criminalizing substance use was clearly linked to colonialist-fuelled racial tensions and provided a handy remedy to the surplus of Chinese labourers imported to build the nation's railroad.[18] Since then, Canada has twinned hyper-criminalized responses to drug use heavily inspired by (if not directly resulting in pressure from) the United States with more medicalized responses inspired by early biopolitical movements in the United Kingdom. The result is a contradictory array of responses to drug use and the drug trade, that weave narratives of drug use and users through clinical/penal mentalities.

Early drug legislation and the formation of benevolent whiteness

Canada's first legislated prohibition arrives in the 1886 Indian Act. Here, Indigenous peoples were banned from buying and selling alcohol. Though, as with most colonial initiatives, the first alcohol prohibition was presented as a benevolent way to save the 'Indians' from themselves, predictably this legislation did nothing more than provide an additional opportunity to exercise sovereign control over Indigenous bodies. While this legislation initially fined those caught selling liquor to 'Indians', amendments made in 1874 were the first in the Commonwealth to criminalize the state of intoxication. The 1874 Act carried a 14-day sentence of incarceration for any Indigenous person found to be intoxicated. Though the Act names liquor directly, opiates, which were in free supply, were also targeted. Importantly, the legislation by 1876 also bans liquor on reserves in treaties 1–6 (the west coast and prairies as well as the north – Canada's frontier lands) and makes clear its intent to protect Indigenous peoples from 'the evil influence of intoxicating liquors'.[19]

This language or protection mixed with punishment is the first legislated example of benevolent whiteness at the start of drug regulation. Tropes of the childlike Indian in need of White protection are familiar.[20] Importantly, this legislation explicitly criminalizes the population, not the substance. Popular wisdom at the time suggested Indigenous people simply could not handle liquor in the same way White settlers could. Thus, so the wisdom goes, Whites had the fortitude to drink alcohol that Indigenous peoples lacked.[21] But if alcohol itself is such an evil substance, why legislate only around Indigenous users and suppliers? Hogarth's famous prints *Beer Street* and *Gin Lane* (1751) were only 115 years old and had certainly made their way into colonial consciousness. *Gin Lane* specifically embodies the evils of alcohol, evils to which White folk were very much subject, at least through Hogarth's eyes located in the centre of empire (Figure 1.1). Gin of course had its own orientalist trappings, making it suspicious especially when compared to the propriety and measure afforded to British ale.[22]

Liquor was evil but its evil nature changed in the colonies. The foreign substance that led to squalor, neglect, infanticide, suicide and ultimate rending of the social fabric (as depicted by Hogarth) meant something different in British North America (later Canada), a signifier of the motherland.[23] At the same time, these early interdictions coincided with the Gold Rush and the building of the Canadian National Railroad, creating a critical mass of 'hard-drinking' culture heavily influenced by the drinking cultures of the American settler West. As such, liquor, including gin, was still a social ill but not one to cause panic. After all, the impacts of liquor on British bodies was already known and accepted as an unfortunate affliction of the lower classes.[24] Indigenous bodies, however, proved different. The loss of inhibition, the reversion to 'savagery', all imagined by Hogarth, were more than social ills in the colonies. In the wrong bodies, inhibition and savagery, two things the colonizers were trying desperately to eradicate from the Indigenous populations when they were not trying to eradicate the populations themselves, amplified the danger of the Indigenous as a threat to settler sovereignty and the project of establishing White supremacy in the colony.[25] These first interdictions are obvious examples of benevolent whiteness as the fragility of White colonial rule is protected against the ever-present threat of the resistant Indian. The ability to control the drunken Indian was undoubtedly the ability to assert and protect whiteness while seeming to be kind and protective by shouldering the 'White man's burden' of civilizing and watching over the savages.

The 1874 Indian Act's criminalization of intoxication is also an important moment in constituting the benevolent whiteness that informs the messily entwined matrix of public health and criminal justice responses to substances in Canada. By criminalizing a mental state as opposed to an act, the intimate potential of law is revealed. Aside from the very real practical questions about how one might define and assess intoxication, apprehending someone through law on the grounds of mental state makes possible all manner of benevolent interventions. If mental state is the criminal event, intervening with that mental state is a reasonable response in an emerging nationhood that is already embracing welfarist tactics. Additionally, criminalizing intoxication makes possible the criminalization of any manner or state of being, laying the foundation for a society already deeply troubled with threatening ontologies.

Before 1908, the government imported opium into Canada by the thousands of pounds, destined for pharmaceutical companies and opium factories in British Columbia.[26] As societal attitudes changed – due, in part, to moral reformers (religious ethics around self-control and sobriety) – and as fears of the foreign Other emerged (Chinese and Japanese men), citizens started to see opium consumption as a threat to the whiteness of the nation. At the turn of the century, following an economic slump and increased resentment towards Chinese and Japanese people in North America, a new surge of anti-immigrant sentiments emerged in Western Canada. With the completion of the Canadian Pacific Railway and the influx of (desirable and decent) White workers to Canada, settlers saw surplus Chinese workers as a menace to White workers who claimed employment rights in the name of whiteness. Chinese men were willing to work for lower wages and in dangerous work conditions, thereby 'stealing' employment from White labourers.[27]

With the increasing influence of moral reformers, White people of British (Protestant) descent were considered more civilized and morally superior to Chinese immigrants; unlike Chinese immigrants, White people were perceived to have the ability to exercise self-control (they could resist the evils of alcohol, at least while in the colonies).[28] Social ills were blamed on drug consumption by Chinese residents, such as smoking opium (seen as the pursuit of pleasure), rather than the opium-based elixirs and patent medicines used by White consumers (seen as the relief of pain). This marks the start of what might be considered the first wave of moral panics over drug use. Following standard tropes of the moral panic,[29] the alleged threats to whiteness as an economic condition posed by the Chinese community served to divert attention away from other social problems at the time. The economic boom that fuelled the construction of the same national rail line built by these same Chinese workers literally ended in Vancouver, a city now overflowing with White settlers from both the rail construction and the Gold Rush as well as the Chinese rail workers, whose economic utility ended with the last spike. Vancouver was in economic crisis and the Liberal government of the time was pressed to find a solution.

Mawani describes how the growing economic tensions in Vancouver targeted the Chinese population through familiar refrains of employment thievery and 'foreigners'.[30] Coupled with growing health concerns over 'Chinese leprosy', Chinese people were framed as an inferior race who brought evil temptations that would corrupt the White population and threaten the (racial) purity of the newly colonized province of British Columbia. To show support for the building of a 'White nation' and to protect a homogenous White society, settlers wore 'White Canada' ribbons and called for the deportation of Chinese people and an end to their immigration.[31] Numerous individuals, municipal politicians, and groups such as the Presbyterian Church in Canada lobbied the federal government for opium control and legislative actions to address 'social problems', usually cited as property crime, compromising the chastity of young White women, undermining Christian 'values' and also posing public health threats through overcrowding and fears of infectious diseases.[32]

On 7 September 1907, in response to fears of the 'yellow peril', the Canadian Asiatic Exclusion League with support from the Vancouver Trades and Labour Council planned a protest and parade holding banners that read 'Stand for White Canada'.[33] As the protesters marched to City Hall, unrest developed and an anti-Asian riot erupted. Following the race riots that ensued, Canadian Prime Minister Wilfrid Laurier appointed the deputy minister of the Department of Labour, William Lyon Mackenzie King, as commissioner to investigate the damages and causes of the riot.[34] In an atmosphere of racist cultural beliefs and interracial hostility, the riot had far-reaching implications, not least of which was to serve as an indicator of the fragility of whiteness that could turn subtle White supremacy into overt acts of supremacist violence, a refrain all too familiar to our present day. Over the next months, Mackenzie King met with foreign officials, including US President Theodore Roosevelt, to discuss how best to gain control of the quickly constructed opium crisis. Over the course of the investigation, the Chinese Anti-Opium League (who believed that opium was a social evil) confronted Mackenzie King about the opium problem in British Columbia.[35] According to Neil Boyd, the meeting had a major impact on the future of drug prohibition in Canada, stating 'in the course of three days government policy regarding psychoactive substances effectively changed.'[36] The most headline-grabbing case made to Mackenzie King concerned the discovery of a 15-year-old White girl in an opium den.[37] After the investigation, Mackenzie King submitted his report, *The Need for Suppression of the Opium Traffic in Canada*, advising of the harms of smoking opium and recommended the prohibition of the drug as 'the most necessary of moral reforms' to protect Canada's citizens from 'evil'.[38]

On 10 September 1908, shortly after Mackenzie King's report submission and with no debate in the House of Commons and Senate, Canada enacted its first federal narcotics law.[39] Although the ostensible purpose of the legislation centred on the criminalization of opium use, the fear and reliance on racist ideas about Chinese immigrants increased the punitive content of the Opium Act towards Chinese residents.[40] The Act passed with the implied assumption that it would not be used against White citizens by focusing on opium smoking – linked directly to Chinese men – and not on elixirs and patent medicines that contained opium, cocaine and marijuana, more commonly used by White settlers.[41] Here the importance of the character 'inherent' in the substance itself is apparent.[42] White modes of consumption (like the newly discovered hypodermic needle) were deliberately excluded from the Act, thereby ensuring that any and all social ills emerging from White addiction remained squarely concerns of the will, medicine and the already White and infirm.[43] In this sense, the Opium Act was crafted to 'carve out White spaces [preserving whiteness] exempt from more punitive approaches', while implementing and leaving intact carceral responses for drug users of Chinese descent.[44] Ultimately, the Opium Act was not about the harmful effects of opium but rather about young White women being vulnerable to Chinese men, economic disparity and fears of contamination of the White body. The benevolent whiteness of these early laws lay in the protection of whiteness through insuring punitive measures and were only extended to particular populations and, most importantly, to protect the fragile White youth from the certain pains of criminal justice.

In the 1920s, following the election of Mackenzie King as prime minister, Canada's drug laws and enforcement powers expanded with the passing of the Opium and Narcotic Drugs Act of 1920 (now including cocaine as a result of panics in Montreal and leaving the door open, through adding 'narcotic', to easily usher in new substances in the future) as well as the establishment of the Narcotic Division. Under the supervision of the Royal Canadian Mounted Police (RCMP), the newly formed Narcotic Division oversaw the enforcement of drug laws – centralizing law enforcement, legal authority and institutional power – along with local police throughout Canada.[45] Clifford Shearing argues that the establishment of the Narcotic Division played a significant role in shaping Canada's drug policy and the treatment of (criminal) addicts alongside shaping ongoing models of policing in Canada.[46]

In the same decade, Britain and the United States (under the Harrison Act, similar to the Canadian 1911 Act) created government-funded drug maintenance programmes to support people addicted to narcotics. The Narcotic Division, by contrast, strongly opposed such programmes, and instead Canada's drug policies encouraged abstinence or imprisonment for violators. Unlike alcohol, treated, as Boyd notes, as an illness and public health problem – used widely amongst White consumers – opium and narcotic addiction was a criminal behaviour matter for which there was no cure.[47] Technologies of addiction treatment were a distinctly post-Second World War phenomena in Canada. Still, inspired by what we could now think of as harm reduction measures in places like the Fens,[48] treatment for what was then understood as hysteria related to opium use (typically infused with the medical induction narrative) was available to some, exclusively White, populations.[49]

Anti-Chinese sentiments continued to rise in the early 1920s with the increasing influence of moral reformers such as Emily Murphy, one of the 'Famous Five' and Canada's first female identified magistrate. A suffragette, Murphy was one of five women who ultimately petitioned the British House of Lords to have women recognized as 'persons' under the British North America Act; she campaigned for the vote for women but also drug prohibition. Murphy's 1920 treatise *The Black Candle* provides a telling window into the emergent benevolent whiteness in whose formation Murphy played such a crucial role.[50] She ran the 'women's court' in Edmonton. It was through this court that she launched her moral campaign against Indigenous women and single mothers. Through her time on the bench, she reached the conclusion that it was the scourge of drug use, a clear flag for non-whiteness, that sat at the centre of the downfall of so many 'well-bred' girls.[51] Unlike fallen women embodied by White drug users – including sex workers and lesbians – or racialized women, White women signified hegemonic pureness, orderliness and chastity.[52] In *The Black Candle*, Murphy demonized specific drugs (including marijuana, argued to cause insanity, addiction and death), and condemned Chinese men whom she depicted as victimizing innocent White women. Chinese men, she argued, threaten not only Canadian womanhood but by extension Anglo-Saxon civilization,[53] since White women, Murphy insinuated, were the bearers of Canada's children and future.[54] As Kate Davy points out, 'white womanhood has long been understood as an ideology of White supremacy.'[55] For example, White women were, according to Murphy, the mothers of the race. Murphy states:

> It is hardly credible that the average Chinese pedlar has any definite idea in his mind of bringing about the downfall of the white race, his swaying motive being probably that of greed but in the hands of his superiors, he may become a powerful instrument to this very end … whatever their motive, the traffic always comes with the Oriental, and that one would, therefore, be justified in assuming that it was their desire to injure the bright-browed races of the world.[56]

Murphy did not limit her xenophobia to the Chinese: 'Some of the Negroes coming into Canada, and they are no fiddle-faddle fellows either, have similar ideas [the downfall of the White race] and one of their greatest writers has boasted how ultimately they will control the white men.'[57]

One can only wonder if Murphy, herself a well-educated woman, had encountered the ideas of Du Bois. For Murphy, whiteness is both powerful and fragile; thus whiteness must be protected from the foreign 'Other'.[58] By reframing the opium crisis as a threat to national identity, whiteness – not drug consumption – becomes the issue. Here we see that the threat to whiteness, articulated through the focus on race (non-White Chinese men), was mobilized as a danger to Canadian society in a time of economic and social anxiety; social times were indeed changing rapidly in ways that Murphy wanted and in ways she abhorred. The expulsion of Chinese men was presented as an antidote to White fragility. As a result, early drug prohibition discourse, couched in racist beliefs of the 'Other', produced what needed to be secured – that is, whiteness and Canadian national identity. Murphy genders benevolent whiteness. For the small cost of Chinese extermination, Emily Murphy and her contemporaries could 'save' the wayward white women from the unscrupulous Chinese. The point was these women were not criminals, merely victims of racial contamination.

The drug and race panic created by Murphy and other moral reformers put pressure on the federal government to implement stricter and harsher drug and immigration laws. By 1923, Chinese drug users were regarded as a moral contagion and thus, with the enactment of the Chinese Exclusion Act, further measures were taken to regulate the immigration of Chinese people to Canada. The Act enforced stricter drug laws for violators of Chinese descent and prevented Chinese people from entering Canada. In addition, with little public debate or interest, marijuana was added to the Opium and Narcotic Drug Act, which included the provision that immigrants convicted of possession and selling of drugs could be deported.[59] It was not until 1938, during the marijuana scare in the United States, that the government turned its attention back to the criminalization of marijuana with the amendment of the Opium and Narcotic Drug Act, enforcing stronger penalties for unauthorized cultivation of hemp.[60] The marijuana scare faded from political attention following the start of the Second World War, and it was not until the mid-1960s that it re-entered public discourse.

Benevolent whiteness and the carceral state

The post-Second World War period adopted a medical model of punishment,[61] consequently, punitive responses to drug use were called into question while national resolve to maintain punitive control of the drug trade remained intact. Ernest E. Winch, a member of British Columbia's provincial legislature, argued that Canada should adopt the 'British system' or a narcotic maintenance treatment approach that included prescribing heroin and morphine to people addicted to narcotics, rather than punishment.[62] Winch was not alone in his ideas. In 1952, the Ranta report, *Drug Addiction in Canada: The Problem and Its Solution*, released by a group of experts in Vancouver, recommended that drug policies should move away from criminal sanctions – arguing that incarceration would not solve drug use or trafficking – to a health perspective by treating drug addiction as a medical problem. The report urged the federal government to establish narcotic clinics to address and find remedies for drug addiction.[63] The federal government and the RCMP rejected all recommendations, including other international and national reports supporting similar approaches.[64] Dr George Stevenson (a psychiatrist at the University of British Columbia who led studies on heroin users at the Oakalla Prison Farm) supported the RCMP's rejection – calling for total abstinence enforcement – and publicly voiced that people who use drugs were addicts with personality disorders; thus, narcotic clinics would not help.

The landscape of drug control in Canada, as a result of these post-war changes, looks only partly reformed. Drug laws have fluctuated in severity with their present punity comparable to Australia or the UK. Mandatory minimum sentences and the aftermath of a decade of 'tough on crime' strategies led to a massive rise in incarceration rates, almost solely related to drug offences. White people are the only underrepresented group in the prison system. Hopeful immigrants and refugee claimants are regularly detained and deported for drug charges. At the same time, the thread of public health runs strong both within and outside prison walls. Far from correcting health and social concerns coterminous with drug use (and poverty), these interventions maintain a toehold in criminal justice as criminalization remains an ever-present threat for those participating in state-sanctioned treatment.

Further, this adoption of the medical model served to amplify the powers of criminal justice. The Oakalla Prison Farm serves as a clear example of the benevolent whiteness that remains stuck[65] to users and substances. Oakalla was the first therapeutic community prison in Canada. Coutts sums up the penality of Oakalla in her study of the women's unit: 'The prison has five primary tasks: custody, internal order, self-maintenance, punishment and reformation. Verbal priority is given to reformation, but custody and internal order take precedence in actual practice.'[66]

Coutts's observations lay the foundation for contemporary benevolent whiteness. The carceral response is justified on the basis that prisons can offer 'more', especially in terms of reforming the individual. Addiction treatment is a major focus of these reforms, as Oakalla was generally accepted to be the addict's prison though the intentionality of building in an addiction focus was nowhere near as deliberate as the establishment of the Narcotic Farm in Lexington. Still, Oakalla represented the needed face saving during a political era in which the use of incarceration and its racist tendencies were increasingly coming under scrutiny.[67] The penitentiary was, after all, built to reform people. This notion of reform (and its rebirth as rehabilitation) set a script of Protestant redemption through a narrative of what it means to be 'good' embedded in a meta-narrative of doing good. Incarcerating addicts was not punitive, it was benevolent. It also marked the start of an explosion of therapeutic community prisons in Canada, almost all of them oriented to addictions.

An industrial complex of benevolent whiteness emerged from these basic mentalities. A group of psychologists began work in the 1970s on the actuarial model of risk/need assessments. James Bonta and D. A. Andrews's *The Psychology of Criminal Conduct* (PCC) became the bible of penal-based treatment and set out a model for understanding and treating criminality that has now been exported around the world.[68] Actuarialism is another foundational tool of contemporary benevolent whiteness. The promise of the actuarial tools developed by Andrews and Bonta and their followers was to accurately assess the risks posed by an individual as well as their individual 'needs', as defined by what is needed in order to curtail future criminal behaviour.

This actuarial model promises efficient and effective punishment and rehabilitation through evidence-based assessment tools. Addiction/substance use is one of the seven 'criminogenic' factors identified by Andrews and Bonta, and the discovery of an individual's 'need' for addiction treatment is nothing less than rote. The tools themselves are designed in such a way as to guarantee the finding of a substance-use problem.

Scholars of actuarialism were quick to critique the empirical promises of truth and reliability attached to the PCC.[69] While PCC's champions were holding it up as a way to make meaningful differences in the lives of people in conflict with the law, critics of actuarialism pointed to faulty logics of the regime.[70] Standardization lies at the centre of this critique. The actuarial tools deployed in the establishment of a risk/need profile reflected the experiences of the majority of the prison system. While Canadian incarceration rates maintain overrepresentation in familiar ways, the population is still overwhelmingly White and male. The baseline population then, either empirically or representationally, inscribed norms of whiteness into the assessment tools. The effect here was staggering and became the subject of at least one human rights complaint and many lawsuits. Women and non-White people were disproportionately ranked as higher need and thus higher risk. When held up against an unacknowledged baseline of male whiteness, any deviation becomes dangerous. Non-White and female prisoners were being held in higher security, for longer periods and with less chance of gaining parole and a higher chance of suffering institutional punishments because their behaviours could not meet the standard of whiteness established in the tools.

These critiques bore out in the successful human rights complaint launched by the Canadian Association of Elizabeth Fry Societies in 2004. The complaint cited sex- and race-based discrimination and revealed that the actuarial tools were targeting women, and especially Indigenous women, disproportionally. Still, these tools were a commodity of the broader, benevolent project of rehabilitation that forms the basis for popular conceptions of Canadian criminal justice. After all, a nation so invested in helping people could not possibly harm them at the same time. Punishment and rehabilitation, however erroneously, are imagined to be antithetical.

To this day, treatment remains entrenched in the Canadian criminal justice system. Canada pioneered drug treatment courts (a distinctly different cousin to the American drug courts – not the absence of treatment) that continue to serve as a post-plea social services triage mainly for racialized peoples who will never successfully complete the programme.[71] Even Canada's seemingly progressive legal exception allowing for safe injection sites comes with the stick of criminal justice and treatment.

In July 2000, the Ontario Court of Appeal ruled that the prohibition of cannabis violated the *Charter of Rights and Freedoms*, forcing the federal government to reconsider its policy on the medical use of cannabis in *R. v. Parker*. One year later, the federal government responded by implementing the *Marihuana Medical Access Regulations* – later ruled unconstitutional by the Supreme Court of Canada for failing to provide a legal source of marijuana to patients – making Canada the first country to adopt a system regulating the medicinal use of marijuana. In April 2002, the Senate Special Committee on Illegal Drugs issued a paper on cannabis, which challenged long-standing myths and drug prohibition policies.[72] In the same year, without federal approval, two supervised injection sites opened in Vancouver (Insite and the Dr. Peter Centre).

Again, Canada looks good and progressive. But the apparent progress of *Parker* must be tempered with the troubling decisions in *R. v. Clay* (2003) and *R. v. Malmo-Levine* (2003). Heard in the same year, both cases challenged the Controlled Drugs and Substances Act scheduling of marijuana on the grounds that denying access to a recreational substance was an infringement of s. 7 *Charter of Rights and Freedoms* right to life, liberty and security of person. The argument in *Clay* focused in part on the notion that facing imprisonment for engaging in harmless leisure activity was an affront to basic human rights.

Then Chief Justice McLaughlin writes for the majority: 'The liberty right within s. 7 of the *Charter* touches the core of what it means to be an autonomous human being blessed with dignity and independence in matters that can properly be characterized as fundamentally or inherently personal. This does not include smoking marihuana for recreation.'[73]

The court justifies its reasoning here in denying the right to 'self-intoxicate' as part of an inherent right to privacy and liberty. This is an odd conclusion to be sure and its direct clash with laws around alcohol, tobacco and all manner of pharmaceuticals is never considered. McLaughlin CJ continues on to reason that removing marijuana possession from the Controlled Drugs and Substances Act would promote further harm, insofar as

> The members of at least some of the vulnerable groups and chronic users could not be identified in advance. In any event, the effects of a psychoactive drug like marihuana on users in the acute phase, where for example operation of motor vehicles or other complex machinery by any user constitutes a public danger, provide a rational basis for extending the prohibition to all users.[74]

While she never identifies these 'vulnerable groups', they have become the ground zero for ongoing resistance to marijuana legalization. As we write this, the Cannabis Act received Royal Assent on 21 June 2018 and was poised to become law on 17 October, a few months later than the promised legalization date of 1 July. The delays were due in large part to concerns in two areas. First, emerging largely from the medical community, worries were raised about the impact of marijuana, especially on the teenage brain. Second, voiced largely by law enforcement, were concerns over driving under the influence and maintaining a control over the drug trade.

For its part, the Liberal government who put forward the bill justifies it as follows,

> Canada's current system of marijuana prohibition does not work. It does not prevent young people from using marijuana and too many Canadians end up with criminal records for possessing small amounts of the drug.
>
> Arresting and prosecuting these offenses is expensive for our criminal justice system. It traps too many Canadians in the criminal justice system for minor, non-violent offenses. At the same time, the proceeds from the illegal drug trade support organized crime and greater threats to public safety, like human trafficking and hard drugs.
>
> To ensure that we keep marijuana out of the hands of children, and the profits out of the hands of criminals, we will legalize, regulate, and restrict access to marijuana.
>
> We will remove marijuana consumption and incidental possession from the Criminal Code, and create new, stronger laws to punish more severely those who provide it to minors, those who operate a motor vehicle while under its influence, and those who sell it outside of the new regulatory framework.
>
> We will create a federal/provincial/territorial task force, and with input from experts in public health, substance abuse, and law enforcement, will design a new system of strict marijuana sales and distribution, with appropriate federal and provincial excise taxes applied.[75]

Despite the declaration to legalize cannabis consumption and possession, the new Cannabis Act does not stray from the criminalization of cannabis; it merely insures that the right populations will be criminalized. Whiteness was protected under the old laws through both the implementation of MME (Medical Marijuana Exemptions) and uneven law enforcement. The new laws continue to protect whiteness by insuring that any threats to whiteness (that is, the mythological fear of increasing consumption amongst youth) especially through biopolitical worries about damaging the White brain, are met with stark reprisal (the rising of sanctions against those caught selling to youth). The point is made apparent in comparing the Cannabis Act's penalties for selling to youth with those of laws governing alcohol and tobacco. The Cannabis Act includes maximum sentences of up to 14 years in prison for selling to a minor or growing more cannabis plants than otherwise authorized (four is the current limit). By comparison, selling tobacco or alcohol to a minor, shown to be much more harmful, carries fines up to $10,000 and (for the sale of alcohol) up to one year in jail.[76] Young people (age 12–18) would also face criminal penalties if found possessing more than five grams of cannabis.

Unlike the United States, Canada does not collect and release race and crime statistics, making it difficult for researchers to access official data on people's race and reasons why people are stopped and searched by the police.[77] Despite this lack of data, research conducted in Montreal and Toronto shows that street youth, particularly racialized youth, are more likely to be stopped and searched, and receive more fines for minor offences, increasing their risk of incarceration.[78] Other studies show that particularly in western parts of Canada, Indigenous people are shown to be frequent targets of racial profiling.[79] Similarly, research conducted in Colorado since the decriminalization of cannabis shows that enforcement related to cannabis use still disproportionately affects racialized people. Already, the Canadian federal government has promised to flow funds to provinces to increase police budgets so that they can take measures to enforce the Cannabis Act. Accompanying the Cannabis Act, Parliament also passed the Impaired Driving Act, introducing stiffer penalties for anyone driving under the influence of marijuana. More abuse of police power will have detrimental effects on racialized people. In this sense, the prevailing carceral enforcement regime for drug possession and use of cannabis, under the Act, may continue to serve as a gateway drug – to the school-to-prison pipeline – for young marginalized users.[80]

In fact, in advance of legalization, Canada has still not decriminalized cannabis, and law enforcement continues to arrest (marginalized) people for the sale and possession of cannabis while carefully self-policed, (marked as) responsible dispensaries operate in a legal blackout, selling high-end designer cannabis products under the guise of medical need. This means that those with access to an educated physician willing to provide a MME have quality marijuana readily available in some cities, for a price. The dispensaries themselves continue to exist at the pleasure of the local police, assigning the shop owners to be responsible for regulating out potentially undesirable clientele.

Similar to the Opium Act of 1908, which restricted opium use and production to elixirs and patent medicine used mainly by White consumers, the new Act also restricts the production of cannabis to certain subjects. A licence to grow cannabis is expensive. To date, licensed cannabis producers (for medical purposes) must grow indoors and are required to have high-security measures, such as secure fencing, reinforced walls and CCTV monitoring.[81] Small individual producers and dispensaries may not have access to the funds (for example, bank credit) to meet such requirements. Furthermore, the government has stated that, under the current Act, it will refuse to issue licences to sell and produce cannabis to anyone who has a prior conviction or is believed to have contravened the Controlled Drugs and Substances Act or the Food and Drugs Act in the past ten years (article 17 of the Act). Since racialized people are more frequently targeted, convicted and arrested for crimes,[82] Black, Indigenous and people of colour will be disproportionately excluded from the legal production and sale of medical or recreational marijuana. As a result, the Act helps the government to continue to hide behind its benevolent whiteness and neoliberal ideology, blaming deviant behaviour as a justification to reject subjects from social and economic inclusion, rather than seeing excluded subjects, and the spaces they inhabit as already embedded in social, political and economic disadvantage. The criminal ban also ensures that those with experience in cultivation are less likely to be the ones able to capitalize on the proposed legislation. Instead, as is currently occurring, the now extremely lucrative market for marijuana regulation is being taken over by the pharmaceutical industry.[83]

Research conducted in Washington also shows that since cannabis is taxed heavily, access to legal marijuana may not be affordable for poor and low-income minority populations.[84] Marginalized subjects may still turn to the black market that remains criminalized, thereby excluding them from both the selling and buying of legal marijuana.[85] As a result, despite legalization, criminal sanctions around marijuana usage will continue to disproportionately affect racial minorities and criminalized subjects, while wealthy (mostly White) entrepreneurs and consumers benefit from legalization. Yet this phenomenon is not new. Courtwright shows that governments and wealthy individuals throughout history have found creative ways to circumvent and cultivate profit versus prohibition, and that legalization or decriminalization has served the interests of the wealthy and powerful.[86] Cannabis production and consumption, under the new Act, thus straddles the boundaries of economic and moral inclusion and exclusion by creating morally proper (White) subjects, who can freely produce and use, and immoral (racialized) subjects, who continue to be excluded from social advances and economic gains of production.

While the federal government stated that the current enforcement of laws surrounding marijuana disproportionally impacts minority communities[87] – making race a central issue – the government's plan to decriminalize some parts of the sale and possession of cannabis leaves intact much of the architecture of racialized surveillance and punishment.[88] Yet by making race a central issue of the Cannabis Act, the current government appears progressive and is seen to be addressing racialized inequality – fitting in with Canada's benevolent whiteness narrative – while at the same time producing racialized subjects that are governed in other ways. At the same time, there are numerous debates and media reports about growing racial inequality across the United States, underlying anxieties about White fragility in Canada which go unspoken. Canada is seen to have progressed, it has moved on, racism lies in the past, 'in another time (centuries ago), or in another place (the United States)'.[89] The Cannabis Act, guided by racial biopolitics, is visible and in plain sight, but it is obscured by Canada's benevolent statehood and reputation as an upholder of human rights that is committed to liberalism, multiculturalism and equality.

The Cannabis Act is the teleological signature of benevolent whiteness. A tacit recognition that racial injustice might be written into extant laws, the face value of the law suggests a correction. Still, law reform cannot escape White fragility and so the White youth must yet again be protected by insuring that those who attempt to interfere with their superiority will be punished. That factors such as hunger, stress, exposure to violence and lack of attentive education might also contribute to encumbered adolescent brain development is notably absent from the debate. These, after all, are not signifiers of whiteness and thus of no great concern. What is presented as an Act of social justice ultimately extends the power of law further into the lives of the vulnerable (not in McLaughlin's sense of the term).

Conclusion

Whiteness as a colonial project can be described as a grand narrative only so far. Colonialism manifests in different ways, some less obvious than others. Re-reading both historical and contemporary attempts to regulate substances in Canada with the starting point of whiteness as the problem to be managed has something to teach us about the particular ways in which whiteness emerges and sustains itself as a mechanism for

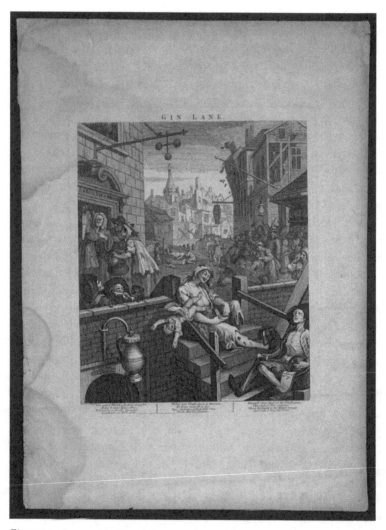

Figure 1.1

governance. Specifically, we shed light on benevolent whiteness, a trope of superiority and protectionism that relies on the blending of health and criminal discourses in order to selectively apply criminal justice while simultaneously making it appear as though even the violence of criminal law may well be in someone's 'best interest'.

There is a political importance to recognizing the iterations of whiteness particular to Canada. Canada is perceptually good. This is a sentiment we encounter even in the most 'progressive' of international spaces. The comparator of the United States makes the project of revealing Canada's particular expressions of colonial violence difficult to identify. While we can point to explicit racisms of the past such as the Indian Act and the Opium Act, the cloak of benevolence is thickening, making it hard to see the tropes of White supremacy that lie beneath.

Notes

1 See Virginia Berridge, *Demons* (Oxford: Oxford University Press, 2013); H. Wayne Morgan, *Drugs in America: A Social History, 1800–1980* (Syracuse, NY: Syracuse University Press, 1981), and David F. Musto, *The American Disease: Origins of Narcotics Control* (New Haven, CT: Yale University Press 1973).

2 Ruth Frankenberg, *White Women, Race Matters: The Social Construction of Whiteness* (Minneapolis, MN: University Of Minnesota Press, 1993). Although, scholars such as Mike Hill point out that in an era of pushback against globalization where Whites feel 'anachronistic and displaced', whiteness is now an increasingly marked category: Mike Hill (ed.), *Whiteness: A Critical Reader* (New York: New York University Press, 1997), p. 173.

3 David R. Roediger, *The Wages of Whiteness: Race and the Making of the American Working Class* (London: Verso, 1991); Hill (ed.), *Whiteness*.

4 Thomas K. Nakayama and Robert L. Krizek, 'Whiteness: A strategic rhetoric', *Quarterly Journal of Speech* 81.3 (1995): 291–309.

5 Robin DiAngelo, 'White fragility', *International Journal of Critical Pedagogy* 3.3 (2011): 54–70 (p. 56).

6 Frantz Fanon, *Black Skin, White Masks*, trans. Charles Lam Markmann (New York: Grove Press, 1967).

7 Robin DiAngelo, *White Fragility: Why It's So Hard for White People to Talk About Racism* (Boston, MA: Beacon Press, 2018), p. 2.

8 According to the Canadian Centre for Justice Statistics, 2018, while Indigenous people make up only around 4 per cent of Canadian society, they are over-represented in correctional services by 28 per cent. This figure is even more troubling for Indigenous youth who account for 8 per cent of the general youth population in Canada but accounted for 46 per cent of admissions to correctional services in 2016/2017: Jamil Malakieh, 'Adult and youth correctional statistics in Canada, 2016/2017', 28 June 2018, www150.statcan.gc.ca/n1/pub/85-002-x/2018001/article/54972-eng.htm [accessed 12 November 2018].

9 Michelle Alexander, *The New Jim Crow: Mass Incarceration in the Age of Colorblindness* (New York: The New Press, 2012); Carl Hart, *High Price: A*

Neuroscientist's Journey of Self-Discovery That Challenges Everything You Know About Drugs and Society (New York: Harper, 2013); Loïc Wacquant, Punishing the Poor: The Neoliberal Government of Social Insecurity (Durham, NC: Duke University Press, 2009).

10 W. E. B. Du Bois, 'The souls of white folk', in Darkwater: Voices from Within the Veil (New York: Harcourt, Brace and Howe, 1920), p. 29.

11 Du Bois, 'The souls of white folk', p. 30.

12 Sara Ahmed, 'A phenomenology of whiteness', Feminist Theory 8.2 (2007): 149–168 (p. 165).

13 John Murray Gibbon, Canadian Mosaic: The Making of a Northern Nation (Toronto: McClelland & Stewart, 1938); Robyn Maynard, Policing Black Lives: State Violence in Canada from Slavery to the Present (Halifax and Winnipeg: Fernwood, 2017).

14 Eva Mackey, The House of Difference: Cultural Politics and National Identity in Canada (Toronto: University of Toronto Press, 2002).

15 Kristin Lozanski, 'Memory and the impossibility of whiteness in colonial Canada', Feminist Theory 8.2 (2007): 223–225.

16 Dionne Brand, Thirsty (Toronto: McClelland & Stewart, 2002).

17 Bruno Latour, We Have Never Been Modern, trans. Catherine Porter (Cambridge, MA: Harvard University Press, 1993); Dawn Moore, Criminal Artefacts: Governing Drugs and Users (Vancouver: UBC Press, 2007).

18 Neil Boyd, 'The origins of Canadian narcotics legislation: The process of criminalization in historical context', Dalhousie Law Journal 8 (1984): 102–136; P. J. Giffen, Shirley Endicott and Sylvia Boorman, Panic and Indifference: The Politics of Canada's Drug Laws (Ottawa: Canadian Centre on Substance Abuse, 1991); W. Peter Ward, White Canada Forever: Popular Attitudes and Public Policy towards Orientals, third edn (Montreal and Kingston: McGill-Queen's University Press, 2002).

19 University of Saskatchewan Native Law Centre, Liquor Offences under the Indian Act, Report No. 19 (1983), p. 2.

20 Bill-Ray Belcourt, 'Animal bodies, colonial subjects: (Re)locating animality in decolonial thought', Societies 5.1 (2014): 1–11; Glen Sean Coulthard, Red Skin, White Masks: Rejecting the Colonial Politics of Recognition (Minneapolis, MN: University of Minnesota Press, 2014); Mackey, House of Difference.

21 Renisa Mawani, '"Half-breeds," racial opacity, and geographies of crime: Law's search for the "original" Indian', Cultural Geographies 17.4 (2010): 487–506; Mariana Valverde, The Age of Light, Soap, and Water: Moral Reform in English Canada, 1885–1925 (Toronto: McClelland & Stewart, 1991).

22 See Elizabeth Einberg and Judy Egerton, The Age of Hogarth: Vol. 2: British Painters Born 1675–1709 (London: The Tate Gallery, 1988).

23 Valverde, Age of Light.

24 Einberg and Egerton, Age of Hogarth.

25 Roediger, Wages of Whiteness.

26 Boyd, 'Origins'.

27 Susan Boyd, Busted: An Illustrated History of Drug Prohibition in Canada (Halifax and Winnipeg: Fernwood, 2017).

28 Valverde, Age of Light.

29 See Erich Goode and Nachman Ben-Yehuda, 'Moral panics: Culture, politics, and social construction', Annual Review of Sociology 20 (1994): 149–171.

30 Mawani, '"Half-breeds"'.

31 Ward, *White Canada Forever*.

32 Giffen et al., *Panic and Indifference*.

33 John Price, *Orienting Canada: Race, Empire and the Transpacific* (Vancouver: UBC Press, 2011); Ward, *White Canada Forever*.

34 Giffen et al., *Panic and Indifference*; Price, *Orienting Canada*.

35 Giffen et al., *Panic and Indifference*.

36 Boyd, 'Origins'.

37 Giffen et al., *Panic and Indifference*.

38 W. L. Mackenzie King, 'Report on the need for the suppression of the opium traffic in Canada. Printed by order of Parliament' (Ottawa: Printed by S. E. Dawson, 1908), p. 9. See also Giffen et al., *Panic and Indifference*, and Boyd, *Busted*.

39 Giffen et al., *Panic and Indifference*.

40 Shirley J. Cook, 'Canadian narcotics legislation, 1908–1923: A conflict model interpretation', *Canadian Review of Sociology/Revue canadienne de sociologie* 6.1 (1969): 36–46; Boyd, *Busted*.

41 Robert Solomon, and Melvyn Green, 'The first century: The history of non-medical opiate use and control policies in Canada, 1870–1970', in Judith C. Blackwell and Patricia G. Erickson (eds), *Illicit Drugs in Canada: A Risky Business* (Scarborough, Ont.: Nelson Canada, 1988), pp. 88–104.

42 Boyd, *Busted*; Giffen et al., *Panic and Indifference*.

43 Moore, *Criminal Artefacts*.

44 Julie Netherland and Helena Hansen, 'White opioids: Pharmaceutical race and the war on drugs that wasn't', *Biosocieties* 12.2 (2017): 217–238 (p. 218).

45 Boyd, *Busted*; Giffen et al., *Panic and Indifference*.

46 Clifford Shearing, 'Nodal security', *Police Quarterly* 8.1 (2005): 57–63.

47 Boyd, *Busted*; Ward, *White Canada Forever*.

48 Berridge, *Demons*.

49 Giffen et al., *Panic and Indifference*.

50 Emily F. Murphy, *The Black Candle* (Toronto: Thomas Allen, 1922).

51 Murphy, *The Black Candle*.

52 Kimberlé Crenshaw, 'Whose story is it anyway? Feminist and antiracist appropriations of Anita Hill', in Toni Morrison (ed.), *Race-ing Justice, En-Gendering Power: Essays on Anita Hill, Clarence Thomas, and the Construction of Social Reality* (New York: Pantheon Books, 1992), pp. 402–440; See also Hill (ed.), *Whiteness*.

53 Catherine Carstairs, 'Deporting "Ah Sin" to save the white race: Moral panic, racialization, and the extension of Canadian drug laws in the 1920s', *Canadian Bulletin of Medical History/Bulletin Canadien d'Histoire de la Medecine* 16.1 (1999): 65–88; Catherine Carstairs, *Jailed for Possession: Illegal Drug Use, Regulation, and Power in Canada, 1920–1961* (Toronto: University of Toronto Press, 2006); Giffen et al., *Panic and Indifference*; Murphy, *The Black Candle*.

54 Anne McClintock, *Imperial Leather: Race, Gender, and Sexuality in the Colonial Contest* (New York: Routledge, 1995).

55 Kate Davy, 'Outing whiteness: A feminist lesbian project' in Hill (ed.), *Whiteness*, p. 213.

56 Murphy, *The Black Candle*, p. 188.

57 Murphy, *The Black Candle*, p. 189.

58 Edward Said, *Orientalism* (New York: Random House, 1978).

59 Another force behind the prohibition of cannabis was the lobbying of cotton-growers (for paper and textiles) in the US, who feared the hemp plant might create competition. See Barney Warf, 'High points: An historical geography of cannabis', *Geographical Review* 104.4 (2014): 414–438.

60 Reginald Whitaker, *Drugs and The Law: The Canadian Scene* (Toronto: Methuen, 1969).

61 See Moore, *Criminal Artefacts*.

62 Giffen et al., *Panic and Indifference*.

63 Boyd, *Busted*.

64 Gordon H. Josie, *A Report on Drug Addiction in Canada* (Ottawa: Edmond Cloutier, 1948); Alfred R. Lindesmith, *Opiate Addiction* (Bloomington, IN: Principia Press, 1947).

65 Ahmed, 'Phenomenology of whiteness'.

66 Dorothy Mae Coutts, 'An examination of the social structure of the women's unit, Oakalla Prison Farm'. Unpublished MA diss., University of British Columbia (1961), p. 1.

67 Boyd, 'Origins'.

68 James Bonta, and D. A. Andrews, *The Psychology of Criminal Conduct*, sixth edn (London and New York: Routledge, 2016).

69 See, for example, Kelly Hannah-Moffat and Pat O'Malley (eds), *Gendered Risks* (New York: Routledge, 2007); Malcolm M. Feeley and Jonathan Simon, 'The new penology: Notes on the emerging strategy of corrections and its implications', *Criminology* 30.4 (1992): 449–474.

70 Hannah-Moffat and O'Malley (eds), *Gendered Risks*; Feeley and Simon, 'The new penology'.

71 Moore, *Criminal Artefacts*.

72 Colin Kenny and Pierre C. Nolin, *Cannabis: Our Position for a Canadian Public Policy: Report of the Senate Special Committee on Illegal Drugs* (Ottawa: Senate Special Committee on Illegal Drugs, 2002).

73 *R v Clay* [2003] SCC 75, p. 736.

74 *R v Clay* [2003] SCC 75, p. 736.

75 Liberal Party of Canada, *Marijuana* (2014), www.liberal.ca/realchange/marijuana/ [accessed 6 August 2018].

76 Today, the sale, possession and consumption of tobacco and alcohol are legally regulated rather than criminalized in Canada. According to Susan Boyd and other scholars, this is mostly due to commercial interests and the wide use of alcohol and tobacco by the mostly (White) diverse population, rather than confined to racialized or marginalized groups.

77 Scot Wortley and Akwasi Owusu-Bempah, 'The usual suspects: Police stop and search practices in Canada', *Policing and Society* 21.4 (2011): 395–407.

78 Bill O'Grady, Stephen Gaetz and Kristy Buccieri, *Can I See Your ID? The Policing of Youth Homelessness in Toronto*. The Homeless Hub Report #5 (Toronto: Justice for Children and Youth, and Homeless Hub Press, 2011); Justin Douglas, 'The criminalization of poverty: Montreal's policy of ticketing homeless youth for municipal and transportation by-law infractions', *Appeal* 16.1 (2011): 49–64; Maynard, *Policing Black Lives*.

79 *Paying the Price: The Human Cost of Racial Profiling. Inquiry report* (Ontario Human Rights Commission, 2003). In November 2017, the Ontario Human

Rights Commission announced that it would launch an investigation into racial profiling and racial discrimination by the Toronto Police Service.

80 Steven W. Bender, 'The colors of cannabis: Race and marijuana', *University of California, Davis Law Review* 50 (2016): 689–706; Maynard, *Policing Black Lives*.

81 Bender, 'Colors of cannabis'; Susan C. Boyd and Connie Carter, *Killer Weed: Marijuana Grow Ops, Media, and Justice* (Toronto: University of Toronto Press, 2014); Boyd, *Busted*.

82 Bender, 'Colors of cannabis'; Maynard, *Policing Black Lives*; Malakieh, 'Adult and youth correctional statistics in Canada'.

83 Bender, 'Colors of cannabis'; William Garriott (ed.), *Policing and Contemporary Governance: The Anthropology of Police in Practice* (New York: Palgrave Macmillan, 2013); Malakieh, 'Adult and youth correctional statistics in Canada'.

84 Bryan Adamson, 'Washington's marijuana laws and social justice: Our clinical work at Seattle University School of Law', 30 October 2015, www.linkedin.com/pulse/washingtons-marijuana-laws-social-justiceour-clinical-bryan-adamson [accessed 6 August 2018].

85 Adamson, 'Washington's marijuana laws'; Bender, 'Colors of cannabis'.

86 David Courtwright, *Forces of Habit: Drugs and the Making of the Modern World* (Cambridge, MA: Harvard University Press, 2001).

87 Ashifa Kassam, 'Justin Trudeau: Father's influence made my brother's marijuana charge "go away"', *Guardian*, 25 April 2017, www.theguardian.com/world/2017/apr/25/justin-trudeau-brother-marijuana-charge-dismissed-canada [accessed 11 March 2018].

88 Jordan T. Camp, *Incarcerating the Crisis: Freedom Struggles and the Rise of the Neoliberal State* (Oakland, CA: University of California Press, 2016); Jordan T. Camp and Christina Heatherton (eds), *Policing the Planet: Why the Policing Crisis Led to Black Lives Matter* (London and New York: Verso, 2016); Maynard, *Policing Black Lives*.

89 Maynard, *Policing Black Lives*, pp. 9–10.

2

Policing the 'Black party': racialized drugs policing at festivals in the UK

Tanzil Chowdhury[1]

'How many drugs did you lot seize in the run up to Glastonbury or we only doing tweets like this for black events?'

Stormzy[2]

This chapter examines the features of antonymous drug policing strategies in two popular cultural and music events – Notting Hill Carnival (NHC) and the Secret Garden Party (SGP) – contending that both are racialized, though differently, and that the drug policing operations used at NHC are one strand of a holistic policing stratagem disciplining events of mass, Black, politico-cultural expression. Unravelling Stormzy's acerbic and pointed tweet speaks to the starkness in these operations, particularly at festivals that are inscriptions of blackness.[3] The lauded music artist was responding to a photograph tweeted by the Metropolitan Police[4] in which they claimed to have seized a kilogram of uncut heroin in the run-up to Carnival. This was part of a coordinated series of pre-emptive raids undertaken in 2016 within Greater London that were then tenuously attributed to the forthcoming Notting Hill Carnival.[5] Notably, the raid took place in Catford, over ten miles from the carnival – antipodal within London's geography. By comparison, at Glastonbury in 2016, attended by less than a tenth of those that frequent Notting Hill Carnival, nearly four kilograms of drugs were seized by the police, though only 21 people were arrested (albeit not pre-emptively).[6] In the same year at NHC, a festival of around 1.5 million revellers, a proportionately lower number of 169 drug-related arrests were made,[7] though this did not disrupt the persistent negative media representations of the carnival – or the police perceiving a need for pre-emptive arrests. The sensationalist press response, combined with the anticipatory drug arrests that were nominally linked to NHC, all form part of the ways in which music festivals are differentially policed along racial lines. To put it plainly, music festivals with origins in or association with Black communities are subject to over-policing.

This chapter begins by detailing the respective histories of NHC and SGP. NHC, having traversed different periods – from showcasing a 'working-class poly ethnic amity'[8] to becoming a prominent signifier of West Indian identity[9] – has been fundamentally rooted in 'a process by which a group engaged in confrontation mobilises its culture and its communal relationships to coordinate its corporate action in the struggle for power'.[10] In contrast, SGP has been framed by the popular press as 'an escapist fantasy for plenty of middle-class kids … steeping them in a performative hedonism tied to fancy dress while never ambling too far from the event's aristocratic roots'.[11] The following section then details the drug policing operations deployed at the two festivals. These juxtapose over-policing deployed at NHC – characterized by pre-emption and a heavy police presence – versus a pioneering Multi-Agency Safety Testing (MAST) scheme, which allows drug users to submit samples for analysis and receive results as part of a confidential, reduction package – that was launched at SGP. The differences in drug policing strategies are initially explained by how these antonymous approaches frame drug use as a criminal justice matter and a public health/harm-reduction issue respectively. The chapter then goes on to posit that these framings are racialized. Probing the drug policing strategy at NHC is enriched by drawing insights from post-colonial theory and Gilroy's 'archaeology of representations of black law-breaking',[12] specifically its articulation through the 'Black Party'.[13] The chapter ends by arguing how these representations follow a trajectory of policing Black culture – from the disciplining of West Indian entertainment venues, house parties and shebeens,[14] to the 'risk assessment form 696' used to shut down grime raves,[15] and the recent censoring of Brixton Drill Music. Establishing the link between culture and politics illustrates how racialized drugs policing is a particularly potent strand of a holistic policing stratagem of disciplining mass, Black politico-cultural expression.

London as Babylon and 'Tree Hugging Hippy Shit':[16] the respective histories of NHC and SGP

A brief exegesis of the histories of these events is particularly important in presaging the later discussion around how the police and drug enforcement agencies construct the subjectivities of these festivals' participants and, ultimately, how this informs the conflicting drug policing strategies. While the discussion linking the politics of these festivals to their aesthetic forms is discussed later, a unique and telling feature of the history of NHC is the almost necessary entanglement of these two elements. In other words, the history and aesthetics of NHC are deeply entwined with its politics of disrupting British state repression. Indeed, 'official opposition to Carnival has been a consistent feature of its history both in Trinidad and in Britain.'[17] In contrast, issues of policing simply do not feature in any rendering that charts the development of the SGP.

While an exhaustive history[18] of NHC is neither possible nor imperative here, it is worth recalling its embryonic stages during the early 1800s in the British Colony of Trinidad. The link to the Trinidad carnival is not only relevant to the later dominance of the Carnival in the 1970s by the West Indian community and its aesthetic articulations, but also because of the repressive responses that the event invited from the British state. Prior to the abolition of slavery, the Trinidad carnival was exclusively celebrated by the elite White French colonial-settlers with Black people present only as observers.[19] It was not until the rebellions and subsequent emancipation of enslaved peoples that carnival was reclaimed as a medium of celebration. Not surprisingly, the carnival attracted the ire of the British imperial authorities, with local colonial governors passing laws limiting the playing of drums in public places and the banning of wearing masks in the street; the staple of the Black Trinidad Carnival.[20] Thus the imminence of state repression has always been intimately linked with the event.

While the first carnival in the UK was established by the radical activist and 'mother of the Caribbean Carnival in Britain', Claudia Jones, following the 1958 Notting Hill 'Race Riots' – in which White 'Teddy Boys' attacked West Indian homes – it was Rhaune Laslett, a daughter of Russian and Native Indian parents, who began what was considered the first Notting Hill Carnival. The idea originally addressed issues of structural violence[21] that impacted the community while celebrating the multi-racial complexion of the area. The logistics of planning such an event combined well with Laslett's presidency of the local London Free School, which provided the platform to mobilize the first NHC. Furthermore, the carnival was not merely a celebration of Caribbean culture, but also a struggle for urban space, with opposition to local government policies, such as housing, voiced at the event.[22] However, its tone was largely 'a caricature of the carnival in Trinidad, reflecting the organiser's perceptions of Black culture in Britain as that of a passive, fun-loving people'.[23] While it fomented some class solidarity across racial lines,[24] it was assimilationist in its normative outlook.[25] However, the carnival shifted in its control, politics and aesthetics with the arrival of a large West Indian population in the 1970s.[26] The building of the A40 flyover, which cleaved the urban geography of the area, was exploited and capitalized on by the far right in separating once harmonious multi-racial communities. The Mangrove Restaurant Case in August 1970, in which police arrested several prominent West Indian activists in a violent confrontation, was another critical juncture in the carnival's history. This compelled Laslett to try to cancel the event, but by then it had taken on a momentum of its own, consolidating the power of West Indian ownership, and the aesthetic and politics of NHC. The most recent change in the dynamic of the carnival, however, began a few years later with the ascendancy of the British-born second-generation West Indians, presaging the rise of the counter-culture movement, Rastafari and reggae music.[27] In addition to the revelry and costume of the Trinidad carnival of old, there were also overtly pan-African and Black nationalist themes.[28] Though the carnival had always attracted opposition from the authorities and local groups, NHC reached a crucial pivot in 1976. In the previous year, the carnival had been policed by 60 officers but in '76, it was patrolled by 1,200 Bobbies, and scuffles with Black youth ensued. This was a 'watershed in the history of conflict between blacks and the police',[29] marking the period of the state's rendering of collective Black criminality.[30] The British media provided a litany of largely inadequate explanations for the confrontations of 1976 but more importantly, it structured the internal politics of the carnival and the repressive state responses to it.

SGP was an infant by comparison, having started in 2004, with its final soirée in 2017. The festival initially began when its founder, the 'Head Gardener' and Etonian Freddie Fellowes, launched the 500-person strong party in Abbots Rippon, Cambridgeshire. It initially began as a private event, not announcing its location till later on, until finally opening its doors to the public in 2017. Since its inception, it has grown in capacity and popularity with their 2017 valediction attracting over 30,000 participants.

SGP billed itself as a '"professional party" for its wild hedonism, creativity, and immersive audiences in fancy dress'.[31] It drew on some of the more established music festivals in the US, such as Burning Man, shifting away from an exclusive focus on music and instead celebrating 'participatory'[32] 'mixed arts',[33] where attendees were encouraged to take ownership of the fun they had, with everything from paint fireworks and champagne fights to mud wrestling. An ethos, inscribed in its website, similarly affirmed the attendees' ownership of the party,[34] rebutting the large corporations whose logos often saturate the horizons of other festivals. Indeed, adding to the carefree, quirky and avant-garde aesthetic, SGP even subscribed to the code of conduct made during the 1889 National Hobo Convention, which largely embraces the principles of individual responsibility, civic duty and a respect for nature.[35]

There was also a prestige attached to SGP, often having been attributed as creating the template for the 'boutique festivals' market.[36] In a 2008 article in the *Independent*, Simon Usborne wrote about how 'the nation's landed gentry, ever eager to diversify as maintenance fees soar and farming profits plummet, are turning over their gardens and fields to promoters looking to buy a slice of the booming market for alternative festivals.'[37] Indeed, the site of the SGP just so happens to be at the bottom of Fellowes' father's Georgian farm land, which is the family seat of the 4th Baron de Ramsey. Another recent publication, in which it claimed that SGP 'made festivals palatable for posh people', stated that it

became an escapist fantasy for plenty of middle-class kids looking for a good time each summer ... By repackaging both participation and giddy indulgence as some sort of life-changing dream world, it transformed British festivals, steeping them in a performative hedonism tied to fancy dress while never ambling too far from the event's aristocratic roots.[38]

Thus, while the aesthetic of the festival drew from a bohemian, hippy culture with its attendant immersive and interactive décor, its material origins were firmly embedded in the aristocratic echelons. Interestingly, the contrast in the class and racial location of the two festivals' genealogies are particularly telling, as they speak to broader representations of how drug taking is framed in communities of colour – as civilizational threats, undermining the moral fabric of society – as against drug taking within (always White) English nobility – as presaging the Romantic imagination, where consumption is attributed with hedonism, mysticism, inviting voyeuristic curiosity rather than condemnation.[39] Both draw from a rich past of how racialized and classed subjects' use of drugs have typically been framed and this necessarily informs the divergent ways in which these events are policed.

Drug policing strategies: racializing public health v. criminal justice approaches

The chapter now examines how the contrasting conceptualizations of these festivals inform the differing policing strategies employed at each, especially in relation to drug supply and consumption. This section argues that despite the comparatively low level of drug arrests at NHC, the drug policing strategy deployed by law enforcement is a variant of a criminal justice model of over-policing, characterized by *pre-emption* and *saturated police presence*. Over-policing, it is argued, is deployed against racialized communities. 'Racialized policing' therefore, is the rendering of communities racialized as Black and Asian as passive, docile. Furthermore, docility is taken to mean a body that may be subjected, used, transformed and improved,[40] and is typically achieved through a strict regime and disciplinary acts. The 'justificatory discourse' for racialized over-policing is pre-figured by an 'archaeology of black law-breaking', specifically the representation of the 'black party'. This section then goes on to demonstrate how the drug policing strategy deployed by law enforcement at SGP is one framed as a public health/harm-reduction issue, where the festival's participants are 'patients not criminals'.[41] In effect, the foundations of the differential drug policing strategies are racialized such that they make presumptions about the subjectivities of the festivals' participants.

It is worth briefly trying to understand why ephemeral events, which are typically contained, attract such policing. Various studies on drug consumption have shown that people at music festivals are more likely to consume drugs.[42] Further, outdoor music festivals 'elevate drivers for use due to multiple factors, including the type of music played, the high cost of alcohol within venues, and because social bonding and connectedness is an important part of participation in music festivals'.[43] Cases of death from drug overdose or emergency room admissions, though a minority and typically embellished by a moralistic media, have also prompted such police operations. However, as it is later explained, these are certainly not the only reasons festivals such as NHC are policed in the manner in which they are.

The debate on how to respond to drug use (and, in particular, addiction) oscillates between the adoption of a criminal justice approach and those that centre public health (also known as 'harm-reduction') as the paramount orientation. The UK approach to drug use, supply and production is largely governed by two statutes. The Psychoactive

Substances Act 2016 criminalizes those who 'produce, supply or import any drug that acts on the central nervous system to change mental functioning or emotional state'. Confusingly, it is not an offence to possess substances that fall under this Act, unless it is banned under the Misuse of Drugs Act 1971. The Misuse of Drugs Act 1971 prevents the non-medicinal use[44] of potentially harmful drugs. It divides banned substances into three classes as determined 'according to their accepted dangers and harmfulness in the light of current knowledge'.[45] However, a 2016 report by the Royal Society for Public Health concluded that while attempting to protect public health, the UK's exclusive criminal justice orientation has largely failed as a deterrent to drug use, production and supply.[46]

A public health/harm-reduction approach

> refers to policies, programmes and practices that aim to reduce the harms associated with the use of psychoactive drugs in people unable or unwilling to stop ... based on the recognition that many people throughout the world continue to use psychoactive drugs despite even the strongest efforts to prevent the initiation or continued use of drugs.[47]

It thus treats drug users 'as patients, not criminals'.[48] The United Nations Office on Drugs and Crime acknowledges the 'growing recognition that treatment and rehabilitation of illicit drug users are more effective than punishment'.[49] While this certainly heralds a rhetorical shift from the criminal justice approach to framing drug use as a public health issue among some of the organs of the UN, many countries, such as Russia, Indonesia, the Philippines and the US continue to take up the prohibitive and prohibitionist criminal justice baton.[50]

Drawing from a study conducted at music festivals in Australia, the varied typologies of drug policing are identifiable: High Visibility Policing (HVP), Riot Policing (RP), Policing with Drug Detection Dogs (DDD), Collaborative Policing (CP), No Police.[51] HVP involves a high presence of plain-clothes and uniformed police. RP would be the equivalent of deploying the Police Support Unit in the UK – that is, officers who have undergone training in public order and riot control. DDD would involve the presence of so-called 'sniffer dogs' and finally, CP would involve the integration of health care professionals on site to help people suffering from drug overdoses.

Before detailing how the different approaches materialize concretely in drug policing strategies, it is worth rehearsing what the number of drug arrests made at NHC and SGP were. The table below illustrates the number of *drug arrests* based on FOI requests in the period 2014–17 at both SGP and NHC.[52] The row 'SGP (scaled up)' multiplies the number of offences to roughly correlate with the number of attendees at NHC. It takes the number of SGP attendees as 30,000 based on rough estimates of its final festival in 2017, and the number of NHC attendees as 1,500,000.

Festival	2014	2015	2016	2017
SGP	12	14	32	14
SGP (scaled up)	600	700	1600	700
NHC	85	170	169	58 (60)*

* additional arrests were made for psychoactive drug offences but were recorded as separate from 'drug offences arrests'

The chairman of the Police and Crime Committee at the London Assembly, Steve O'Connell, stated in a recent report that the positives associated with the carnival 'are overshadowed each year by the level of crimes that take place' and 'the very real risk to public safety'.[53] However, what is immediately telling from the figures is that NHC has a considerably lower proportion of drug arrests than the SGP, despite police and local state authorities claims and contestations to the contrary. Despite the lower number of drug arrests, in 2016 there were 7,000 police officers[54] occupying the carnival; as well as the pre-emptive drug arrests which are almost unique in their application to NHC. Further, a 2017 article in *VICE* magazine compared NHC to a host of other popular festivals and, after scaling up, found that without exception, NHC had fewer overall arrests. This also included Latitude Festival, voted the 'Best Family Festival' in 2012, which has an attendance roughly equal to SGP, but had twice the number of drug-related arrests.[55]

This may appear to run antithetical to the claim that drugs policing at NHC is racialized – that is, predicated on a criminal justice model – as it would have produced more drug arrests than at SGP. However, it is important to note that drug arrests only form part of the number of overall arrests and don't necessarily constitute the only manifestation of over-policing. Over-policing, as was the case at NHC, can be characterized by *pre-emption* and *saturated police presence*. Further, these figures are only illustrative once they are 'scaled up', ignore other types of arrests, and ignore the other forms of technologies and governance techniques used at NHC, such as facial recognition. What is additionally revealing as to the racialized nature of these drug policing strategies, however, is how an innovative public health-centred model was recently deployed at SGP.

In 2016, a national drug community interest company, known as 'The Loop', launched a pioneering harm-reduction programme known as Multi Agency Safety Testing (MAST) at the SGP. MAST is described as:

> a form of drug safety testing (or 'drug checking') whereby individual service users submit samples for analysis and receive their results as part of a confidential, individually tailored harm reduction package delivered by experienced substance misuse practitioners. In contrast with 'back of house' testing of police seizures and 'halfway house' testing of emergency service samples, the added value of this model of 'front of house' testing is that it facilitates a dialogue directly between individual customers and members of the Loop's harm reduction team, enabling the vital connection to be made between presumed and actual drug contents.[56]

The MAST approach was supported by the local authorities and the police and was described by The Loop's director and co-founder, Professor Fiona Measham, as the UK's first ever *de facto* decriminalized drugs space.[57]

Both these approaches can be situated within different typologies of drug policing strategies described above. The collaborative policing strategy adopted at the SGP was predicated on a progressive, public health approach and contrasted sharply with the drug policing strategy deployed at NHC, which could be said to be a combination of HVP, RP and DDD. Indeed, NHC clearly adopts an austere version of a criminal justice model, designated here as racialized drug policing that is characterized by pre-emptive arrests, facial recognition technologies, and a saturated police presence.

Commendable though it was that a more pragmatic, evidenced-based approach to drug use was deployed at SGP, it is telling that this was not piloted at a festival such as NHC. One may speculate as to the public and media response had such an approach been used at NHC.

More broadly, the tensions between the criminal justice and public health models are themselves racialized, where Black subjectivity is pathologized and White subjectivities are constructed as patients in need of care. There are rehearsals of this in the past and present. Indeed, the claims that the foundations of Nixon's 'War on Drugs', as an austere, militarized criminal justice approach to drug production, use and supply were racist have been well-documented.[58] These manifested in discriminatory enforcement, prosecution and mass incarceration under drug laws against communities of colour for low-level, non-violent drug 'crimes' and have been described as the 'new Jim Crow' in the US,[59] and the legacies of these crimes have often inhibited individuals and their ability to work or find housing.[60] Drawing useful parallels, in the UK, despite the fact that Black people use drugs less than their White counterparts, they are still six times more likely to be stopped and searched for suspected drug offences – and Black people who are arrested for cocaine possession are more likely to be charged than cautioned.[61]

Drawing from post-structuralist thought, a genealogical analysis of drugs and drug use reveals how its formation has always been racialized and therefore structured by power – whether it was Chinese men using opium to lure White women into prostitution or the cocaine-bloated 'uppity Southern blacks and race-mixing drug parties'.[62] In 2016, US President Donald Trump mobilized his administration to confront the growing opioid epidemic, providing – among other things – expanded access to telemedicine services and dislocated worker grants – a clear harm-reduction approach.[63] This can be contrasted to the crack cocaine epidemic, the majority of addicts of whom are African American, which instead produced incredibly punitive crackdowns focused on harsher prison sentences and militarized police tactics – a continuation of Nixon's aberrant war.

Drug policing at music festivals, it has been argued, is similarly racialized. The drug policing strategy deployed by law enforcement at SGP is one foundationally framed as a public health issue and takes measures to reduce the harm to 'patients' who consume drugs. NHC, in contrast, is predicated on a criminal justice model characterized by, among other things, pre-emption and saturated police presence. The next section draws insights from post-colonial theory to unravel the 'archaeology of black law-breaking' upon which NHC's racialized drug policing strategy is predicated, specifically the representation of the 'Black party'.

The 'Black party' and policing mass, Black politico-cultural expression

Gilroy claims that the 'Myth of Black Criminality'[64] is often deployed by some academics, policy makers and commentariat in attempting to explain the correlation between national decline and race. It focuses on how a 'unified national culture articulated around the theme of legality and constitution' is alleged to have been violated by 'Black criminality', illustrating how Black criminality disrupts the obedience for law and the ubiquitous threat to British culture which blackness poses.[65] His *archaeology of Black criminality* or law breaking describes how 'the representation of black crime has taken several quite different forms ... the changing pattern of portrayal as law breakers and criminals, as a dangerous class or underclass, offer an opportunity to trace the development of the new racism for which the link between crime and blackness is absolutely integral.'[66] Gilroy's focus therefore is 'concerned with the history of representations of black criminality and in particular with the elaboration of the idea that black law-breaking is an integral element in black culture'.[67] The riots at the 1976 NHC, in particular, are seen as presaging the mass criminalization of Black people and the subject-formation of 'Black youth' as implicitly male, homogenous and a hostile ground.[68] The deference to pathologizing the Black community, a bedrock of drug policing strategies at NHC, is re-articulated through different representations which are contingent on the powers that set the rules of how those subjectivities are constructed. For example, the epithet of the 'Black mugger'[69] was particularly pervasive until 'White muggers' began to be caught[70] and this consequently presaged new articulations of Black criminality.

One particularly important rendition of this archaeology is the 'Black party' which Gilroy describes as 'an entrenched sign of disorder and criminality, of a hedonistic and vicious black culture which is not recognisably British'.[71] Hedonism and dangerousness were important elements in the 'Black criminality' repertoire. Black parties and shebeens were seen as hubs of anti-police violence, when in fact, at their absolute worst, they were places that may have infringed bureaucratic licensing laws.[72] The disorderly 'Black party' discourse has had its earlier rehearsals as far back as the Trinidad carnivals of the 1800s, tying together Black musicality, sexuality and social unrest.[73] When the liberated slaves reclaimed the carnival, it caused one observer to describe it as having 'degenerated into a noisy and disorderly amusement for the lower classes'.[74] Hal Austin, in his reflections on carnival, wrote how NHC had provided the material for the book *Jungle West 11* – written about the 1958 Notting Hill Riots – in which it provides a 'sordid account of sexual promiscuity, venereal disease and illicit drug taking'.[75] Even progressive writers have veered toward a crude essentialism that reproduces this fantastical rendition of Black law breaking more generally. Indeed, Gilroy levels criticism at them, saying that even environmental explanations of 'Black criminality' and the policing it attracted were underwritten by latent racisms that parroted reactionary representations of indifferent familial structures within the West Indian household.[76] Even Cohen, while deeply sympathetic to the carnival, at times toed the line of the 'Black party' by saying how the West Indians generally loved loud pop music and were used to staying up until the early hours of the morning.[77]

Interestingly, while the Black community were accustomed to 'culturally expressing themselves' privately during the 1950s, '60s and '70s,[78] this did not immunize them from police harassment, whether in the shebeens, house parties, or eating venues. Frank Crichlow's Mangrove Restaurant, for example, was the beating heart of the West Indian community in Notting Hill, as well as being a thriving nexus for activists and intellectuals from the surrounding area. However, it was also the target of 12 raids in 19 months. The police rehearsed the fiction that the restaurant was a 'drug den', despite fruitless raids producing no evidence to validate their claims. Similar examples included the Metro 4, the Swan Disco 7,[79] the New Cross Fire in 1981, the Four Aces Club, the Burning Spear Club or the Carib Club, in which 13 people were violently arrested and charged following raids by the police.[80] More contemporary examples provide further coordinates that extended this trajectory. The 'Risk Assessment Form 696', a document that used to be issued by the Metropolitan Police to request information about performers and audience members at gigs,[81] were accused of targeting garage and grime events.[82] The original form asked 'Is there a particular ethnic group attending? If "yes", please state group.' It also required the genre of music to be stated as well as details of the musicians. Several weeks later, the question stating ethnicity of audience members had been removed. While the forms were removed in 2017, similar attacks on the Chicago-inspired, Brixton-born Drill Music – considered the 'new sound of the disenfranchised as they make sense of a neglectful nation'[83] – have emerged following a spate of knife attacks in Greater London. The Metropolitan Police Commissioner Cressida Dick blamed the rise in violent crime on the genre and had YouTube remove over thirty videos.

These renditions of the 'Black party' – which are part of the mythological 'Black law-breaking' taxonomy – upon which the racialized drug policing strategy at NHC is predicated, are in fact one strand of *disciplining mass, Black, politico-cultural expression.*[84] What is meant by 'politico-cultural expression' is not a reductionist rendering of a cultural superstructure to an economic base but explains how politics and culture are mediated through a dialectical relation.[85] Cohen explains the reciprocity between culture and politics that underwrites NHC:

Carnival is discussed as a two-dimensional movement, involving a continual interplay between cultural forms and political relations. Cultural forms are evolved to express the sentiments and identity of people who come together as a result of specific economic-political conditions and at the same time they serve to mobilise other people as well. These in turn develop more elaborate cultural forms.[86]

While the structural incongruity[87] of NHC has historically allowed it to oscillate between ambivalence to the state or resistance to it,[88] Pryce swings to the latter, describing carnival as

the two days of the year when black people in the United Kingdom consider themselves to be in the majority. It is essentially an occasion when black people come together to assert their presence culturally, politically, socially, and, if needs be, violently, in symbolic affirmation of the mood of agitation endemic to the existence of black people in an overwhelmingly white milieu.[89]

The 'politics' of carnival, therefore, comes not *just* from the overt expressions critiquing structural violence, or the piercing command of reggae lyricism, or the Black youth resistance to police violence in 1976, but also in the very aesthetic form itself. Indeed, Jackson describes how the *Carnivalization of Life* is resented by the force of law and order and how the aesthetic form sits 'outside of and contrary to all existing forms of the coercive socioeconomic and political organisation'.[90] Carnival then is a flouting of these socially constructed boundaries which are reified as 'normative'. NHC is, by its very nature, disruptive, in that it produces mass Black space in public. It provides the grounds to explore 'the intersection of culture and politics in the creation of a specific geography of protest or resistance'.[91] Indeed, the Trinidad carnival was a potent symbol of Black resistance, emancipation and triumph and NHC shares in that ancestry.

Conclusion

Drug policing strategies at festivals can illustrate how antonymous approaches are oriented around racialized subjectivities, where Black subjectivities are pathologized as criminals, while White subjectivities are constructed as hedonistic patients, posing no threat to the moral fabric of society and in need of care. Indeed, SGP draws from a long association between hedonism, Romanticism and aristocracy in the English cultural memory[92] and, like Henri Bergson's *durée*, this memory cannot be disconnected from the present representations and strategies that constitute the types of drug policing strategies deployed at such festivals. These representations of Dionysian living through the consumption of opiates are consistent with the old English literati, such as Samuel Taylor Coleridge in the preface to his poem *Kubla Khan* and Thomas de Quincy's *Confessions of an English Opium-Eater*. These narratives of drug taking induced a voyeuristic fascination with drugs that operates in stark contrast with consumption by 'natives', which are typically framed as a moral malaise, in need of extermination.

Further, the general presumption that drug policing strategies deployed at festivals are primarily because drug consumption is higher is also a partial misnomer – at least to the extent of the number of drug arrests. More specifically however, the strategies at NHC demonstrate how racialized drug policing is a part of a grander disciplining regime of mass, Black politico-cultural expression, articulated through its explicit political voice but also through its aesthetic form, which fundamentally challenges the repressive practices of the British state. Indeed, rehearsals of such repression from the state have existed since time immemorial. While drug policing is a microcosm of the 'global colour line', NHC is a unique rendition of resistance to that. While there may be some sense that NHC has become defanged as Europe's biggest street party where 'authentic culture and heritage' becomes a unique selling point, its location in what is now an economically affluent area, still threatens the elite atmosphere of Notting Hill with the scourge of the spectre of the Black party. To that end, NHC, in its overt political articulations and aesthetic renditions, will continue to push back against the manifestations of British state repression – whether through racialized drug policing or otherwise.

Notes

1 Tanzil Chowdhury is a Lecturer in Public Law at Queen Mary, University of London. He would like to thank Kojo Koram, Adam Elliot-Cooper, Nayeli Urquiza Hass, Remi Joseph-Salisbury, Waqas Tufail, Mike Salinas, Becky Clarke as well as the reviewers and the attendees at 'The War on Drugs and the Global Colour Line' workshop for their help. Tanzil.chowdhury@qmul.ac.uk.

2 Stormzy, https://twitter.com/Stormzy1/status/899959361572921344. [Accessed 30 August 2017].

3 See also Cecil Gutzmore, 'Carnival, the state and the black masses in the United Kingdom', in Winston James and Clive Harris (eds), *Inside Babylon: The Caribbean Diaspora in Britain* (London: Verso, 1993), pp. 207–230; Abner Cohen, 'A polyethnic London Carnival as a contested cultural performance', *Ethnic and Racial Studies* 5.1 (1982); Abner Cohen, 'Drama and politics in the development of a London carnival', *Man*, 15.1 (1980).

4 Metropolitan Police, https://twitter.com/metpoliceuk/status/899914758866051072 [accessed 30 August 2017].

5 Patrick Headman, 'Here's a list of festivals that have more crime than carnival', *VICE*, 23 August 2017, www.vice.com/en_uk/article/zmmy89/proof-carnival-has-less-crime-than-the-uks-other-big-summer-events [accessed 23 August 2017]. Indeed, anticipatory drugs policing operations and their tangential connection to NHC follow a precedent with similar operations having taken place as far back as 2014. See also Netpol, https://twitter.com/policemonitor/status/899924389986058240 [accessed 30 August 2017], and Hal Austin, 'Carnival: Reflections on a community', *New Community* 7.1 (1978): 115.

6 Avon and Somerset Constabulary, 'Drug seizures at Glastonbury Music Festival 2014–2016', 22 February 2017, www.avonandsomerset.police.uk/about-us/freedom-of-information/previous-foi-requests/glastonbury-festival/drug-seizures-at-glastonbury-music-festival-2014-2016/ [accessed 22 February 2017].

7 Metropolitan Police, 'Statement from police commander for Notting Hill Carnival 2016', 30 August 2016, http://news.met.police.uk/news/statement-from-police-commander-for-notting-hill-carnival-2016-182480 [accessed 8 June 2018].

8 Cohen, 'Drama and politics', p. 67.

9 Cohen, 'Drama and politics', p. 68.

10 Cohen, 'Drama and politics', p. 67.

11 Tshepo Mokoena, 'How Secret Garden Party made festivals palatable for posh people', *Noisey*, 7 March 2017, https://noisey.vice.com/en_uk/article/ez8npw/how-secret-garden-party-made-festivals-palatable-for-posh-people [accessed 2 February 2018].

12 Paul Gilroy, *There Ain't No Black in the Union Jack* (London: Routledge, 2002), p. 86.

13 Gilroy, *There Ain't No Black*, p. 130.

14 Gutzmore, 'Carnival, the state and the black masses', pp. 208, 214.

15 Lambros Fatsis, 'Grime: Criminal subculture or public counterculture? A critical investigation into the criminalization of Black musical subcultures in the UK', *Crime, Medial, Culture: An International Journal*, 28 June 2018.

16 Secret Garden Party, 'Ethos', www.secretgardenparty.com/ethos [accessed 9 May 2018].

17 Peter Jackson, 'Street life: The politics of carnival', *Environment and Planning D* 6.2 (1988): 215.

18 See also Everton Pryce, 'The Notting Hill Gate Carnival – Black politics, resistance, and leadership 1976–1978', *Caribbean Quarterly* 31.2 (1985); Gutzmore, 'Carnival, the state and the black masses'; Abner Cohen, 'A polyethnic London Carnival as a contested cultural performance', *Ethnic and Racial Studies* 5.1 (1982); Cohen, 'Drama and politics'; Jackson, 'Street life', p. 215.

19 Jackson, 'Street life', p. 215.

20 Jackson, 'Street life', pp. 214–215.

21 See also Johann Galtung, 'Violence, peace and peace research', *Journal of Peace Research* 6.3 (1969); Iris Marion Young, 'Five faces of oppression', in Ann Cudd and Robin Andreasen (eds), *Feminist Theory: A Philosophical Anthology* (Oxford: Blackwell Publishing, 2004), pp. 91–104.

22 Cohen, 'A polyethnic London Carnival', p. 27.

23 Pryce, 'The Notting Hill Gate Carnival', p. 35.

24 Cohen, 'Drama and politics', p. 67.

25 Gutzmore, 'Carnival, the state and the black masses', p. 215.

26 Cohen, 'A polyethnic London Carnival', p. 31; Cohen, 'Drama and politics', p. 75.

27 Pryce, 'The Notting Hill Gate Carnival', p. 37.

28 Cohen, 'A polyethnic London Carnival', p. 33.

29 Gilroy, *There Ain't No Black*, p. 117.

30 Jackson, 'Street life', p. 217.

31 Elisa Bray, 'Secret Garden Party: Why a pioneering festival wants to change the format', *Independent*, 6 June 2017, www.independent.co.uk/arts-entertainment/music/features/secret-garden-party-freddie-fellowes-crystal-fighters-kate-tempest-metronomy-glamping-festival-a7775361.html [accessed 9 June 2018].

32 Roxy Robinson, 'No spectators! The art of participation, from Burning Man to boutique festivals in Britain', in George McKay (ed.), *The Pop Festival: History, Music, Media, Culture* (London: Bloomsbury, 2015), pp. 171–174.

33 See also Roxy Robinson, *Music Festivals and the Politics of Participation* (London: Routledge, 2015).

34 Since then however, it had grown to have over 15 stages with its final festival attracting over 30,000 participants.

35 Secret Garden Party, 'Ethos', www.secretgardenparty.com/ethos [accessed 9 May 2018].

36 Bray, 'Secret Garden Party'.

37 Simon Usborne, 'Poshstock generation: The entrepreneurial aristocrats who are creating a whole new summer season of festivals', *Independent*, 11 May 2008, www.independent.co.uk/arts-entertainment/music/features/poshstock-generation-the-entrepreneurial-aristocrats-who-are-creating-a-whole-new-summer-season-of-823497.html [accessed 9 June 2018].

38 Mokoena, 'How Secret Garden Party made festivals palatable'.

39 See also Alethea Hayter, *Opium and the Romantic Imagination* (London: Faber and Faber 2009).

40 Michel Foucault, *Discipline and Punish* (New York: Vintage Books, 1975), p. 136.

41 This does not necessarily mean public health approaches, carte blanche, are inherently more progressive. Indeed, the governmentality of public health approaches can be just as racially violent as the criminal justice approach. See Peter Skrabnek, *The Death of Human Medicine and the Rise of Coercive Healthism* (Edmonds, Suffolk: The Social Affairs Unit, 1994).

42 M. Hesse and S. Tutenges, 'Music and substance preference among festival attendants', *Drugs and Alcohol Today* 12.2 (2012): 82–88.

43 Caitlin Hughes et al., 'The deterrent effects of Australian street-level drug law enforcement on illicit drug offending at outdoor music festivals', *International Journal of Drug Policy* 41 (2017): 92.

44 Misuse of Drugs Regulations 2001 allows for the supply and possession of certain controlled substances.

45 For a critical exegesis on the drug nomenclature, see also Toby Seddon, 'Inventing drugs: A genealogy of a regulatory concept', *Journal of Law and Society* 43.3 (2016).

46 Royal Society for Public Health, *Taking a New Line on Drugs*, 2016, p. 17, www.rsph.org.uk/uploads/assets/uploaded/68d93cdc-292c-4a7b-babfc0a8ee252bc0.pdf [accessed 15 February 2018].

47 Harm Reduction International, 'What is harm reduction?', 2016, www.hri.global/what-is-harm-reduction [accessed 3 March 2018].

48 Joanne Csete and Daniel Wolfe, 'Seeing through the public health smoke-screen in drug policy', *International Journal of Drug Policy* 43 (2017): 91.

49 United Nations Office on Drugs and Crime, *World Drug Report 2012*, www.unodc.org/doc/wdr2016/WORLD_DRUG_REPORT_2016_web.pdf [accessed 10 January 2018]. See also Royal Society for Public Health, *Taking a New Line on Drugs*.

50 International legal prohibitions on drugs often shape UK law and policy. See also Royal Society for Public Health, *Taking a New Line on Drugs*, p. 19.

51 Hughes et al., 'The deterrent effects of Australian street-level drug law enforcement', p. 93.

52 NHC 2012–2015, www.whatdotheyknow.com/request/294154/response/743308/attach/html/3/ELFITURI%20Data.xls.pdf.html; NHC 2016, http://news.met.police.uk/news/statement-from-police-commander-for-notting-hill-carnival-2016-182480; NHC 2017, http://news.met.police.uk/news/notting-hill-carnival-arrests-257013 [all accessed 23 August 2017]; SGP 2014–2017, www.cambs.police.uk/assets/Cambs-FOI/FOI-2018/January-2018/FOI201701585-Jan2018.pdf [accessed 3 November 2018].

53 London Assembly: Police and Crime Committee, 'Notting Hill Carnival: safer and better', 2017, p. 4, www.london.gov.uk/sites/default/files/pcc_report_-_notting_hill_carnival_safer_and_better.pdf [accessed 5 June 2018].

54 London Assembly: Police and Crime Committee, 'Notting Hill Carnival', p. 5.

55 Headman, 'Here's a list of festivals that have more crime than carnival'; two additional arrests were made for psychoactive drug offences but were recorded as separate from 'drug offences' arrests.

56 The Loop, https://weareatheloop.org/mast/ [accessed 23 August 2017].

57 Henry Fisher and Fiona Measham, 'How one patch of grass became the UK's first ever decriminalised drugs space', *Politics.co.uk*, 28 July 2016, www.politics.co.uk/comment-analysis/2016/07/28/how-patch-grass-uk-first-decriminalised-drugs-space [accessed 10 June 2018].

58 Michael Tony, 'Race and the war on drugs', *University of Chicago Legal Forum* 1.4 (1994); Gabriel Chin, 'Race, the war on drugs, and the collateral consequences of criminal conviction', *Journal of Gender, Race and Justice* 6 (2002).

59 Michelle Alexander, *The New Jim Crow: Mass Incarceration in the Age of Colorblindness* (New York: The New Press 2012).

60 Bruce Western, 'The impact of incarceration on wage mobility and inequality', *American Sociology Review* 67.4 (2002): 526–546.

61 Niamh Eastwood et al., 'The numbers in black and white: Ethnic disparities in the policing and prosecution of drug offences in England And Wales', *Release*, 2013, www.release.org.uk/sites/default/files/pdf/publications/Release%20-%20Race%20Disparity%20Report%20final%20version.pdf [accessed 3 March 2018].

62 Seddon, 'Inventing drugs', p. 409.

63 Donald Trump, 'President Donald J Trump is taking action on drug addiction and the opioid crisis', White House, 26 October 2017, www.whitehouse.gov/briefings-statements/president-donald-j-trump-taking-action-drug-addiction-opioid-crisis/ [accessed 10 June 2018].

64 Paul Gilroy, 'The myth of black criminality', in Phil Scranton (ed.), *Law, Order and the Authoritarian State: Readings in Critical Criminology* (Milton Keynes: Open University Press, 1987), pp. 47–56.

65 Gilroy, *There Ain't No Black*, p. 91.

66 Gilroy, *There Ain't No Black*, p. 89.

67 Gilroy, *There Ain't No Black*, p. 90; See also Stuart Hall et al., *Policing the Crisis: Mugging, The State, and Law and Order* (London: Macmillan, 1978).

68 Jackson, 'Street life', p. 214.

69 Hall, *Policing the Crisis*, pp. 3–7.

70 Gilroy, *There Ain't No Black*, p. 125.

71 Gilroy, *There Ain't No Black*, p. 130.

72 Gilroy, *There Ain't No Black*, p. 129.

73 Jackson, 'Street life', p. 215.

74 Jackson, 'Street life', p. 214.

75 Austin, 'Carnival: Reflections on a community', p. 114.

76 Gilroy, *The Myth of Black Criminality*, pp. 52–53.

77 Cohen, 'A polyethnic London Carnival', p. 28.

78 Gutzmore, 'Carnival, the state and the black masses', p. 214.

79 Gilroy, *There Ain't No Black*, p. 116.

80 Gutzmore, 'Carnival, the state and the black masses', p. 208.

81 A failure to respond could result in a 6-month sentence or a £20,000 fine.

82 Dan Hancox, 'Public enemy no 696', *Guardian*, 21 January 2009 www.theguardian.com/culture/2009/jan/21/police-form-696-garage-music [accessed 15 March 2015]; See also Fatsis, 'Grime: Criminal subculture or public counterculture?

83 Yemi Abiade, 'Inside UK drill, the demonised rap genre representing a marginalised generation', *Independent*, 15 April 2018, www.independent.co.uk/arts-entertainment/music/features/drill-music-london-stabbings-shootings-rap-67-abra-cadabra-comment-government-a8305516.html [accessed 2 November 2018].

84 Peter Fryer, *Staying Power: The History of Black People in Britain* (London: Pluto Press, 1988), pp. 391–399.

85 See also Walter Benjamin, 'The work of art in the age of its technological reproducibility', in Michael W. Jennings, Brigid Doherty and Thomas Y. Levin (eds), *The Work of Art in the Age of Its Technological Reproducibility and Other Writings on Media* (Cambridge, MA: Harvard University Press, 2008).

86 Cohen, 'Drama and politics', p. 67.

87 Cohen, 'A polyethnic London Carnival', p. 37; Jackson, 'Street life', p. 222.

88 Cohen, 'A polyethnic London Carnival', p. 35.

89 Pryce, 'The Notting Hill Gate Carnival', p. 36.

90 Jackson, 'Street life', p. 225.

91 Jackson, 'Street life', p. 224.

92 Hayter, *Opium and the Romantic Imagination*.

3

Racism and drug policy: criminal control and the management of Black bodies by the Brazilian State

Evandro Piza Duarte and Felipe da Silva Freitas[1]

Introduction

The drug policy in Brazil has been driven by racism through a system of political, economic and cultural power.[2]

Through criminalization processes regarding drug use, possession and trafficking in Brazil, racial hierarchies delimit the political framework of the debate, colonizing even the forms of legal definition concerning who are the users and the dealers of illicit drugs.

In this chapter, we offer initially an overview of Brazil's drug policy and the racialization of the country's justice system since the 1990s. Based on the international demands of the drug policy, a) its legislative design, b) its institutional dimensions and c) its effects, we describe the legislative patterns of increasing punishment and restriction of rights. In this context, we note the importance of the emergence of right-wing political movements and the idea of 'Whiteness'[3] in making this model effective, and we present the main data on incarceration and deaths caused by the State, primarily carried out by the police. We point out that the patterns of mortality, disappearance and incarceration of young people, mainly Black and poor, consolidate a process of extermination and impact on how the data on incarceration can be interpreted.

The chapter's central proposal is to demonstrate how the Brazilian Judiciary collaborates in producing negative effects of the drug policy. In this context, we highlight two central mechanisms: a) interpretative patterns which maximize the legislation's punitive character, by using procedural measures of incarceration when incarceration sentences cannot be used; b) procedural patterns for the evaluation of evidence produced during the investigation phase, incorrectly validating information that has been produced illegally, or is not supported by evidence.

Hence, when considering the racialization patterns of the Brazilian Judiciary's composition, and the singular processes and speeches produced by its members, we thematize the construction of Whiteness and institutional racism. However, we argue that the responsibility of the Judiciary can only be understood when it is articulated with their relations with the police. Therefore, we intend to discuss the relationship between the police and the Judiciary in the formation of Brazil's drug policy and its negative effects on the Black population.

In this chaper, we primarily use the data produced by the National Justice Council and from surveys on policing approaches and the impact of the drug policy on Black and poor youth that we have developed since 2014 with the Ministry of Justice.[4]

The 1988 Constitution and the role of the drug policy in the perpetuation of an authoritarian legal tradition

The Brazilian Constitution of 1988 is traditionally presented as the basis of a humanistic model of legal integration, with a view to promoting human dignity and overcoming myriad forms of discrimination.[5] However, the Constitution remained stuck in a compromise: it did not represent any revolutionary rupture with the earlier values and ideas of the country's Law, but did imply an alignment with progressive features on the concepts of equality, democracy and human rights. By ending the long period of military governments inaugurated by the 1964 civil-military coup, the Constituent Assembly (1987 and 1988) brought together different Brazilian social and political actors. Such a judicial political arrangement had been produced by and reiterated successive agreements between the still influential leaders of the military regime and new and old civil leaders drawn mainly from Brazilian society's socially elite sectors.[6]

This contradictory situation of permanence/rupture can be observed in the constitutional text itself. In the chapter focused on fundamental rights and guarantees, the innovations should formally consolidate a criminal justice system which respects broad guarantees of substantive and procedural criminal law rights for the accused, based on the presumption of innocence, strict legality and human dignity.[7] The Federal Constitution's provisions, as a whole, propose the principle of minimum intervention of criminal law as the guideline on lawmaking.

However, in the article that established the rights of the accused, the category of 'heinous crimes' was included, for which the constituent is determined to the legislator to provide a differential treatment.[8] It was in this context that the punitive discourse attached, in the constituent process, drug trafficking to the vague idea of 'heinous', making possible the legislative creation of a criminal law of exception.

The model of guaranteed rights contrasted with the paradoxical continuity of an authoritarian model in the institutional structure of 'public security', that is, in policing and judicial practices.[9] The mass incarceration of the 2000s, also an important part of the 1964 dictatorship's legislation, is rooted in the 1930s and, even earlier, in the forms of control of the mass of slaves in the 'black cities'.[10]

In addition to the important warnings of critical criminology concerning the undeclared roles of prison and sentencing and their negative effects on social subjects and realities,[11] what we see in Brazil is even more peculiar, with serious deformations of the punitive apparatus, as evidenced in crowded prisons, practices of torture and ill-treatment, and arrests expressly contrary to the legal order, especially in scenarios where policing practices resemble war zone strategies, with high mortality rates.[12]

The available data[13] reveal that as of June 2016, the Brazilian prison population was 726,712 with 689,510 people in the correctional system; 36,765 in police stations and 437 people serving sentences in the federal prison system. These data show that the country has a deficit of 358,663 places, with a prison occupancy rate of 197 per cent, placing it among the top five countries with the largest prison populations in the world.

Brazil has experienced a boom in hyper-incarceration over the last 26 years (1990–2016), represented by a 707 per cent increase in the prison population compared to the total recorded in the early 1990s, with progressive increases in the number of remand prisoners (prisoners without conviction) and successive increases in both the number of incarcerated people and places available in prison system units. Even though there have been announcements of public spending increases in prison construction, expansion and renovation, these are outflanked by increases in incarceration rates at levels higher than the public capacity to construct and manage the facilities.

Figure 3.1 shows the evolution of the prison population from the 1990s to 2016, in hundreds of thousands of people.[14]

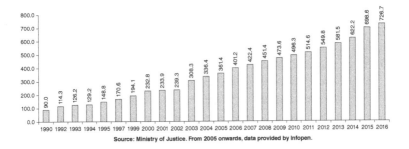

Figure 3.1 Progression of persons deprived of liberty from 1990 to 2016

Figure 3.2 indicates that between 2000 and 2016, the imprisonment rate increased by 157 per cent in Brazil: 'In 2000, there were 137 people incarcerated for each group of 100 thousand inhabitants. In June 2016, there were 352.6 people incarcerated for every 100 thousand inhabitants.'[15]

As we show below, Figure 3.2 indicates a trend in case law of increasing pre-trial detention and increasing flexibility in terms of criminal and procedural safeguards in detaining custodial measures.[16] In an empirical study to monitor the application of Brazil's Drug Law, conducted by the University of Brasília and the Federal University of Rio de Janeiro, in 2009, and coordinated by the Secretariat for Legislative Affairs of the Ministry of Justice,[17] it is possible to note, based on the judgments of the Courts of Justice of Rio de Janeiro, the Federal District and the Federal Supreme Court that there is great discretion for police action that decisively influences the criminalization of trafficking and often exceeds the selective framework of the accused, which disproportionately harms Blacks, poor people and residents of socially deprived urban areas. At

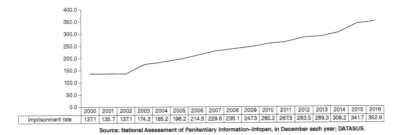

Figure 3.2 Progression of the incarceration rate of Brazil from 2000 to 2016

the same time, the amount of drugs seized or the agent's role in the drug trade's hierarchy is of little relevance in the process of fixing the sentence for the crime of trafficking, since in the analysed cases the increase has little or no reasoning at all.[18]

This picture has been confirmed in similar studies carried out over the last thirty years. Such studies were carried out under the strong influence of civil society organizations and government agencies addressing legislative issues,[19] and have provided an overview of the challenges for the criminal justice system with regard to the implementation of the Drug Law.[20]

Drug policy is one of the main causes for these deformations of the criminal policy that we examine here. In the National Penitentiary Survey (2017), drug trafficking is the most recurrent crime resulting in incarceration in Brazil. Among men, 26 per cent of those deprived of their liberty were incarcerated on charges of drug trafficking, while among women this figure rises to 62 per cent, with each new national survey expressing rates of rapid and persistent growth.

This phenomenon is the product of a series of legal provisions and case law understandings which have moved Brazil from its own constitutional provisions in terms of guarantees for the accused and prisoners.[21] The War on Drugs is the political aspect of a process of penal hardening, which, based on the cognitive foundation of racial representations, produces and maintains hyper-incarceration as a formula for controlling and managing populations in urban spaces.[22]

Brazil's drug policy, as in most countries of the world, consists of false pathologized and stigmatizing images, which reinforce, support and organize every war-like narrative upon which the country's criminal policy and the – war-like – strategies of public security are based. Based on a model adopted by the international conventions, Brazil has sought to deal with drugs legally categorized as illicit through normative standards of criminalization,[23] with deprivation of liberty.

Prohibitionism was originally initiated in the US, which was then disseminated into the international forums as the policy of control of the criminal use, production and trade of drugs. This doctrine spread widely into other countries' social and political life, guiding not only other nations' lawmaking, but also directing the understandings of the Magistracy, organizing public security management strategies, influencing media coverage, and, particularly, presiding over the public interpretations regarding the issue of psychoactive substances designated as illegal. This prohibitionist doctrine rapidly evolved into a 'War on Drugs' policy, justifying massive militarized police operations, based on the belief that state violence can contain the increase in the number of users.[24]

In addition to extremely high incarceration rates, the 'War on Drugs' policy has generated very high homicide rates, murders committed by the police forces as well as those arising from the disputes between drug trafficking groups pursuing territorial control. The War on Drugs is increasingly a source of violence and urban insecurity far more potent than trafficking itself, as a high homicide rate offers no economic benefit for the traffickers, as Maria Lúcia Karam points out:

> The 'war on drugs' is not exactly a war against drugs. It is not a war against things. Like any other war, it is a war against people – the producers, dealers and users of prohibited substances. But, not exactly all of them. The preferred targets of the 'war on drugs' are the most vulnerable among these producers, dealers and users of prohibited substances. The 'enemies' in this war are the poor, the marginalized, the nonwhite, the powerless.[25]

The rhetoric of the War on Drugs is a narrative of moral values, disregarding the cultural, anthropological, political and social dimension of drug use in the history of different societies, and thus making it impossible to construct an approach which permits the discussion of the issue in terms of public health, risk reduction, abuse, and, particularly, discussion about the conditions of a social coexistence less socially harmful concerning drug use and trafficking. Criminalization bans more refined discussions on the subject and prevents the formation of policies of inclusion, defence of public health and the guarantee of the rights of people who use drugs.

Drug policy in Brazil: racialized institutional dynamics

Understanding the distance between a constitutional rights-guaranteeing project and actual authoritarian practices involves understanding the racialized dynamics of legal institutions.

The crimes listed in the Drug Law (2006) fall under the jurisdiction of 'Federal Justice' and 'State Justice'. The State Justice has a Court of Justice, a second-tier body, in each of Brazil's 27 states, with first-tier bodies, generally corresponding to one municipality, spread across the districts. The State Justice is competent to judge drug use and domestic trafficking crimes. The Federal Justice has five Federal Regional Courts, which as a rule comprise the large regions in which the country is divided, including several states, as well as first-tier bodies corresponding to the grouping of some municipalities. The Federal Justice is competent to prosecute drug trafficking offences with an international dimension (article 109 FC). The State Criminal Justice has a greater territorial applicability; a higher number of judges are responsible for almost all criminal cases and criminal law places more importance in its operation.[26]

However, State Justice carries significant differences. The most evident is between small, medium and large courts.[27] Among the state courts, the Tribunal de Justiça of São Paulo (TJ/SP) is the largest court of all, with 25,943,503 cases processed. In second place, the Tribunal de Justiça of Rio de Janeiro (TJ/RJ), with 13,448,660 cases processed. Third, the Tribunal de Justiça of Minas Gerais (TJ/MG), 6,048,754 cases processed. Fourth, the Tribunal de Justiça of Rio Grande do Sul (TJ/RS) with 4,491,617 cases processed. Fifth, the Tribunal de Justiça of Paraná (TJ/PR) with 4,137,586 cases processed.[28] These five state courts accounted for 61.12 per cent of those arrested in Brazil: 240,061 (TJ/SP), 50,219 (TJ/RJ), 68,354 (TJ/MG), 33,868 (TJ/RS) and 51,700 (TJ/PR). Therefore, there is an evident concentration of incarceration in the Justice of five states of the Southern and Southeastern regions.

In Brazil, the accusatory body is the Public Prosecutor's Office, the public body for the defence of poor defendants is the Public Defender's Office, and the judicial police are composed of chiefs of police, all with separate careers in Federal and State Justice. Entry into these careers is determined by placement on a series of civil service exams, but occupancy of the higher positions in the hierarchy depends on internal corporate (peer), external (legislative) validation, and appointment by the executive branch. Criminal advocacy depends, in addition to a specific course common to all legal careers, on passing the standard qualifying test. In some situations, the defence of poor defendants can be made by lawyers who are funded by the state; free legal advice is unusual.

In the few data available on the subject, the following gender and race profiles are found. Regarding the Public Defender's Office, in 2015 at the state level, of 5,512 defenders, 2,697 answered the survey; among them 49 per cent were women and 51 per cent men. Of the total, 76.4 per cent are

White, 21.4 per cent are Black (19.2 per cent are Brown and 2.2 per cent are Black), 1.8 per cent are Yellow and 0.4 per cent are Indigenous.[29] At the federal level, of the 550 defenders, 354 answered the survey; 32 per cent were women and 68 per cent were men, 73.7 per cent were White, 23.5 per cent were Black (21 per cent Brown and 2.5 per cent Black), 3 per cent Yellow and 0.6 per cent Indigenous.[30]

As for the Public Prosecutor's Office, in 2017 there were 5,114 female prosecutors and attorneys and 7,897 male prosecutors and attorneys – that is, 39 per cent women and 61 per cent men. There was no data collection by race.[31]

As for the chiefs of police in 2002, IDESP, based on a sample of 1,228 chiefs of police working in the states of Amapá, Bahia, Goiás, Paraná, Pernambuco, Rio de Janeiro, Rio Grande do Sul, São Paulo and the Federal District, 82.9 per cent of the interviewees were male and 17.1 per cent female; 83.7 per cent were White, 11.4 per cent were Brown, 3.1 per cent Black, 1.3 per cent Yellow/Indigenous and 0.3 per cent did not state colour.[32]

According to the Brazilian Bar Association (OAB), there are 1,095,339 registered lawyers, 51.4 per cent men and 48.6 per cent women, with no mention of race/colour.[33] In the data referring to the VII up to the XIII Examinations of the OAB there were 833,100 enrolled candidates (64.7 per cent White, 32.5 per cent Black and 2.8 per cent Indigenous and Yellow). Of this total, 135,900 candidates (16.3 per cent) were approved, 53.8 per cent of whom were women; 68.9 per cent were White, 28.7 per cent Black and 2.4 per cent Indigenous/Yellow.

As for the positions of higher hierarchy in the Judiciary (which depends on political appointments), Fragale, Moreira and Sciammarella show the disparity in the positions of management, presidency, vice-presidency and the comptroller's office regarding gender. In 2011–12, 29.44 per cent, and in 2013–14, 28.33 per cent were women occupying these positions.[34]

As for the judges' profile, according to the Census of the Judiciary (data from 2012–13, published in 2014), 82.8 per cent of the judges were White, 15.6 per cent Black (14.2 per cent Brown and 1.4 per cent Black), 1.5 per cent Yellow and 0.1 per cent of Indigenous. In the State Justice, 82.8 per cent were White, 15.6 per cent were Black (14.2 per cent Brown, 1.4 per cent Black), 1.5 per cent Yellow and 0.1 per cent Indigenous. In the Federal Justice, 85.7 per cent were White, 13.13 per cent Black (12.4 per cent Brown, 0.9 per cent Black); 0.9 per cent Yellow, and 0.1 per cent Indigenous.[35] In relation to the judiciary employees, 69.1 per cent of the judiciary's public servants were White, while 28.8 per cent were Black (24.7 per cent Brown, 4.1 per cent Black), 1.9 per cent Yellow, and 0.3 per cent Indigenous.[36]

The disparity between race/colour and gender among judges is even more relevant when we take into consideration the five main State Courts. In the TJ/SP, 68.2 per cent were men; of the total number of judges, 96.6 per cent were White, 3.2 per cent Black (3 per cent Brown and 0.2 per cent Black), 3.4 per cent Yellow, and 0.1 per cent Indigenous. In the TJ/RJ, 53.7 per cent were men; of the total number of judges, 91.3 per cent were White; 8.2 per cent Black (6.7 per cent Brown and 1.5 per cent Black), 0.3 per cent Yellow and 0.2 per cent Indigenous. In the TJ/MG, 72.3 per cent were men; of the total number of judges, 87.4 per cent were White and 12 per cent Black (0.5 per cent Black and 11.5 per cent Brown), 0.5 per cent Yellow and 0.2 per cent Indigenous. In the TJ/RS, 56 per cent were men; of the total number of judges, 97.1 per cent White and 1.7 per cent Blacks (1.3 per cent Brown and 0.4 per cent Black), 0.8 per cent Yellow and 0.4 per cent Indigenous. In the TJ/PR, 63.5 per cent were men; of the total number of judges, 90.4 per cent were White, 5.6 per cent Black (4.8 per cent Brown and 0.8 per cent Black); 3.8 per cent Yellow and 0.0 per cent Indigenous.[37]

In summary, the legal careers involved in criminal prosecution are mostly occupied by White men and women, and as far as these institutions' hierarchies are concerned, White men prevail. In addition to the low Black presence to begin with, the presence of more Browns than Blacks in this group seems to indicate the processes of 'whitening', with institutional preferences for the lighter skin tones. Among the five major courts which have incarcerated more people, the disparity between the racial profiling of the population, the racial profiling of the judges and the prisoners is more evident. In these cases, it can be said that the most common scenario is a White man judging the lives of poor young Blacks and Whites.

In turn, the public security system is an important element of Brazil's drug policy. Two judicial police forces are constitutionally responsible for investigations taken to the Judiciary: the federal police and the civil police. In Brazil, the responsibility for urban crime prevention activities belongs to the military police – that is, in everyday life, citizens come face to face with a militarized form of policing. Its management is apparently answerable to the state administration, since these police officers are integrated with the state public security departments, as well as with the civil police. However, the military police are also subject to the structure of the Brazilian Army, since they are an auxiliary and reserve force of the army. In practice, the military police work as a corporation, with national guidelines and interests negotiated with the state administrations responsible for paying their salary.[38] In addition, one characteristic of the 'system' is the competition and conflict between the various agencies.[39] The two police forces are each responsible for half the volume of drug trafficking cases within the State Justice's jurisdiction. Although usually prisoners are arrested with only small amounts of drugs, the two police forces compete in the media to demonstrate their greater 'effectiveness' in the seizure of large volumes of illicit drugs.

During the civil-military dictatorship of 1964, the legitimation of the military forces was carried out by the diffusion of the Doctrine of National Security – that is, political persecution of internal political enemies, who were identified with the communists.[40] The regime imposed new militarized forms of urban patrolling and associated the idea of urban (racialized) disorder with the idea of crime.[41] At the end of the civil-military dictatorship in 1985, with the suspension of Cold War tensions and the emergence of Mercosur,[42] the Brazilian Army and Military Police were strategically deployed in the formation of a national system of repression and prevention of drug trafficking. Although the Military Police do not have the constitutional competence to act as investigative police, there are military police officers who are responsible for investigations into common crime, and especially internal structures and procedures similar to the Civil Police's, but which are not made public. In fact, the regulatory norms of several of these procedures in the states are subject to criteria of secrecy due to 'public security needs'. The legal debate is simplified. It is argued that if someone is arrested during a drug seizure and the Military Police testify regarding the circumstances of the arrest, there is no need to question the legality of the chain of investigation.[43] However, the external control mechanisms of both the Military and Civil Police are inefficient. There is, in fact, no transparency about the prevention and punishment of corporate members who violate citizens' fundamental rights.[44]

Police structures are racialized, as in the Judiciary, with an internal hierarchy between management activities versus policing activities, and between higher positions in the hierarchy (chief of police) and everyday investigative duties (police officer). There is disproportionality between the racial composition of prisoners, and the population's racial composition. In public security,[45] Whites are in the management activities, but the presence of Black (especially Brown) people[46] in the activities of enforcement is increasing.

In Brazilian institutions' public discourses, the racialized dimension arises in the way in which representations are distributed concerning the value of one's own work in the face of society's or the victims' criticisms. The most common discourse in everyday institutional responses by the Judiciary is to hold the police officers who carry out urban policing activities accountable for their violence, especially due to lack of training; and by the Police Commands, to hold the police officers who would be the 'bad apples' accountable for the violence,[47] especially if they bring violent or dishonest behaviours inside the corporations from their places of social origin. Therefore, spaces of 'Whiteness', which correspond precisely to the most prestigious spaces, possessing social and economic capital, are rendered immune to interference while being vested with greater institutional power to manage the security system and to alter collective patterns of behaviour.

Mechanisms of incarceration: The Sentence Compliance Scheme and procedural arrests for 'heinous' criminals

Criminal enforcement was administered under only local regulations until Law No. 7,210/1984 Criminal Enforcement Law (LEP) was established. This first national law emerged in a climate of criticism of the dictatorship, with the collaboration of politicians who had been arrested by the regime and especially by sectors of the Catholic Church that had reported institutional violence.[48] The LEP emphasized the progressive system and constituted rules for protection of prisoners' rights, which had never been applied in the penitentiary system, determining that a prisoner could be transferred to a less strict regime once they had completed one-sixth of their sentence imposed by the previous regime. The Federal Constitution of 1988, influenced by such reforms, stipulated that the law should regulate the 'individualization of punishment', expressly referring to alternative penalties, such as 'alternative social benefit' and 'suspension or ban of rights'.

However, the inclusion in the Constitution of the principle of the individualization of punishment and other rights (prohibition of torture and cruel punishment, the right to silence, inviolability of the home, etc.) was accompanied by some tension between prospects for the guaranteeing of rights and punitive demands in the Constituent Assembly, tension manifested in the creation of a category for 'exceptions', on the topic where individual guarantees were established, as will be seen later.[49] Faced with the demands to increase the punishment for certain crimes (homicide, for example), and especially as a political strategy to displace the public debate about the punishment of the dictatorship for crimes of torture, the Constituent Assembly established that 'heinous and similar crimes' should be specified by the ordinary legislator.[50]

In the following two years, two laws marked the punitive escalation of the 1990s. First, under pressure from sectors of the police forces, which were said to have no tools to combat crime because they were forbidden to arrest people without judicial authorization and without reasonable suspicion (that is, they could not make arbitrary arrests to investigate or check), Law 7960 (1989) was passed. The Preventive Detention Law (LPT) creates a kind of 'precautionary' arrest, which is unconstitutional, since it does not meet the usual parameters (precautionary arrest can last five days and is extendable to another five, to 'facilitate investigation' of someone who is not yet suspected of a concrete action), even if it is decreed by the judge at the request of the Public Prosecution Office or the police authority. Then, under the alarmist climate predicting an increase in urban crime, Law 8072 (1990), the Heinous Crimes Law (LCH) was enacted. The LCH selected certain crimes,[51] labelled them 'heinous', increased their sentences and the term of preventive detention (30 days, extendable for another 30), created federally administered maximum security facilities and, in this context of preventive incarceration without justification, introduced the plea bargain. The legislation was decisive for drug policy, as it consolidated the association of drug trafficking crimes with the label of 'hideousness', restricting rights in 'block', emphasizing the notion of crimes 'equated with heinous'.

The opportunity was taken to extend, beyond constitutional provision, the list of rights which should be 'lost' by perpetrators of these 'heinous' crimes. No symmetry existed between the rights restricted by the law and those listed as subject to restriction by the CF. The Constitution provided that these crimes would be 'inviolable and insusceptible of pardon or amnesty'.[52] The LCH provided that the 'amnesty, pardon and reprieve' of 'bail' and 'probation' should be prohibited, established that the sentence should be 'fulfilled in full in closed conditions', increased the term for eligibility to two-thirds of the original sentence, and prohibited probation for specific recidivists.

Therefore, the LCH attacked the progressive system of the application of sentence, forcing the condemned to complete their full sentence in the most burdensome and closed conditions. This is because the LCH partially revoked the LEP regarding the right of downgrading in 1/6 (art. 112). Therefore, in practice, first offenders would be housed with repeat offenders, since the concrete gravity of their actions was not taken into consideration to differentiate them regarding their prison conditions, especially in an already overcrowded structure. At the same time, their behaviour in prison was less and less important in modulating the fulfilment of their sentence, since transferring to a lesser security prison was no longer an option.

The LCH practically ended the possibility of freedom in the course of the process, and in fact transformed the nature of the provisional detention, which became 'officially' a 'sentence without process'. In our system, defendants who are incarcerated, wrongly accused, because they have been acquitted or because they have been disqualified for crimes without deprivation of liberty, do not receive compensation. When we take into consideration that this occurs in a large number of cases, the nature of incarceration is transformed. From a legal point of view, it is a return to the 1941 Code's system – which had been abolished in 1977 – of compulsory procedural arrest for certain offences, regardless of reasonable justification. So, if charged by the police, the defendant would be incarcerated until being sentenced without bail. In addition, the LCH reversed the logic of the impossibility of serving time before the final sentence of the conviction be ruled, by establishing that the judge should explain the grounds for freeing the defendant who had appealed against the sentence.

For almost two decades, many attempts have been made to expose the apparent unconstitutionality of the LCH. The Anti-Torture Law (No. 9,455), for example, was only enacted in 1997 and provided that only the initial conditions would be closed.[53] In practice, a first-time dealer, arrested for possessing a small amount of drugs, would be treated more severely than a chief of police who tortured a defendant in their custody. These punitive politics had well-defined targets and the 'monstrous' label of heinous was selectively applied.[54] Even in the face of the evident inequality in the legal treatment given to similar crimes, the Superior Courts to their shame supported the law's constitutionality. In 2006 alone, the STF (Supremo Tribunal Federal) declared the unconstitutionality of the compliance with the closed conditions, guaranteeing a convict the downgrading of the conditions according to the rules previously in force in the Penal Code, and emphasizing that the downgrading of the conditions had 'as a greater reason the resocialization of the prisoner who will eventually return to social life' (HC 82959). However, because this was declared in the light of diffuse constitutional control, it would be useful, according to a conservative reading of constitutionality control in criminal matters, only for the complainant.[55] A movement has begun, sometimes not so silent, in the Judiciary and in the Public Prosecutor's Office, so as not to extend to the other prisoners the same right. That is, each of those illegally incarcerated should sue, first in the lower instances, and after being able to process at least three appeals, this should reach the Court. In practice, this prevented many convicts from actually obtaining the same right until 16 December 2009, when the Summary 471 of the STJ and the Binding Precedent 26 was published.[56]

Before the performance of the punitive bench, and mediated by the President of the Court, the new Law n. 11464/2007 was enacted to 'solve' the problem of the unconstitutionality of differential treatment for 'heinous' crimes, realigning the legal strategies. The new LCH stated that, as in the Anti-torture Law, the sentence should initially be enforced in closed conditions. The 'novelty' was in the increase of the differentiated quantitative criteria for the downgrading of two-fifths of the sentence, if it was a first-time offence, and three-fifths, if it was 'specific recidivism in crimes of this nature', and two-thirds of the sentence for probation.

The New LCH provoked the continuation of the debates: first, whether the quantitative parameters could be applied to heinous crimes which had already been commited before the New LCH. In 2007, one of the STF courts ruled that it was impossible to be applied because of the express constitutional prohibition of retroactivity of the criminal law, except to benefit the defendant (article 5, XL, of the CF) (HC 92709). Thus, for the previous cases, the downgrading of compliance conditions would respect the parameter of one-sixth of their sentence. Despite the absurdity of the hypothesis of retroactive application of the Criminal Law, the debate served, in practice, to postpone the downgrading of several defendants.

Second, there was a debate about whether the imposition of initial conditions, provided for in the New LCH, would not violate the principle of individualization of the sentence, since it does not allow the judge to analyse the concrete situation of the defendant. If the legislator could not impose the fully closed conditions scheme, could it impose the initial closed conditions scheme?

The issue was even more problematic because in the course of debates over the unconstitutionality of the Heinous Crimes Law, the New Drug Law (NLD) was passed and resumed and extended in the specific legislation the unconstitutionalities of the old LCH.

The unconstitutionalities of the New Drug Law are at the basis of increased incarceration by the end of the decade. According to the NLD, in drug-trafficking offences: a) bail, amnesty and pardon would be prohibited (prohibitions provided for in the CF); b) a pardon (prohibition not expressly provided for in the CF and similar to that in the old LCH and declared unconstitutional) would be prohibited; probation would be prohibited (prohibition not provided for in the CF and similar to that in the old LCH and declared unconstitutional); c) the conversion of sentences in restriction of rights (article 44) would be prohibited; d) it was mandatory that detention in prison be a requirement for the admissibility of an appeal by a defendant who was not a first-time offender and with a good track record (the rule repeated part of article 594 CPP (the Federal Procedural Code) that would be revoked in 2008 due to contrary court decisions since 1999).

For ten years, there were isolated judgments of the aforementioned unconstitutionalities: a) In 2009, the STF declared unconstitutional the requirement of being imprisoned in order to launch an appeal (HC 90279); b) In 2010, the STF declared the unconstitutionality of the prohibition of substitution for a restrictive rights sentence. For the court, 'in the context of international treaties and conventions, approved and promulgated by the Brazilian State, differential treatment is given to illicit trafficking of narcotics which is characterized by its lower offensive potential. This differential treatment aims to enable alternatives to incarceration' (HC 97256); c) In 2012, the STF declared the unconstitutionality of the prohibition on granting probation (HC 104339); d) Only in 2012, the STF declared unconstitutional the *ex lege* setting of the initial conditions in the case of heinous and similar crimes (HC 111.840/ES). This was again an incidental declaration;[57] e) In 2016, the STF stated that trafficking committed by a first-time offender, on a one-off basis, with no previoius track record and no link with a criminal organization, could not be considered a 'heinous' crime (HC 118533).

Between 2006 and 2012, there were decisions in which the Court upheld the Drug Law especially in relation to the New Law of Heinous Crimes, maintaining the restriction of rights that had already been surpassed by the Court in relation to heinous crimes since 2006. Therefore, in what was an absurd reasoning, Drug Policy was sometimes more repressive because it was considered subject to the parameters of the Heinous Crimes and sometimes was more repressive than the Heinous Crimes Law because it was Drug Policy. In the end, from the point of view of the relations between the Legislative Power and the Judiciary, it can be noted that in the historical review of debates on the use of an 'exception' criminal law,[58] the Heinous Crimes category was used more extensively for drug offenders than other perpetrators. If the crime of drug trafficking was initially only 'tolerated', after nearly three decades, it had become the flagship of punitive politics.

This 'unconstitutional mutation' of the meanings of the constitutional 'exception' promoted by the Superior Courts, and the uses of the criminal procedure as a strategy to deny rights to the defendants, were two central mechanisms for the juridical production of the hyper-incarceration and social legitimation of the institutions that had developed throughout the dictatorship, such as the military police forces, to control urban space in a racially unequal society.

In this context, the fact that 40 per cent of the prison population is still awaiting trial is not just the result of a slow-moving and deficient justice system. It also constitutes a work pattern that must be understood in the context of unfounded accusations and the strategic use of the appeal system (by police, judges and prosecutors) as a way of transforming the exceptional nature of procedural arrest into a mechanism of racialized management of both punishment and urban space.

The survey 'Provisional Incarceration and Drug Law', analysed the arrests of those caught in the act between November 2010 and January 2011 in the State of São Paulo and concluded that there is a certain pattern in the in flagrante drug trafficking arrests:

a) The caught in the act arrests are performed by the Military Police, on public streets and during routine patrols; b) Only one person is arrested in each event and there is only the witness of the police authority who performed the arrest; c) The average of the common arrests was 66.5 grams of drugs; d) The accused have no defence in the police phase; e) The person arrested was not carrying the drug; f) The events of caught in the act arrests of drug trafficking do not involve violence; g) The accused represent a specific part of the population: men, young people aged between 18 and 29, browns and blacks, with up to elementary school education and without criminal records; h) The defendants are defended by the Public Defender's Office; i) They wait for trial in custody; j) The accused are sentenced to less than five years; k) Convicts shall not be given the right to appeal out of custody.[59]

What are the possibilities for defending such prisoners? The reference to the higher Courts is relevant, since local judges, who have constitutional guarantees (article 95, CF), are not forced to follow the parameters of the Superior Courts' decisions.[60] Their decisions will be altered, but this may take years. One of the fundamental mechanisms of the parameters of material illegality of arrests in Drug Policy is the systematic maintenance of decisions that will ultimately be declared illegal or unsubstantiated. As a rule, procedural arrests in Brazil have no time limit.[61] Therefore, the standards of correction of its bases are well differentiated regarding the local courts and the Superior Courts.

One of the serious problems is when the procedural arrest turns out to be longer and/or more serious than the sentence provided for by law, by the judge in the sentence or by the Superior Courts. Superior Courts only consider illegality due to excessive deadlines in extreme cases, and this again involves more delays. It is not unusual to find news of 'lost' prisoners within the penitentiary system, that is, those whose reason for arrest is no longer known by the administrative and judicial authorities. In practice, the average prison time is served in more burdensome prison conditions than was received in the sentence, or it is difficult to grant downgrading conditions benefits. Therefore, the procedural arrest and detention becomes, in many cases, materially the main sentence.[62]

Public security and criminal procedure: the effects of drug policy in Brazil and its impacts on Black people

Let's see how the drugs policy's effects are articulated and how they impact on Black people in Brazil. The country's drug policy produces a series of negative effects on Brazilian society as a whole. From the point of view of public health, these effects are manifested in terms of the expanded use of low-quality and unsupported psychoactive substances by the public health system for cases of dependence and abusive use.[63] In public security, this translates into expansive levels of incarceration and deaths resulting from militarized police action, with costs both in economic and ethical terms of guaranteeing life and preserving human dignity.

One impact of drug policy (and punitive discourse in general) on Black people is the forms of police approach and urban policing practices which result from how public security professionals construct their representations of suspects. In Brazilian law, some ideas are important for understanding the concept of suspicion and its legal and social derivations: the judicial suspect, the criminal suspect, the suspect individual, suspicious activity and suspicious situation.

a) The judicial suspect: that is, before the fact that is contrary to the legal order, which is apparently characteristic, and after that moment, there is the attempt to identify the agent, that is, the suspect of the committed act, based on the evidence found of the fact.[64] The vague CPP definitions of situations of suspicion; the existence of a doctrine that denies the rights of the accused in the police phase, keeping the constitutionalization away from the criminal process; the fact that such a perspective has allowed inquisitorial investigation to be used as one of the bases of condemnation; the presence of a theory of nullity which validates the vices of the police inquiry, on the grounds that it would not be an 'essential element' of the conviction, even though it may be used to convict; almost no application of the theory of unlawful evidence in situations where there is no discussion of problems concerning 'real proprietary citizens', that is, violations of rights occurring in urban areas of intense circulation and in peripheral areas against Black people, corroborate the indiscriminate use of this concept in police practices.[65]

b) The criminal suspect: individuals who had some criminal involvement at an earlier moment in their lives, which mark their social reputation, that is, those who have somehow 'started' in criminal activities. They are viewed by both police officers and society in general as marked and reprehensible individuals, since it is expected that they will commit crimes again.[66] It is, therefore, an effect of the penal system labelling process. In the case of Brazilian police practices, mere suspicion, formalized in a police record without investigation, has consequences often equivalent to condemnation or death inside the prison. Therefore, police practices consistent in the arrest and statements taken on the street without effective investigation that results in the production of material evidence, extend the labelling process. This process distances itself from the very selectivity that could exist within the framework of legality and establishes a selectivity which lacks legality but that is based on the power of 'authority'.[67]

c) The suspicious individual: the notion of a suspicious individual is closely related to the control of the individuals' bodies, that is, the police officer tries to identify the disorder or order in the bodies of those observed, trying to distinguish the discrepant cultures from the dominant culture. Hence there are bodily signs, signs of discipline, which identify the individual as suspicious or vulnerable. Along with the corporeal control comes the control of the movement and the clothes of such individual.[68] As we have pointed out below, it is not only a filter relative to social class, the suspect is identified based on a racialized filter.

d) The suspicious activity: this category deals with the act, the behaviour of the individual. Certain activities, movements, behaviours are categorized by the police as suspicious. An example is the act of 'circulating', which in police language means to reveal through gestures, looks, or any other activity what could not be shown, that is, something that the subject is hiding. In addition, the social roles, that is, those kinds of behaviour that are socially expected of certain people with certain characteristics, have a strong influence on the categorization of suspicious activity, since if these expectations are met, suspicion is raised.[69] As we point out later, what gives meaning to suspicious action is racialized social expectation.

e) The suspicious situation: the suspicious situation encompasses the control of the place or situation in which the social actors are inserted. It is mainly the image that the police officer has of a certain locale and beyond this, the affinity between individual and place, hence the actors' bodies need to be in tune with where they are. Thus, if someone wearing so-called 'kit peba' clothing (items typically worn by criminals and/or those of low quality) is walking in an upper-class neighbourhood, he will appear to be out of place, therefore, he will become a suspect. A similar situation arises when police observe a poor-looking individual driving a high-value car.[70]

These ideas of suspicion are articulated within the structurally selective character of the penal system. In a scenario where the 'opportunities' for criminalization are virtually unlimited, as is the case with the production/distribution/consumption market of drugs, in which the number of involved individuals exponentially exceeds the overall capacity of the penal system of incarceration, the attribution of a criminal status also tends to derive from characteristics of the penal system itself – that is, the system's ability to identify, investigate and repress certain behaviours. This is an interesting demonstration of how drug policy impacts on the Black population overwhelmingly.

The racialization of social expectation concerning just who are the suspects can be observed in police practices from different perspectives.

The first one is the analysis of the discourses of the subjects involved (interview technique and focus group), aggressors, victims and witnesses.

The surveys in this regard confirm: a) the existence of explicit race-based discourses by civil servants, with verification of internal police regulations that favour the approach of Black people, or that direct police detachments to the Black urban areas;[71] b) discourses by victims citing verbal aggression, in which racial attributes are highlighted in cases that often lack any judicial acknowledgement of the existence of racism;[72] c) in addition, by implicit discourses that can be perceived as racialized based on their contextual linkage and their consequences – for example, the police officers deny racial discrimination in their approaches and state that they consider the individual is suspect due to the discrepancy between his expensive apparel and his 'social class', in this case the unspoken parameter of inadequacy between one of the signs of social status and clothing rests, in fact, on the racialized hierarchy of wealth, that is, the prohibition of Black individuals being able to rise socially without being subjected to forms of social control); d) In Brazil, the main thrust in publicizing the victims' perspectives came from the Black social movement during the dictatorship period and by several cultural movements that have elaborated reports against the racism of police violence for at least a century; In the same way, surveys of perception concerning police violence always indicate that the Black population perceives themselves as more closely monitored and registers a greater number of approaches by the police.[73]

The second perspective concerns the consequences of both police practices and, above all, their institutional management. Surveys of the death rate involving confrontations with the police are revealing. In Brazil in 2017, an average of 14 people were killed per day in police interventions, more than 70 per cent of whom were Black, young and male;[74] these were in police operations mainly organized under the pretext of combating drug trafficking and focused in the peripheral communities of Black and poor people. The number of deaths are constantly being reported by human rights organizations,[75] especially deaths due to the lack of transport to hospitals for the wounded, and the lack of emergency medical assistance. To these deaths, add the countless deaths attributed to harmful drug policies, and since these also have more impact on the Black population than on other social groups, they are ignored by public managers and legislature.[76] The racial pattern of the death rate of young Blacks shows how often being subjected to unfair criminal procedure does not apply to poor Whites. The increased incidence of young Blacks among the dead when provisionally arrested, as well as sentenced prisoners and ex-cons, represents a distinctive form of selectivity. Therefore, the selectivity of Brazil's penal system cannot be considered in terms of incarceration alone, since it is linked to the processes of institutionalized death. The legal system officially rejects the death penalty, but produces, throughout its selection processes, the arrival at the most serious end in terms of violation of rights.

A third perspective is the way in which police institutions and police practices respond to different forms of reporting racism. In the face of constant reports against the police, especially the Military Police, the innumerable discursive and institutional strategies of these institutions in not controlling such practices is disturbingly effective. On the contrary, Brazilian police produce a preventive discourse against the reports that, more often than not, are combined with symbolic and real persecution of victims of institutional violence.[77]

Other social controls are in line with the cognitive process of constructing police suspicion. The geographical division and social demarcation of the urban space contribute to the police's construction of the suspect and the direction of the police actions. In this way, actions of social control and 'hygiene' are carried out 'rationally' in different places with different individuals. Therefore, there is an interchange between the construction of the 'social suspect', made in everyday life, in the media, and in social interactions marked by the physical and symbolic exclusion of certain groups and the 'police suspect'. 'Racial profiling' can directly occur both within the internal police sphere and outside in 'society', especially of those who use the security services (such as those who phone the call centres), or those who have the political capital to influence police actions, either through official mechanisms such as 'community representatives' or through informal mechanisms, building demands for protection.

As we pointed out in the survey 'Who is the suspect in drug trafficking?' one of the fundamental questions for social institutions dealing with conflict is to know how they can overcome the stereotypes of victim and aggressor which reproduce social prejudices. The acknowledgement of an internal filtering similar to social filtering does not exclude institutional accountability for the reproduction of patterns that violate fundamental principles which should guide the work of these social institutions, equal treatment in particular. In concrete terms, from the viewpoint of the victims of discriminatory practices – which is the viewpoint of preserving the rights that should be conferred on all citizens – the fact that discriminatory action is 'socially accepted' does not excuse its discriminatory character. Institutional inertia or aversion to victim discourse can be instrumental in legitimizing discriminatory practices.[78]

A final aspect of these punitive agendas against Black people concerns the Judiciary's role in confirming an argumentative pattern that integrates the conclusions of police work, validating the testimony given by these public agents to define what reasonable suspicion is and corroborate the processes of stereotyping Black women and men:

> A striking feature of the whole process of drug trafficking cases is the inertial dynamic present in the relations between public security and justice organizations ... there is little disagreement regarding the work of these organizations when it comes to reviewing and prosecuting a crime. What happens, from the police performance to the trial by judges of law, is a continuity in the way they comprehend the facts, based on the lack of questions and the low quality of evidence.[79]

There are few judgments concerning the elements of the founded suspicion. However, the courts have upheld the understanding that the officer could act without a warrant and, if he subsequently found drugs, his behaviour was legally adequate. It is important to remember that no police officer is administratively liable if drugs are *not* found. In turn, the Superior Court of Justice has decided on the matter directly related to the debate on the 'objective character of the founded suspicion', accepting vague references, made only by police officers' testimony, that there would be an anonymous report about the suspect or in that area. The validity of anonymous reports, sometimes only referred to as existing by police officers and of generic content in relation to the facts, has not been contested by the Superior Courts (HC 83.830/PR, 2009; REsp 1256968/SP, 2012).

The courts remain indifferent, validating a typical practice found in war zones, and common in Brazilian cities: the generic personal search made under the pretext of supposed crime prevention. For this reason, young Blacks using public transport are often subjected to humiliating and violent searches by heavily armed police officers, with no specific purpose (only the generic claim).

Contrary to the situation in other countries, the submission of police action to the Judiciary is not guaranteed in the investigative acts, since in our legal discourses, the fact that someone may possibly be in possession of a quantity of drugs, although small, would justify both a personal search and a residential search, at any time and without a warrant, given the permanent nature of the crime of drug trafficking and in the face of 'founded reasons' (RE 603616/STF). In practice, such understandings make constitutional guarantees almost nonexistent for a population without political power to oppose the police's institutional power. The power to stop, search and arrest, without prior authorization by the Judiciary, in a democratic State, should at most be an exception for cases of concrete risk to a legal right. However, in Brazil's case, since the nineteenth century, these powers are implemented daily in cities, where Black individuals are subject to arbitrary police violence.

Finally, throughout Supreme Court case law, although an initial concern for the subjective nature of a possible definition of founded suspicion is noted, it is possible to see that the existence of the 'anonymous report' and the 'permanent' character of the crime of drug trafficking have served to legitimize the definition of suspicion, personal search and home invasion.

The courts' argumentative standard is to accept the description of the police officers' work in cases of caught-in-the-act arrests and the determination of the hypotheses of suspicion from the validation of their testimonies without an effective confirmation with bureaucratic records of police work or other evidence (HC 67648, 1989; RHC 66359, 1988). The courts repeat that:

> The value of the witnessing testimony of police officers – especially when rendered in court, under the guarantee of the adversary – is of unquestionable probative effectiveness and cannot be disqualified by the mere fact of emanating from commissioned state agents, due to official duty of criminal repression. The witnessing testimony of the police officer will be of no value unless it is shown that this state servant, because it reveals a particular interest in the criminal investigation, acts factually or when it is demonstrated – as with other witnesses – that the statements are not supported nor, do they harmonize with other suitable evidence. (HC 73518, 1996)

In fact, the courts comprehend the problems concerning the police investigation as issues related to the theory of nullities present in the CPP (1941). Based on two premises: a) that the records of the investigation are not probative acts, but at the same time, paradoxically, they have probative value, so their vices are irrelevant, since they can be addressed in the judicial phase; (b) that errors committed in the police inquiry, in particular in the case of caught-in-the-act arrest warrants, are merely formal devices which have repercussions only at that stage, with the consequent invalidation of the caught-in-the-act arrest. However, in less common criminal cases – white-collar crimes, for example – these two premises are replaced with the adoption of the doctrine of exclusion of the unlawful evidence that is explicitly provided for among fundamental rights as cited in article 5.[80]

In summary, the case law reflects the ambiguity experienced by the common criminal investigation practices. Throughout the decades after the 1988 Constitution, the requirements for police testimony to be considered valid were loosened. Initially, the case law indicated that the defendant should prove that the sentence was based exclusively on those elements, that there was no other evidence collected in the investigation or in the judicial phase. However, after 1988, it was simply stated that it was impossible to discuss the nullity of the police investigation and the presumption of veracity of the public agents' testimony.

Thus, paradoxically, insofar as the theory of exclusion of illicit evidence being incorporated into the constitutional text, as advanced in other situations, it failed to discuss what the necessary requirements would be for, on the one hand, the probative, albeit indicia, production in the police investigation and the requirements for using such evidence in the grounds of the decisions. Instead, the Court relied on a defensive case law that precludes the analysis of the concrete facts brought to its analysis, especially on the ground that it is a matter of fact but not of law. In these terms, the STF tends to deny a prosecution of the procedures adopted by the police in the investigation phase (concerning common crimes), contrary to what has happened in a long tradition of judicial analysis of police investigation and approach procedures as found, for example, in the US Supreme Court.

Added to this is the 'inertia' pattern (toward criminalization) of judges who do not even consider the lack of plausibility of the narratives contained in the cases, replacing the contradictory with the common sense, openly stating that those individuals arrested by the police are all guilty. Investigations only record the tip of the Police State's iceberg that moves into exception practices. The restrictive interpretation of the existence of the rights of the accused at the investigation stage validates the way in which the Judiciary remains distant but not equidistant in the control of institutional violence. In practice, this same model is responsible for the validation, without a constitutional filter, of evidence collected under duress, since subjectively, although not always explicitly, the judges are associated with valorizing the activity of the persecution of criminals (the 'others' racialized) and, bureaucratically, they say nothing about the daily routine of investigations.[81]

This picture corroborates a model of criminalization of Black people's presence in the public space in an inexhaustible combination between drug policy, racism and punitivism. It is a complex legal-political imbrication that is based on a series of social representations which condemn, interdict and exterminate Black life.

Conclusions: the anti-Black genocide as the basis of drug policy – death, politics and violence in Brazil

Such a picture is anchored in what Black social movements and intellectuals have called 'anti-black genocide'[82] to refer to the deep, systematic and permanent violence against Black people in the colonial *continuum*.[83] In Brazil, in 1978, Abdias do Nascimento in 'The genocide of the black Brazilian: a process of masked racism' indicates the extent to which racism had formed the national identity and at the same time how such a process could be described theoretically based on the category of genocide. The author refers to the multiplicity of physical, symbolic, political and cultural processes, which prevent the existence of Black people in Brazil (and in diaspora), stating:

> In case it is impossible to appeal to the Brazilian conscience, we believe that human conscience can no longer remain inert, endorsing the revolting oppression and collective clearance of Afro-Brazilians, which we are documenting on these pages, both more effective and insidious, diffuse and evasive. Brazilian racism is characterized by a mutable, multipurpose appearance that makes it unique; however, in order to face it, it is necessary to wage the characteristic fight of any and all anti-racist and anti-genocidal combat. Because its uniqueness is only on the surface, its ultimate goal is the obliteration of blacks as a physical and cultural entity.[84]

The subject was also addressed by Ana Luiza Pinheiro Flauzina in her work 'Corpo Negro caído no chão: o sistema penal e o projeto genocida do estado brasileiro':

> Taking racism as the core of this whole endeavor is, in the end, to assume openly that the armed wing of the State is programmed to exterminate the black population. And this kind of statement, we are aware, not only produces shocks and fissures in the building of racial democracy, but also becomes a definitive end in this kind of reading of our racial relations.[85]

From the political point of view, the War on Drugs is perhaps the most explicit and evident demonstration that any discourse about racial democracy is unsustainable in Brazil. As many researchers and activists of the Brazilian Black movement have stated, it is impossible to defend the idea of a society without hierarchies and racial barriers in Brazil, as we have tried to demonstrate throughout this chapter, there is much evidence that Blacks and Whites have accessed rights and opportunities unequally throughout the country's history and that these inequalities have ultimately resulted in lethal consequences for Brazil's Black population. According to the data from the Brazilian government itself, the possibility of a Black person meeting a violent death is at least twice as high as a White person of the same sex and age.

In the context of the drug war, these consequences are demonstrated quantitatively. Surveys show that young Blacks are imprisoned on drug trafficking charges even though they are carrying only very small quantities of illicit substances,[86] with a higher incidence of physical violence and torture against Black people by the police,[87] and, finally, reiterated and repeated complaints of racial profiling in trials and approaches of Black people accused of drug trafficking in Brazil.[88]

As noted by Ana Flauzina:

> The consolidation of such brutal ways of working by the criminal justice systems is only justified by the existence of a perspective which excludes the black pain from the ethical horizon. Whether it be in the foundations of US democracy, which incorporates discriminatory practices in a legalistic way, or through the ill-finished paths of an institutionality which approves of barbarism, as in the Brazilian case, what can be perceived is that black bodies are managed by state policies which regard them as fungible and disposable.[89]

There is a broad process of deconstruction of Black people's humanity which supports and justifies the discriminatory and violent practice of illegal arrests, torture and extermination of Black people.[90] This long and systematic process of dehumanization involves a permanent renewal of the slave experience[91] and the repetition of negative representations of Black people, which are articulated in the drug war's hyper-punitive dimension to promote Black people's arrest, corporal punishment and death.

The connection between the image of the 'junkie' – irrational and violent – and the ex-slave – dangerous and hostile – reveals the cognitive foundation around which judges, police officers, prosecutors, and public authorities in general, organize their activities and form their understanding of the idea of public order and the control of urban scenarios. Over the years, the drug wars policy has become, on the one hand, an economic policy of moving illegal financial assets to maintain the political power of small groups, and on the other hand, a strategy to control the cities through the mobilization of law-and-order discourses as an argument for the proliferation of authoritarian and anti-democratic measures.

The Brazilian Judiciary, managed from 'Whiteness' by validating a genocidal security policy, has been balancing itself on an ambiguous strategy. On the one hand, by means of constitutional decisions with a lot of symbolic investment, it validates affirmative action policies, which in fact were built by social disputes and were already consolidated almost a decade ago. On the other hand, it seeks to exempt itself from its responsibility for the current 'state of unconstitutionality' of the prison system. At the same time, the Judiciary corroborates a genocidal security policy in everyday life, through procedures which are only superficially neutral. The management of urban Black bodies is a central mechanism for the reproduction of racial hierarchies in relation to work and wealth.[92]

Obsession with the Black body has historically fuelled irrational desires and fears. The imagination of the elites has always been occupied with a paranoia regarding the Black body. Such paranoia sustained the racial terror of Brazil-Cologne, the eugenics theories of the nineteenth century, the territorial configuration of our cities, the emergence of the police apparatus and the contemporary narratives of urban violence which are still deeply 'racialized'. White paranoia concerning the Black body cultivates a range of meanings not only of the Black body per se, but also of the predominantly Black spatial territories. The slum appears in the racist imagination as a bad place, as the space reserved for criminals. In this sense, the racialization of fear in the news media is based on stereotypes of Blackness: the Black family as pathological, the Black man as a criminal, the Black woman as promiscuous and degraded. With such a script in mind, it is easy to contextualize the premature deaths of young Blacks in urban Brazil.[93]

Finally, what is at stake before the strategies of criminal control of drugs is the control of Black people's lives and the reiteration of a practice of extermination. Unveiling the racial dimension of this phenomenon seems to us, for various reasons, a necessary initiative to promote justice and freedom as legitimate expectations for a significant proportion of Brazil's citizens who have been cast aside as the 'garbage of society' for so many years.[94]

Notes

1 We thank the research assistants Gustavo Costa, Lucas Araújo Alves, Vitor Lages and Ariadne Souza and Gisela Aguiar for reviewing the judicial decisions. Dr Duarte thanks the Coordination of Improvement of Higher Education Personnel (CAPES), which through the granting of a postdoctoral research fellowship (2018–19), allowed the preparation of this text as part of the ongoing research at the University of Pennsylvania, at the Population Studies Center under the guidance of Professor Tukufu Zuberi.

2 Dora Lucia de Lima Bertúlio (1989) wrote the first academic work in the area of law, *Law and Race Relations: A Critical Introduction to Racism*, linking the criminal system to institutional racism, beginning the criticism of the uses of the ideology of Racial Democracy by Brazilian jurists: Dora Lúcia de Lima Bertúlio. *Direito e relações raciais: uma introdução crítica ao racismo*. Dissertação de mestrado em direito (Florianópolis: UFSC, 1989).

3 Lourenço Cardoso, 'A Branquitude acrítica revisitada e a Branquidade', *Revista da ABPN, Florianópolis* 6.13 (mar./jun. 2014): 88–106; V. Ware, 'O poder duradouro da branquidade: um problema a solucionará', in idem, *Branquidade: identidade branca e multiculturalismo* (Rio de Janeiro: Garamond, 2004), pp. 7–40.

4 Evandro C. Piza Duarte et al., 'Who is the suspect of drug trafficking? Notes of the dynamics of racial and social prejudice in the definition of the conduct of users and drug dealers by the military police officers of the cities of Brasília, Curitiba and Salvador', in Cristiane Lima, Gustavo Baptista and Isabel Figueiredo (eds), *Public Security and Human Rights: Transversal Themes* (Brasília: Ministry of Justice, 2014), pp. 81–118.

5 Menelick de Carvalho Netto, 'A hermenêutica constitucional sob o paradigma do Estado Democrático de Direito', *Notícia do Direito Brasileiro. Nova Série* 6 (jul/dez 1998) (Brasília: UnB, 2000); Menelick de Carvalho Netto, 'A hermenêutica constitucional e os desafios postos aos direitos fundamentais', in José Adércio Leite Sampaio (ed.), *Jurisdição constitucional e os direitos fundamentais* (Belo Horizonte: Del Rey, 2003).

6 Marcos Nobre, *Imobilismo em Movimento: da abertura democrática ao governo Dilma* (São Paulo: Compania das Letras, 2013); Francisco Weffort, *Porque democracia* (São Paulo: Brasiliense, 1984).

7 Gisela Aguiar Wanderley, 'Entre a lei processual e a praxe policial: características e consequências da desconcentração e do descontrole da busca pessoal', *Revista Brasileira de Ciências Criminais* 128.25 (2017): 115–149.

8 'Despite the confrontation operated by the doctrine and by the case law in relation to the unconstitutionality of art. 2, paragraph 1 of Law no. 8,072/90, only in 2006, the Plenum of the Federal Supreme Court declared that the prohibition of downgrading conditions conflicts with the guarantee of individualization of the sentence (article 5, XLVI, of the Federal Constitution). The Supreme Court's slow analysis of the matter – which in many respects is regarded as negligence – has allowed for a radical change in the foundations of the national punitive

system throughout the 15 years of the obstruction of downgrading conditions ... The possible conclusion, therefore, is that the Law of the Heinous Crimes was the first turn of the national punitive system in the sense of adherence to the neoconservative foundations of punishment that characterize the international scenario of the 1990s': Salo Carvalho, *Penas e medidas de segurança no Direito penal Brasileiro* (São Paulo: Saraiva, 2015), p. 305.

9 The most common argument in the Brazilian doctrine is that the 1941 CPP reproduced the inquisitorial model by repeating the model of Fascist Italy. However, the vision of a continuity with a medieval tradition loses, as it could not be otherwise, the modernity of the Inquisition and, specifically, the insertion of the Inquisition into modernity, with its contradictory and colonial dimensions: Evandro Piza Duarte and Tiago Kalkmann, 'Por uma releitura dos conceitos de sistema processual penal inquisitório e acusatório a partir do princípio da igualdade', *Revista Brasileira de Ciências Criminais* 142 (2018): 171–208.

10 Evandro C. P. Duarte, Marcos V. L. Queiroz and Paulo H. A. Costa, 'A Hipótese Colonial, um diálogo com Michel Foucault: a Modernidade e o Atlântico Negro no centro do debate sobre Racismo e Sistema Penal', *Universitas Jus* 27 (2016): 1; Ana Luiza Pinheiro Flauzina, 'Apresentação', in Michele Alexander, *A nova segregação: racismo e encarceramento em massa* (São Paulo: Boitempo, 2017), pp. 11–17.

11 Alessandro Baratta, *Criminologia crítica e crítica do direito penal* (Rio de Janeiro: Revan, 2002); Vera Regina Pereira de Andrade, *A ilusão da segurança jurídica: do controle da violência à violência do controle penal* (Porto Alegre: Livraria do Advogado, 2003); Vera Malaguti Batista, *Introdução crítica à criminologia brasileira* (Rio de Janeiro: Revan, 2012); Gabriel Ignácio Anitua, *História dos Pensamentos Criminológicos* (Rio de Janeiro: Revan, 2008), and Nilo Batista, *Introdução crítica ao direito penal brasileiro* (Rio de Janeiro: Revan, 1990).

12 Torture, abuse and violations of law are systematic in the Brazilian prison system, as the Federal Supreme Court recognized in the scope of the MC in ADPF 347, which declared the unconstitutional state of the prison system establishing emergency precautionary measures aimed at combating the system's serious human rights violations.

13 The data on Brazil's prison system are produced primarily by the National Justice Council (CNJ), a body that monitors the activities of the Judiciary, and by the National Penitentiary Department (DEPEN), a body linked to the Federal Government and responsible for monitoring penitentiary management in Brazil. However, the data produced by these two organs are very limited because: a) they are not updated with any regularity, b) their attempts to elicit information from prisons are usually ignored, c) they lack permanent monitoring and supervision. Recently, the National Council of Justice sought to correct some of these problems and on 28 February 2018 published the map of implementation of the National Registry of Prisoners, which, on 20 June 2018, reported a registration level of 51 per cent, corresponding to 490,291 people deprived of their liberty (https://tinyurl.com/y826mszn). This registry assigns a unique identification number for each detainee in Brazilian prisons and can be accessed by any citizen online and in real time, according to news from the CNJ website (www.cnj.jus.br/news/cnj/86259-prisoner-of-prisoners-of-cnj-contributes-to-overcome-crisis-of-security). However, this

data is not yet consolidated in technical terms and, therefore, we will continue analysing the data from the last survey of the Brazilian prison population (INFOPEN), released by the National Penitentiary Department and by the Ministry of Justice and Public Security in 2017, referring to the period up to June 2016. This National Survey of Penitentiary Information (2017) indicates that there are 726,712 prisoners in the Penitentiary System (689,510) in the Secretariats of Security (36,765) and in the Federal Penitentiary System (437), representing an occupation rate of 197.4 per cent and a rate of imprisonment of 352.6 people imprisoned for every 100,000 inhabitants. The total percentage of prisoners without conviction is 40.2 per cent, with some states exceeding the 60 per cent mark, such as Sergipe (65.1 per cent) and Amazonas (64.4 per cent), with occupancy rates, respectively, of 236 per cent and 483.9 per cent: CNJ (Conselho Nacional de Justiça), INFOPEN, 2017. *Justiça em Números*, 2017. Mapa de implantação do Cadastro Nacional de Presos. Vetores Iniciais e Dados Estatísticos. Censo do Poder Judiciário 2018. Departamento Penitenciário Nacional. *Levantamento Nacional de Informações Penitenciárias – Atualização Junho de 2016* (Brasília, 2017), pp. 7–8.

14 CNJ, 2017, p. 9.

15 CNJ, 2017, pp. 9–12.

16 Julita Lemgruber and Márcia Fernandes, 'Tráfico de drogas na cidade do Rio de Janeiro: prisão provisória e direito de defesa', in Barbara Mourão, Julita Lemgruber, Leonarda Musumeci and Silvia Ramos (eds), *Polícia, Justiça e Drogas: Como anda nossa democracia?* (Rio de Janeiro: CESeC, 2016); Luciana Boiteux, 'Tráfico de Drogas e Constituição. Um estudo jurídico-social do tipo do art. 33 da Lei de Drogas diante dos princípios constitucionais-penais', Série Pensando o Direito (Brasília: Ministério da Justiça, março de 2009); Maria Gorete Marques Jesus et al., *Prisão Provisória e Lei de Drogas – Um estudo sobre os flagrantes de tráfico de drogas na cidade de São Paulo* (São Paulo: NEV/ USP 2011); Julita Lemgruber et al., *Usos e abusos da prisão provisória no Rio de Janeiro. Avaliação do impacto da Lei 12.403/2011* (Rio de Janeiro: ARP/ CESeC/ Ucam, novembro de 2013), and Beatriz Vargas Ramos Gonçalves de Rezende, 'A Ilusão do proibicionismo: estudo sobre a criminalização secundária do tráfico de drogas no Distrito Federal'. Tese de Doutorado em Direito pela Universidade de Brasília, 2011.

17 Boiteux, 'Tráfico de Drogas e Constituição'.

18 Boiteux, 'Tráfico de Drogas e Constituição'.

19 Within civil society, the work of the organizations articulated by the Brazilian Drug Policy Platform – PBPD (http://pbpd.org.br); Black Initiative for a New Drug Policy – INNPD (https://pt.br.facebook.com/innpd/); National Network of Antiprohibitionist Feminists – RENFA (https://pt-br.facebook. com/renfantiproibicionistas/), among others, fostered research on the effects of drug policy in Brazil and on alternatives for regulating psychoactive substances through non-criminal channels. In the governmental sphere, the work of the Secretariat for Legislative Affairs and the National Secretariat of Public Security, which between 2005 and 2015 financed numerous researches on the subject of criminal justice in Brazil, also contributed significantly to the accumulation of knowledge about drug policy and its main challenges. Among others are the exploratory works of Salo de Carvalho, Maria Lucia Karam, Luciana Boiteux, Ella Wiecko de Castilhos and Beatriz Vargas Ramos.

20 Following the impeachment of Brazilian president Dilma Rousseff in 2016, a series of investigations were interrupted by the Secretariat for Legislative Affairs and the National Secretariat of Public Security of the Ministry of Justice. On the subject of the interruption of the presidential term, see André Singer, *O Lulismo em crise: um quebra cabeça do período Dilma (2011–2016)* (São Paulo: Companhia das Letras, 2018).

21 Since the 1990s, there have been numerous legislative changes in criminal matters aimed at aggravating sentences and hardening the criminal procedure. According to Ferreira, between the 1990s and 2000s, 203 laws were passed, most of them aimed at increasing penalties, new penalties and aggravating circumstances: Carolina Costa Ferreira, *O Estado de Impacto Legislativo como estratégia de enfrentamento a discursos punitivos na execução penal*. Tese de Doutorado em Direito, Estado e Constituição (Brasília: UnB, 2016).

22 Laís da Silva Avelar and Bruna Portella Novaes, 'Há mortes anteriores à morte: politizando o genocídio negro dos meios através do controle urbano racializado', *Revista Brasileira de Ciências Criminais* 135.25 (2017): 343–376 (São Paulo: Ed. RT); Naila Ingrid Chaves Franklin, 'O controle social e as mulheres: possibilidades e releituras para a criminologia feminista', *Revista Brasileira de Ciências Criminais* 135.25 (2017): 487–518 (São Paulo: Ed. RT).

23 Criminalization processes are forms of designating who will be protected and who will be prosecuted; thus, crime cannot be defined as an ontological reality but as a social construction and there is an insurmountable distance between the declared and the actual roles of imprisonment and punishment. The number of examples illustrating how criminalization processes – primary or secondary – are arbitrary and violent processes of operationalization of the ruling power, or the actions of those seeking to maintain political, economic and cultural hegemony, are vast: Baratta, *Criminologia crítica e crítica do direito penal*; Andrade, *Vera Regina Pereira de. A ilusão da segurança jurídica*; Anitua, *História dos Pensamentos Criminológicos*; Batista, *Introdução crítica ao direito penal brasileiro*.

24 The drug policy narrative is based on the discourse that drugs are an evil, that the drug trade is the main reason for urban violence, and that state violence itself is the only means of deterring drug dealers and restoring social and political order in today's drug-traffic-dominated communities: Maria Lúcia Karan, 'Legalizar para Respeitar os Direitos Humanos', Conferência de abertura do Seminário Redução de Danos da Universidade Federal da Bahia (UFBA) em agosto 2015.

25 Karan, 'Legalizar para Respeitar os Direitos Humanos'.

26 The number of judges involved in the criminalization processes and the distinction in terms of territorial scope and workload between the two justices can be observed. In 2016, in the Brazilian Judiciary, there were a total of 18,011 magistrates, 15,582 at trial court level and 2,429 at appellate court level (CNJ, 2017, p. 37). In the Federal Justice, there were 1,796 magistrates, 1,658 at trial court level and 138 at appellate court level (CNJ, 2017, p. 44). In the State Justice, there were 12,392 magistrates, 10,681 at trial court level and 1,796 magistrates at appellate court level (CNJ, 2017, p. 40). The majority of the judicial units belong to the State Justice, 49.2 per cent of the Brazilian municipalities are headquarters of the State Justice, while 5 per cent of the municipalities are headquarters of the Federal Justice (CNJ, 2017, p. 30). There are 2,415 trial courts of common justice that touch on the criminal subject, exclusively or not (1,242 are exclusively

criminal courts, 723 civil and criminal courts, 159 exclusively children and youth courts, 123 exclusively criminal enforcement courts, 109 exclusively domestic violence courts, and 59 courts dealing with children and youth that include elderly and/or family) (CNJ, 2017, pp. 30–31). Regarding the number of cases, there were 2,749,153 new criminal cases in the State Justice (13.89 per cent of the total); in the Federal Justice, there are 124,020 new criminal cases (3.26 per cent of the total), in the Electoral Justice, 4,498 new criminal cases (0.46 per cent of the total). In turn, there were 7,564,003 pending criminal cases in the State Justice (11.99 per cent of the total), 214,967 pending criminal cases in the Federal Justice (2.14 per cent of the total), and 10,411 pending criminal cases in Electoral Justice (a branch specializing in electoral integrity) (2.37 per cent of the total). There are also criminal proceedings in the state military courts and military audits of the Union, which together total 4,162 new and 4,188 pending criminal cases. In the High Courts, there are a total of 80,581 new criminal cases (3.39 per cent of the total) and 70,702 pending criminal cases (2.97 per cent of the total): CNJ, 2017, p. 39.

27 According to CNJ, the division between the Courts is based on the following criteria: total expenses; the processes which were processed in the period (downloaded and pending); the number of magistrates; the number of servers (personnel, requested, assigned and commissioned without personnel link), and the number of auxiliary workers (outsourced, trainees, lay judges and conciliators). The consolidation of this information forms a single score, by court, from which it is grouped into three categories, according to their size, namely: large, medium, or small courts: CNJ, 2017, p. 33.

28 CNJ, 2017, p. 34.

29 Ministério da Justiça, 'IV Diagnóstico da Defensoria Pública no Brasil', in *Diálogos sobre Justiça* (Brasília, 2015), pp. 19–20.

30 Ministério da Justiça. 'IV Diagnóstico da Defensoria Pública no Brasil', pp. 83–85.

31 CNMP (Conselho Nacional do Ministério Público), 'Cenários de Gênero. Série Cenários – reflexão, pesquisa e realidade', 2018.

32 Maria Tereza Sadek, *Delegados de polícia* (Rio de Janeiro: Centro Edelstein de Pesquisas Sociais, 2009).

33 Ordem dos Advogados do Brasil (OAB), *Institucional/Quadro de advogados, 2018*, in www.oab.org.br.

34 Roberto Fragale, Rafaela Moreira and Ana Paula Sciammarella, 'Magistratura e gênero: um olhar sobre as mulheres nas cúpulas do judiciário brasileiro', in *E-cadernos ces*, vol. 24, pp. 57–77 (Centro de Estudos Sociais da Universidade de Coimbra, Coimbra, 2015).

35 CNJ (Conselho Nacional de Justiça), INFOPEN, 2015, p. 41.

36 CNJ (Conselho Nacional de Justiça), INFOPEN, 2015, p. 120.

37 CNJ (Conselho Nacional de Justiça), INFOPEN, 2015.

38 Zuenir Ventura, *Cidade Partida* (São Paulo: Companhia das Letras, 1994).

39 Eugenio Raúl Zaffaroni, *Em busca das penas perdidas: A perda de legitimidade do sistema penal* (Rio de Janeiro: Revan, 2001).

40 Nilson Borges Filho, *Os militares no poder* (São Paulo: Editora Acadêmica, 1994); Paulo Sérgio Pinheiro, 'Autoritarismo e Transição' *Revista Usp* 9 (1991): 45–56.

41 Duarte, Queiroz and Costa, 'A Hipótese Colonial, um diálogo com Michel Foucault'.

42 Mercosur is a South American trade bloc established by the Treaty of Asunción in 1991 and the Protocol of Ouro Preto in 1994. Full members are Argentina, Brazil, Paraguay and Uruguay. Venezuela is a full member, though it has been suspended since 1 December 2016.

43 Rafael de Deus Garcia, *O uso da tecnologia e a atualização do modelo inquisitorial: Gestão da prova e violação de direitos fundamentais na investigação policial na política de drogas* (BH: DPlácido, 2015).

44 Ignácio Cano, *Controle de polícia no Brasil* (Trabalho apresentado na Conferência internacional 'Controle da polícia e a qualidade do monitoramento: tendências globais em contextos nacionais') (Haia: Altus, 2005), www.soudapaz.org/upload/pdf/textocanoppc.pdf [accessed 23 July 2018]; C. Zackseski, *Diagnóstico sobre a situação das corregedorias das instituições de segurança pública dos estados da região Nordeste*. Produto 2, Consultoria Especializada Cooperação Programa das Nações Unidas para o Desenvolvimento e Secretaria Nacional de Segurança Pública do Ministério da Justiça (Brasília, DF: PNUD; Senasp-MJ, 2016). Instead, with the use of social networks and new communication technologies, many of these corporations came to act as advocates of 'severe crime' procedures, normalizing scenes of inhumane treatment and acting as 'moral entrepreneurs': Eugênio Raul Zaffaroni and Nilo Batista, *Direito Penal Brasileiro I.* (Rio de Janeiro: Revan, 2003). This normalization can be identified in the last elections of the three 'B' benches in the National Congress: 'ox (boi)' (rural owners, most traditional), 'bible' (members of conservative religious economic groups) and 'bullet' (police and defenders of punitive and corporate guidelines): Evandro Piza Duarte and Leonardo da Silva Santana, *Hasteemos a bandeira colorida: diversidade sexual e de gênero no Brasil* (São Paulo: Editora Expressão Popular, 2018).

45 Data from the report 'Research Profile of Public Security Institutions', produced by MJ/SENASP. The data are limited by the total or partial absence of information about the racial composition of the members. In 2012, information was supplied about race/colour of 43.8 per cent of the entire Military Police force in Brazil. In Minas Gerais, in 2013, information was supplied for about 93 per cent of the total, in Rio Grande do Sul 100 per cent, in Paraná and São Paulo there was none. Only Rio de Janeiro did not provide data related to this criterion. In relation to the Civil Police, it was possible to gauge the racial composition of 59.76 per cent of its total personnel. In SP it was informed about 99.97 per cent of the personnel, in RJ 16.44 per cent, in RS and PR 100 per cent. However, the MG Civil Police did not report the data. The data on the prison population are from the last National Survey of Penitentiary Information for 2016, an annual report produced by DEPEN. However, the data present a sub-representation, since the 2016 report assessed 72 per cent of the information on the race/colour of the Brazilian prison population. In São Paulo and Minas Gerais, this rate is 79 per cent, in Rio de Janeiro 100 per cent, in Rio Grande do Sul 87 per cent, and in Paraná 43 per cent. Regarding the Brazilian population's racial composition, the national data are from the National Household Sample Survey (PNAD) report for 2015, while data by state are from the 2010 population census, both carried out by the Brazilian Institute of Geography and Statistics (IBGE). It is also noted that the category 'non-whites', which corresponds to Black, Brown, Yellow and Indigenous, was used in the table in some data. The name and grouping used in these surveys was then maintained.

46 However, there is a deliberate under-reporting of data on the composition of

these police forces and especially, a lack of data on their performance. In the last two administrations, with the increasing politicization of the racial question and with attempts to implement rational management systems, the states' administrations (state military police) refused to collect the data.

47 Jorge da Silva, 'Fighting police corruption in Brazil: The case of Rio de Janeiro', in Rick Sarre et al. (eds), *Policing Corruption: International Perspectives* (Lanham, MD: Lexington Books, 2005), vol. 1, pp. 247–258.

48 In this context, there was the action of the Unified Black Movement with the campaign 'Prisons, cellars, until when?', cited in *Journal of MNU* 17 (1989) ('React to racial violence') and the work of the Teotônio Vilela Commission (Vilela, 1986).

49 Mateus do Prado Utzig, 'A proibição da tortura na constituinte de 1987–88 entre demandas por justiça e reconciliação nacional. 2015' 121 f. (Brasília: UnB, 2015).

50 Art. 5º, XLVI da CF, Arts. 5º, 8º, 41, XII and 92, single paragraph, II, of the LEP, Art. 34 of the CP.

51 Regarded as heinous, after some changes, the crimes of robbery-murder, extortion qualified by death, extortion by means of kidnapping and in the qualified form, rape, indecent assault, epidemic resulting in death, poisoning of drinking water or food or medical substance, qualified by death, and by genocide, attempted or accomplished (Art. 1).

52 Article XLIII – the law shall consider as non-bailable and not eligible for pardon or amnesty crimes of torture, illicit trafficking of narcotics and related drugs, terrorism and those defined as heinous crimes, by these meaning the mentors, executors and those with foreknowledge who declined to prevent the crime.

53 Such provision has not yet been declared unconstitutional. However, there is an isolated precedent of the STF, and considered contrary to all other decisions, in the sense that it is constitutional: HC 123316/SE (2015).

54 David Garland, *A cultura do controle: crime e ordem social na sociedade contemporânea* (Rio de Janeiro: Revan, 2005).

55 The STF reaffirmed this position in Rcl 4335 (2014), due to non-compliance with HC 82959.

56 Binding Summary 26 STF and Summary 471/STJ.

57 In HC 111.840/ES, the rapporteur summarized the Court's consolidated position: 'If the Federal Constitution mentions that the law will regulate the individualization of the sentence, it is natural that it should exist. Likewise, the criteria for the establishment of the initial prison conditions must be harmonized with constitutional guarantees, and it is always necessary to state the reasons for the conditions imposed, even if it is a heinous or equivalent crime.'

58 Zaffaroni, *Em busca das penas perdidas*; Günther Jakobs and Manuel Cancio Meliá, *Direito Penal do Inimigo* (Porto Alegre: Livraria do Advogado, 2008).

59 NEV, *Prisão Provisària e Lei de Drogas. Um estudo sobre os flagrantes de tráfico de drogas na cidade de São Paulo*, Arquivo Digital (São Paulo: USP, 2012).

60 Even though the Code of Civil Procedure of 2015, in its art. 927 mentioning the precedents of binding effectiveness that must be followed mandatorily by judges and courts, our institutional history is marked by such a perspective. On the other hand, there is an understanding in the STF's 'punitive turn' that the HC filed against the decision to order preventive custody loses the object if the conviction is handed down in which the arrest is held, as there would be a 'renewal of the

title'. Therefore, it would be necessary to file a new HC against the sentence and restart the long journey to the Superior Courts (HC 143333/PR).

61 In Brazil, there are legally two types of procedural arrest: pre-trial detention (with no time limit for termination) and temporary arrest (with a fixed time limit), and a third form of arrest (caught in the act) that should only involve a brief custody period until the court decides on the application of one of those modalities within 24 hours, but which in practice may be wrongfullly extended. Pre-trial detention is ordered in the course of the preliminary investigation or prosecution, including after the verdict. The law provides, although in a vague way, situations of risk that would justify such arrest (article 312 of the CPP). The temporary arrest (Law No. 7.960/89) is a precautionary prison to satisfy the interest of the police, in the course of the investigation, placing the accused at their disposal within the stipulated period (5 days and, in the case of heinous crimes, 30 days, both extendable for the same period). The caught-in-the-act arrest is a precautionary measure, justified in exceptional cases, of necessity and urgency, which are expressly indicated (articles 301 and 302 CPP): A. Lopes, Jr., *Direito Processual Penal* (São Paulo: Saraiva, 2018). In 2016, the National Council of Justice regulated the custody hearings to ensure that the incarcerated person is brought before the court within 24 hours to assess the need to maintain the detention.

62 There are always reports of prisoners who have been overlooked after the issuance of procedural arrests; see www.conjur.com.br/2016-dez-17/reu-obtem-hc-supremo-anos-meio-prison-preventive and https://noticias.r7.com/sao-paulo/homem-concegue-liberdade-apos-dois-anos-esquecido-em-prisao-20042017 [accessed 21 November 2018].

63 J. L. Ratton et al., *Políticas de Drogas e Redução de Danos no Brasil: o Programa Atitude em Pernambuco* (Recife, 2016); T. Rui, M. Fiore and L. F. Tófoli, *Pesquisa preliminar de avaliação do Programa 'De Braços Abertos'* (São Paulo: Plataforma Brasileira de Política de Drogas (PBPD)/Instituto Brasileiro de Ciências Criminais (IBCCRIM), 2016); CESeC, Redes da Maré, '"Meu nome não é cracudo": a cena aberta de consumo de drogas da rua Flávia Farnese, na Maré, Rio de Janeiro', in Barbara Mourão, Julita Lemgruber, Leonarda Musumeci and Silvia Ramos (eds), *Polícia, Justiça e Drogas: Como anda nossa democracia?* (Rio de Janeiro: CESeC, 2016).

64 Silva, 'Fighting police corruption in Brazil', pp. 83–85.

65 Evandro C. Piza Duarte, *Criminologia & Racismo. Introdução à Criminologia Brasileira* (Curitiba: Juruá, 2017); Gisela Aguiar Wanderley, 'Entre a lei processual e a praxe policial: características e consequências da desconcentração e do descontrole da busca pessoal', *Revista Brasileira de Ciências Criminais* 128.25 (2017): 115–149.

66 Silva, 'Fighting police corruption in Brazil', pp. 86–90.

67 Duarte, *Criminologia & Racismo*.

68 Silva, 'Fighting police corruption in Brazil', pp. 97–100.

69 Silva, 'Fighting police corruption in Brazil', pp. 102–105.

70 Silva, 'Fighting police corruption in Brazil', pp. 107–110.

71 In 2013, for example, a rule of command for the Military Police was published in the city of Campinas (SP), which explained the order to prioritize the Taquaral neighbourhood, on the outskirts of the city, and in 'individuals of brown and black colour'. See: 'PM of Campinas leaks order to prioritize approaches on blacks', http://g1.globo.com/sp/campinas-regiao/noticia/2013/01/pm-de-campinas-deixa-

vazar-ordem-par-priorizar-abordagens-em-negros.html [accessed 20 November 2018].

72 In reports of racism, there is a general tendency for the lawsuits to be filed away and ignored, since the institutions tend not to believe the victims' testimony; see Thula Rafaela de Oliveira Pires, 'Criminalização do racismo entre política de reconhecimento e meio de legitimação do controle social dos não reconhecidos', Tese de Doutoramento. Pontifícia Universidade Católica do Rio de Janeiro, 2013; Marta Rodriguez de Assis Machado, Carolina Cutrupi Ferreira and Natália Neris da Silva Santos, 'Legislação antirracista punitiva no Brasil: uma aproximação à aplicação do direito pelos tribunais de Justiça brasileiros', *Revista de Estudos Empíricos em Direito* 2.1 (2015): 60–92; Gislene Aparecida dos Santos, 'Nem crime, nem castigo o racismo na percepção do judiciário e das vítimas de atos de discriminação', *Revista do Instituto de Estudos Brasileiros Brasil* 62 (dez. 2015): 184–207.

73 The greater police surveillance can be measured in the observation of caught-in-the-act arrest rates, that is, those arrests that are due to police action and not a final sentence administered by the justice. In a study carried out in the city of São Paulo, for example, in 2012, while the rate of caught-in-the-act arrests of White people was 14 per 100,000 inhabitants, among the Black population the rate was 34 per 100,000 inhabitants, evidence of greater surveillance and control of Black individuals in urban areas: Jacqueline Sinhoretto, Giane Silvestre and Maria Carolina Schlittler, *Desigualdade Racial e segurança pública em São Paulo: letalidade policial e prisões em flagrante*. Sumário Executivo (São Paulo: UFSCar, 2014).

74 FBSP (Fórum Brasileiro de Segurança Pública), *Anuário Brasileiro de Segurança Pública* (São Paulo: FBSP, 2018).

75 Anistia Internacional, *Brasil: Eles entram atirando: Policiamento de comunidades socialmente excluídas*, 2005; Anistia Internacional, *Você matou meu filho: homicídios cometidos pela polícia militar da cidade do Rio de Janeiro*, 2015; Justiça Global, *Execuções sumárias, arbitrárias ou extrajudiciais: uma aprovação da realidade brasileira*, 2001; Justiça Global, *Relatório Rio: Violência Policial e Insegurança Pública*, 2004; Conectas, *Tortura blindada: como as instituições do sistema de justiça perpetuam a violência nas audiências de custódia* (São Paulo: Conectas, 2017).

76 Ratton et al., *Políticas de Drogas e Redução de Danos no Brasil*; CESeC, Redes da Maré, '"Meu nome não é cracudo".

77 Duarte et al., *Quem é o suspeito do crime de tráfico de drogas?*; Michel Misse (ed.), *Autos de resistência: uma análise dos homicídios cometidos por policiais na cidade do Rio de Janeiro (2011–2011)*. Relatório de Pesquisa (Rio de Janeiro: NECVU-UFRJ, 2011).

78 Silva stresses that changing this framework of positive and negative discrimination requires actions that are beyond the internal controls of police institutions. Even if police power was fully regulated, not allowing legal loopholes or discretion, the symbolic powers, specifically the power to give names would provide symbolic violence. In this sense, Silva affirms that this stems from the observation that it belongs to the same group who produces the 'rules of the game', the laws and the police guidelines or doctrines. Thus, moral values are an integral part of laws and police doctrines that can only be changed with full democratization, that is, with social, legal, political, cultural

and economic democracy: Silva, 'Fighting police corruption in Brazil'.

79 NEV, *Prisão Provisòria e Lei de Drogas*, p. 126.

80 In addition, the procedural reform undertaken by Law 11.690/08 altered the conceptual framework on the probative value of the informative elements collected in the investigation, since in establishing (Article 155 CCP) that the judge could not base their decision 'exclusively on these elements', ended up accepting that those elements constitute evidence. In practice, the confrontation with other evidence produced in the judicial phase is almost non-existent.

81 Garcia, *O uso da tecnologia e a atualização do modelo inquisitorial*; Duarte et al., 'Quem é o suspeito do crime de tráfico de drogas?'

82 J. Amparo-Alves, 'À sombra da morte: juventude negra e violência letal em São Paulo, Rio de Janeiro e Salvador', *Bahia Análise & Dados* 20.4 (2010): 563–578; Ana Luiza Pinheiro Flauzina, 'Apresentação', in Michele Alexander. *A nova segregação: racismo e encarceramento em massa* (São Paulo: Boitempo, 2017), pp. 11–17; J. Amparo-Alves, 'Inimigo público – imaginação branca, o terror racial e a construção da masculinidade negra em "Cidade de Deus"', in O. Pinho and J. H. C. Vargas (eds), *Antinegritude: a impossível sujeito negro na formação social brasileira* (Cruz das Almas: EDUFRB, 2016), pp. 59–80; A. L. P. Flauzina, 'As fronteiras raciais do genocício', *Direito. UnB* 1.1 (2014): 119–146; J. H. C. Vargas, '"Desidentificação": a lógica da exclusão antinegra do Brasil', in O. Pinho and J. H. C. Vargas (eds), *Antinegritude: a impossível sujeito negro na formação social brasileira* (Cruz das Almas: EDUFRB, 2016); J. H. C. Vargas, 'Por uma mudança de paradigma: antinegritude e antagonismo estrutural', in A. L. P. Flauzina and J. H. C. Vargas (eds), *Motim: horizontes do genocídio antinegro da Diáspora*, first edn (Brasília: Brado Negro, 2018), pp. 91–105.

83 Angela Davis, *A democracia da abolição: para além do império, das prisões e da tortura* (Rio de Janeiro: DIFEL, 2009).

84 Abdias do Nascimento, *O Genocídio do Negro Brasileiro* (Rio de Janeiro: Paz e Terra, 1978), p. 105.

85 Ana Luiza Pinheiro Flauzina, *Corpo Negro caído no chão: o sistema penal e o projeto genocida do estado Brasileiro* (Brasília: Brado Negro, 2017), p. 92.

86 Salo Carvalho, 'O encarceramento seletivo da juventude negra brasileira: a decisiva contribuição do poder judiciário', *Rev. Fac. de Direito da UFMG* 67 (2016): 623–652.

87 Brasil, Secretaria de Políticas de Promoção da Igualdade Racial, *Subsídios para o debate: III Conferência Nacional de Políticas de Promoção da Igualdade Racial* (Brasília, 2013).

88 Duarte et al., 'Quem é o suspeito do crime de tráfico de drogas?'

89 Flauzina, 'Apresentação', p. 95.

90 Edson Cardoso, *Negro, não – a opinião do Jornal Ìrohìn* (Brasília: Brado Negro, 2015).

91 Davis, *A democracia da abolição*.

92 Duarte, Queiroz and Costa, 'A Hipótese Colonial, um diálogo com Michel Foucault'.

93 Amparo-Alves, 'À sombra da morte'; Duarte, Queiroz and Costa, 'A Hipótese Colonial, um diálogo com Michel Foucault'.

94 Lélia Gonzalez, 'Racismo e Sexismo na Cultura Brasileira', *Revista Ciências Sociais Hoje*, ANPOCS (1984): 223–244.

4

Necropolitical wars

Ariadna Estévez

Introduction

Mexico currently is immersed in an unprecedented wave of violence in which drug cartels and law enforcement officials sometimes work together in cases of forced disappearance, kidnapping, execution, torture, persecution, feminicide, rape and massacres. While the government claims criminal gangs are solely responsible for these brutalities and it invests important resources in security as well as in judicial and constitutional reform, among other normative changes, it has failed to tackle impunity and corruption, and although the Mexican government claims to have taken measures against these crimes, they continue to occur. Since the so-called 'war against drug trafficking' was launched by former Mexican president Felipe Calderón in 2006, human rights organizations, the press and academics have registered 234,996 killings,[1] 23,800 feminicides,[2] and the forced disappearance of 34,656 people (25,682 men and 8,974 women). Regarding specific violence against women, 41.3 per cent of the total 46,501,740 women in the country (19,216,151) have suffered sexual violence and 66.1 per cent (30,700,000) have been the victims of violence in general.[3] As for displacement, there have been 329,917 people internally displaced in 25 episodes, 60 per cent of which included women and 92 per cent included families, which in turn involved women and girls.[4] As for asylum seekers, by 2016, there had been 98,547 claims.[5]

As we can see, women suffer as much as men in this wave of violence, but sexual violence is somehow invisible and mostly ignored in political interpretations of the conflict. My hypothesis is that this is the case because criminal violence is solely attributed to a war with a political-State dynamic, when in reality we are talking about two wars that do not necessarily involve political control. The analytical interpretation proposed here is that we are seeing two wars, two *necropolitical wars*.

This chapter develops the idea of necropolitical war as a type of conflict that simultaneously explains criminal and sexual violence as part of a continuum of colonial and racialized violence for the securing of criminal markets and the commodification of women's bodies.

Using Mexico as its focal instantiation, this chapter offers a typology of necropolitical wars: the *war for the necropolitical governmentalization of the State* and the *war for the dispossession of women's bodies*. While these wars have different aims – co-opting and reconfiguring the State, on the one hand; and dispossessing women of their bodies for commodification, on the other – they share a common feature: a dysfunctional, permanently corrupt, racist and deliberately deadly legal-spatial site that secures the impunity of their power technologies: massacre, feminicide and forced disappearance. These technologies give agents of war not only the control of drug markets but also of sex trafficking and slavery, while subordinating women to the reproduction of the economy as a whole.

Race, class and gender in the contemporary War on Drugs: the rise of the criminal homo economicus

From the very beginning, the War on Drugs was race oriented. In 1994, John Ehrlichman, President Richard Nixon's assistant for domestic affairs, told journalist Dan Baum, from *Harper's Magazine*:

> 'You want to know what this was really all about?' he asked with the bluntness of a man who, after public disgrace and a stretch in federal prison, had little left to protect. 'The Nixon campaign in 1968, and the Nixon White House after that, had two enemies: the anti-war left and black people. You understand what I'm saying? We knew we couldn't make it illegal to be either against the war or black, but by getting the public to associate the hippies with marijuana and blacks with heroin, and then criminalizing both heavily, we could disrupt those communities. We could arrest their leaders, raid their homes, break up their meetings, and vilify them night after night on the evening news. Did we know we were lying about the drugs? Of course we did.'[6]

In the late 1970s and throughout the 1980s, the War on Drugs expanded its scope internationally, particularly across Latin America, which remained under the US's sphere of influence. In its enactment within Latin America, the War on Drugs continued to be underwritten by the same racialized politics as in its country of origin. Using the War on Drugs as an excuse, the US could militarize security services in Colombia, Nicaragua and other countries, while allowing an umbrella under which governments could criminalize the Marxist opposition for drug production. In Mexico's War on Drugs, the situation is no different: it has colonial objectives and thus a colour line. Socioeconomic inequality caused by neoliberal economics, as well as the criminalization of the drug productive chains, has led impoverished men (frequently dark-skinned, uneducated, Indigenous) to the illegal neoliberal economy in which jobs range from drug, sex and human trafficking, to torture, murder, rape and disposal of bodies.

While in the US the subjects of anti-drug policy and securitization were Black disenfranchised men, and in Colombia impoverished male farmers often from the Indigenous and Afro-Colombian communities, in Mexico the criminal subjects are frequently dark-skinned, unedu-cated, Indigenous, unemployed urban males – often sexist and violent – who have found the illicit economy sector the sole area for potential profitable trade. These males are self-employed as hitmen and drug dealers who are in conflict with each other, *but most importantly, they rape and murder women, and trade with their bodies.* I believe that dif-ferent forms of neoliberal subjectivity are at stake in this version of the War on Drugs, in which there is also a gender and a class line. Specifi-cally, the Foucauldian reinterpretation of the liberal *homo economicus* is useful to look at these forms of subjectivity. Foucault was interested in the modalities of objectification of power through which human beings become subjects. There are three of such modalities: the forms of research that we call sciences; the dividing practices by which the sub-ject is separated within his own body or divided from others, and the techniques through which human beings are willing to become them-selves subjects.[7] *Homo economicus* is a mixture of the three, and it is biopolitics' predominant subjectivity.

Biopower is the type of power emerging from a major shift in the power over life in the seventeenth century, taking two forms: 1) an 'anatomo-politics of the human body', which consisted in treating the human body as a machine, that is, focusing on 'its disciplining, the optimization of its capabilities, the extortion of its forces, the parallel increase of its usefulness and its docility, its integration into systems of efficient and economic controls'; and 2) a 'bio-politics of the population', that is, a power 'focused on the species body, the body imbued with the mechanics of life and serving as the basis of the biological processes:

propagation, births and mortality, the level of health, life expectancy and longevity, with all the conditions that can cause to vary'.[8] Their supervision was affected through an entire series of 'interventions and regulatory controls'.[9]

The subject of biopolitics is, as mentioned above, *homo economicus*, but not that of English liberalism. This *homo economicus* is purely neoliberal in the sense that it is rooted in human capital theory, which in turn brought liberal economic analysis to an entire new field: labour. Neoliberalism's new interest in work not only incorporated the missing part in their approach to economic production – land, capital and labour – but also made human behaviour the object of economic study. However, for neoliberals, labour is not an abstract category – as in Marxism – but a rational decision made by individuals who locate scarce resources. Labour is in fact an economic behaviour, which is practised, implemented and calculated by the person that works.

Looked at this way – assuming, as liberals and neoliberals do, that capital is everything that is the source of future income – then salary is the income resulting from investing in human capital, which is made up of all the physical and psychological factors that allow someone to earn their wages. It has biological elements but also requires proper investment in education and mobility (that is, the decision to migrate). From the point of view of the worker, their labour is their very own capital, a skill inseparable from the person who owns it. The inherent character of human capital makes it only obvious that humans are themselves machines that cannot become alienated, which is the basis of the political and class struggle features of Marxism: workers do not own the means of production – the machines – and can never own the produce of their work. On the contrary, the human seen as a machine means that they produce profit, which is in itself the business. The human is a social and economic unit functioning as a self-producing business. The *homines economici* of neoliberalism are then entrepreneurs of themselves, and they themselves are their own capital, producer, source of profit and generator of their own satisfaction. The new *homo economicus* is both consumer and producer.[10]

As one can expect, the neoliberal *homo economicus* has a dystopian, shadow, illegal and even criminal version, because not all individuals can compete and reach neoliberal standards of investment in human capital. For the people who have been rejected and made disposable by neoliberalism, do they have any 'choices' in neoliberalism? An 'economic decision' could be emigrating to another country, probably without documents, but an alternative option would be becoming themselves a 'successful case' in the illegal and criminal neoliberal economy – that is, drugs and the biomarket, which includes drug, human, sex and organ trafficking. Millions of people – especially men – 'choose' to become entrepreneurs in this economy and invest in necrocapital, such as weaponry and torturing skills. Those who are already pushed out of the legitimate market, such as racial Others excluded because a long history presumes their inability to be as rational, inventive and industrious as the more 'civilized' races, are more likely to be drawn to this criminal neoliberal economy. They become hitmen (*sicarios*) or even mafia leaders (*capos*). This is the necropolitical *homo economicus* that Mexican philosopher Sayak Valencia called the *Endriago* subject.

Cameroon-born philosopher Achille Mbembe first discussed the concept of necropolitics, a post-colonial interpretation of Michel Foucault's biopolitics. He maintained that biopolitics was not enough in itself for an understanding of how life is subordinated to the power of death in its approach to Black bodies. He affirmed that the proliferation of arms and the existence of worlds of death – those places where people are so marginalized they are in effect the living dead – were an indication of the existence of a politics of death (necropolitics) rather than a politics of life (biopolitics), as understood by Foucault. He examined how the sovereign right to kill is reformulated in those societies where a state of exception is permanent. According to Mbembe, in a systematic state of emergency, power refers and appeals constantly to a state of exception and a fictitious idea of an enemy. He also stated that military operations and the right to kill were no longer the exclusive prerogative of the State, and that the regular army was no longer the sole means for executing the right to kill. Urban militias, private armies and security guards also had access to the techniques and practices of death. The proliferation of necro-empowered entities, together with generalized access to sophisticated technologies of destruction and the consequences of neoliberal socioeconomic policies, made concentration camps, ghettos and plantations unnecessary disciplinary devices since they could easily be substituted with massacres, a necropolitical technology that can be executed anywhere and at any time.[11]

As for necropolitical subjectivity, before thinking of necropolitics, Mbembe claimed that neoliberal violence was transforming the subject.[12] Neoliberal restructuring of the economy comprised the thinning of the State and its consequent withdrawal from public services and social security. This led to the entrepreneurship of bureaucrats who sold services to the highest bidder, and to the spread of mercenaries who were hired for war. This social crisis was reflected as a crisis of the regime of subjectivity that in turn produced more violence.[13] For Mbembe, a regime of subjectivity is

> A shared ensemble of imaginary configurations of 'everyday life' imaginaries which have a material basis; and systems of intelligibility to which people refer in order to construct a more or less clear idea of the causes of phenomena and their effects, to determine the domain of what is possible and feasible, as well as the logics of efficacious action. More generally, a regime of subjectivity is an ensemble of ways of living, representing and experiencing contemporaneousness while, at the same time, inscribing this experience in the mentality, understanding and language of a historical time.[14]

However, years later, when Mbembe conceptualized necropolitics, he failed to update his understanding of the regime of subjectivity in the politics of death. However, Mexican philosopher Sayak Valencia did.[15] She theorized about this type of man as part of the cultural features of contemporary criminal capitalism. Valencia argues that while capitalism is a system of production, it is also a cultural construction. Its dynamics create cultural patterns and subjectivities that sustain and reproduce the means of production. The cultural patterns of 'gore capitalism', as Valencia has labelled this phenomenon, build on the subversion of the meaning of work caused by the post-Fordist organization of labour.[16] Valencia argues that the post-Fordist contempt towards labour, culture and the working class in general, subverts the traditional processes of capital reproduction, replacing labour as a meaningful social activity with consumption, even in extremely deprived and marginalized places. Social pressure for consumption, together with widespread frustration among the young who cannot reach the socially demanded levels of consumption, makes the criminal economy and the use of violence a market tool. Given that work is not socially valued, young men who need to feel competent as providers in a hyper-consumption dynamic, look for 'work' in the gore industry: killing, drugs, kidnapping and the sex trade.[17]

Gore jobs become an alternative because there is also a subversion of the humanist project that had prevailed in western and westernized societies. Humanism is replaced by consumerism. Given that goods instead of self-realization through work are more socially accepted, the ethical limitations for engaging in gore activities disappear. In hyper-consumerism, ethics becomes redundant, it's seen as the loser's protection. In other words, the Kantian categorical imperative is replaced by the economic imperative.[18] These cultural changes have also led to a new subjectivity that Valencia calls the '*Endriago* subject'. The Endriago is a mythical character in the book *Amadis de Gaul*, which belongs to Spanish medieval literature. Endriago is a monster, a hybrid of man, hydra and dragon. The Endriago is a tall, strong and agile beast that inhabits infernal lands and produces great fear in his enemies. Valencia borrows the term 'Endriago' to conceptualize the subjectivity of men who use violence as a means for survival, a self-affirmation mechanism and a work tool. Endriagos kill and torture for money, but also to seek dignity and reaffirmation as men through a 'kamikaze logics'. Valencia claims that given the social and cultural conditions prevailing in Mexico, it should not come as a surprise that Endriagos use gore practices in order to fulfil consumerist demands since they are subverting the feeling of failure evinced by material frustration.

The Endriago is the dissident subjectivity resisting power. Resistance, however, doesn't mean legitimate resistance: Endriagos continue to be businessmen who take neoliberalism to its last consequences, resisting the neoliberal State, but in a dystopian way. Endriagos do not dispute the State as such, but biopolitical power – that is, the control of population, territory and security. Endriago subjects hired by the criminals in contemporary Mexico are usually former sportsmen, soldiers, law enforcement officials and private guards. The Endriago subject is usually a male who has been left out of the neoliberal 'global village' – that is, the unemployed, the drug addict, the migrant, and the unskilled worker who has been unable to access the legal means to achieve neoliberal success. In other words, the prototype of this subject is the 'loser' of the neoliberal system. The loser of the system is the corporality of a complex of neoliberal violence informed by subjective, power, structural and cultural issues. The Endriago subject as the necropolitical *homo economicus* in the War on Drugs explains how many racialized and dehumanized men are willing to become *sicarios* and *capos*, and why as part of their human capital they use rape and feminicide against women.

Necropolitical wars

While the term 'necropolitics' is attributed to Achille Mbembe, the definition used here is that offered by Tijuana feminist Sayak Valencia, who 'Mexicanizes' the term and points out that in hyper-consumerist societies, bodies become merchandise, and their care, conservation, freedom and integrity are related products. For Valencia, the cartels exercise an oppressive power analogous to that of the State and they have essentially become a parallel State that reconfigures biopolitics and uses techniques she terms 'necropractices' –radical actions intended to inflict pain, suffering and death. Just like the legitimate State, its criminal counterpart tries to maintain control over its territory, security and the population – that is, to govern by exploiting national resources and people, and the offer of private security. They control the bodies of men and women, transforming them into merchandise for exchange or goods offered on the 'narcomarket'.[19]

As a former Spanish colony and a historical zone of influence for the US, Mexico and its necropower are also defined by what Paul Farmer calls 'structural violence', that is, the 'social machinery of oppression' – a form of necropower dating from the colonial period – which includes death, injury, illness, subjugation, stigmatization and psychological terror, exerted systematically and indirectly by everyone belonging to a specific social order, but affecting mostly those at the bottom of the social ladder (women, racial minorities, the poor). Thus in Mexico, necropolitical actors include cartels but also gangs, politicians, some branches of the army, police officers, and the US government funding the War on Drugs.[20] It is what Banerjee has called 'necrocapitalism', that is, the 'practices of accumulation in (post)colonial contexts by specific economic actors ... that involve dispossession, death, torture, suicide, slavery, destruction of livelihoods, and the general management of violence'.[21]

This interpretation of necropolitics complements the discussion on new wars by Mary Kaldor, who does not explicitly name this criminal violence but does describe it. Kaldor affirms that these new wars are not traditional civil wars or low-intensity conflicts, concepts widely used during the Cold War. Neither are they informal or privatized wars. What they are, she says, are 'postmodern', in the sense that it is impossible to distinguish between the public and the private or the economic motives of politicians.[22] These new wars are waged inside the State rather between States and are the result of the neoliberal dismantling of the State, since they appear in situations where the State's income is reduced due to a weakening of the economy and the growth of criminality, corruption and inefficiency. They allow for the internal demarcation of the State's populations. According to Kaldor, violence is privatized due to the growth of organized crime, the emergence of paramilitary groups and the loss of political legitimacy. The State loses control of sections of its territory as these are taken over by criminal groups. The new wars are an expression of the struggle for 'necropower'. For at their core, these wars often revolve around subjectivity and identity.

With their focus on the struggle for 'necropower', these new wars Kaldor discusses have specific characteristics in the so called 'Third World', where 'necropower' revolves around not only criminality, paramilitaries and mercenaries, but also on the centrality of the Endriago subject and control of the market for bodies and other illicit merchandise. For this reason, I propose naming these as necropolitical wars, of which there are two basic types: 1) wars to form a partnership with the State for the reproduction of criminal capital in general, or wars for the necropolitical governmentalization of the State, in which Endriagos kill each other; and 2) wars waged against women to dispossess them of their bodies for private misogynistic domination and sexual exploitation, or wars for the dispossession of women's bodies.

War for the necropolitical governmentalization of the State

I share with Valencia the idea that 'necropower' is a criminal appropriation of the fundamental elements of biopolitics – territory, security and the population – but I do not agree that a parallel State is established. Evidence provided by empirical studies of the co-opted reconfiguration of the State suggest that, at certain levels of government, 'necropower' and the State are the same thing – that is, criminals serve as the armed wing of State power to regulate death in accordance with the reproduction of criminal capital.[23] Although a relationship has always existed between criminals and the Mexican State, as Flores indicates, the War against Drugs has served to intensify these links since it placed the armed forces and different police bodies in the position of choosing between your money or your life (*plata o plomo*), leading to a war between cartels to win their favour.

I propose to speak here of the necropolitical governmentalization of the State, which implies the delegating of techniques of domination of the population by the State to criminal gangs, so they can control their actions via practices that produce death (murder, torture, persecution, human trafficking and sex trafficking). The necropolitical governmentalization of the State uses political discourses such as the War on Drugs or the security crisis as means to regulate death; the securitization of public spaces is the central strategy, and the criminal economy is the principal motivation.

In the Foucauldian framework, the word 'government' does not refer to the institution of government but 'an activity designed to lead individuals throughout their lives, placing them under the authority of a guide responsible for what they do and what happens to them'.[24] For Foucault, the techniques of government are not exclusive to the State since they constitute a group of actions over the possible actions of other subjects, or the actions exercised to dominate pleasures or desires: 'Government of children, government of souls and of conduct, government of a home, of a State, or of oneself'.[25] To differentiate political governmentality from other forms, Foucault called this the governmentalization of the State.

The necropolitical governmentalization of the State directs the conduct of police and the military towards a situation in which the expert management of the technologies of death becomes an advantage in a context where people receive miserable salaries and ethics is subordinated to the market and consumption. The necropolitical war for the governmentalization of the State implies a war between criminal groups to win the capacity to serve as the indirect private government of the State, as explained by Bunker[26] and Sullivan.[27] These authors state that Mexican cartels are the archetype of a kind of insurgence that in the 1990s was only a theory: criminal insurgence, which is the product of the struggle between criminal gangs for 'necropower'. This competition is not for traditional political participation within State structures – such as political parties – but to free themselves from State control and thereby maximize their illegal profits.

To summarize, what we know as the War on Drugs is a war for the necropolitical governmentalization of the State, that is, a dispute between cartels to receive preferential treatment by the State and its association with the State. However, the war has mutated. While at first it was a war for territorial power and control of the drug market, the economic objectives moved into markets and merchandise with an equal commercial value as drugs, but without the increasing costs in terms of risk and security. This merchandise turned out to be the bodies of women. The commodification of women's bodies, the exacerbation of misogyny, systematic impunity and the growing risks associated with the drugs trade have transformed women into adversaries in another necropolitical war, which is being waged parallel to the 'narcowar' and involves the same men participating in this war as well as many men who have been or could be the object of narco-violence. It is a war in which the victim of the War on Drugs is also potentially the victimizer, since what is in play is not territory or power or control over the illicit drugs market, but the dispossession of women's bodies for their domination and profit through sexual exploitation.

War for the dispossession of women's bodies

Kaldor highlights the use of rape and other sexual crimes as a general feature of the new wars and part of the strategy of domination. Anthropologist Rita Laura Segato[28] agrees with Kaldor, but goes more deeply into the use of torture and sexual slavery which are paradigmatic of the new wars and were exemplified in Rwanda and the former Yugoslavia; Segato says that, in this paradigm, 'aggression, domination and sexual predation are no longer, as they were formerly, the side effects of war, collateral damage, but have become central to war strategy.'[29] For this reason, 'corporate and anomic [violence] is expressed in a privileged way on the bodies of women', since the agents of violence 'write' on their bodies to make them the 'frame in which the structure of war manifests itself'.[30]

While the definitions offered by Kaldor[31] and Segato[32] serve as a point of departure to identify the central role played by women's bodies in the actions of war, they continue to subordinate them to a war strategy with the goal of dominating a territory for reasons independent of those involving the use of women's bodies. In contrast, what is proposed here is that these bodies play a central role as merchandise and an end in themselves. While the necropolitical governmentalization of the State may represent a new war in which the subjects competing for 'necropower' are criminals battling for preferential treatment by the State, violence against women constitutes a dispute for the control of illicit merchandise, only in this case the enemy and the merchandise are the same thing, women and their sexually commodified and objectified bodies. The control of women's bodies is disputed by means of extreme physical and sexual violence, since this is the only way women can be dispossessed of their bodies for their commodification in the sex market. This is a live product that must be dispossessed through torture and death.

In order to analyse the role of women's bodies as merchandise in necropolitical wars, I propose introducing the idea of dispossession developed by Judith Butler.[33] Butler states that there are two types of dispossession: 1) the dispossessed subject in the sense it is decentred from itself, which allows it to form relational connections with others and society; and 2) the deprivation of means of subsistence or 'accumulation by dispossession' which radicalizes the 'originary' accumulation of Karl Marx, referring to 'the depredation, fraud and violence', entailed by this activity that extracts natural resources to privatize them and profit from them.[34]

For Butler, dispossession in the first sense determines the second, for even when we enjoy rights, we are dependent on a type of governance and a legal system that grants us these rights and limits our actions in such a way that even before the possibility of being dispossessed we are outside of ourselves. We are interdependent subjects whose pleasure and suffering depend from the start on a sustainable environment and for this reason, when someone is born in conditions of extreme poverty, their life is already dispossessed. In other words, 'we can only be dispossessed because we are already dispossessed.'[35]

This basic idea of subjective and objective dispossession helps us understand how a misogynistic social environment with structural impunity for sexual and domestic violence creates the possibility for violent and misogynistic subjects to dispossess women of their bodies, so they become slaves, forced by means of physical violence, deceit and depredation to become sexual merchandise.

However, when exactly can we affirm that this dispossession of bodies constitutes a war? The war for the dispossession of bodies is directly related to the violent and self-affirmative violent activities of subjects central to the 'narcowar': they use the same techniques of extraction – that is, murder and forced disappearance. However, the necropolitical war for dispossession is not between criminal groups disputing control of the drugs market and association with the State, but between violent and disenfranchised men, and women who resist being dispossessed of their bodies. The front line in the war for women's bodies is where we find the poorest and most marginalized women of rural areas and urban areas of the big cities.

These bodies are taken from their owners by means of physical and sexual brutality, so they are enslaved and stripped of their will by means of threats against them or their children, torture and forced migration. After this dispossession, their bodies are used in slavery for sexual commerce or to control them for domestic or sexual subordination. The war for the dispossession of women's bodies is a war whose existence is reflected in the data but has been rendered invisible through structural and selective impunity that shows contempt for women and minimizes their suffering to the point of complete inexistence.

Characteristics of necropolitical wars

Human trafficking and feminicide were practiced prior to naming the anti-drug policy 'the War on Drugs'. The facts they explain commenced before the 'narcowar', but that necropolitical wars can be used as a framework to interpret and name events that began many years ago and have shared characteristics that have been emphasized and intertwined in such a way in recent years that they can be named in this way. The proposal is not to analyse them separately but show that they refer to a type of war (necropolitics) with different objectives and use this basis for the proposal of a typology. Necropolitical wars are such because they share at least three characteristics: 1) the law operates to maintain impunity and conditions in which human rights violations are 'invisibilized', especially in the case of women; and 2) the use of forced disappearances, massacres and feminicide constitute techniques of capital accumulation (drugs in the case of the criminal war and women's bodies in the war for dispossession).

Invisibilization of human rights violations

Human rights violations in necropolitical wars occur in a nebulous area between the private and public; in the war for the dispossession of women's bodies, the structural impunity affecting the entire legal system obscures the magnitude of these violations. The invisibilization of human rights violations has two basic causes: a) the spatial collapse of the public/private dichotomy for the purpose of identifying State attribution in responsibility for human rights; and b) structural impunity.

COLLAPSE OF THE DISTINCTION BETWEEN PUBLIC AND PRIVATE
Human rights violations as a legal concept are the product of a process of legal interpretation in which certain events are constructed as human rights violations and others are not. The key point is that violations occur in the public domain, that is, the political-State arena. Criminal activities are not considered public to the extent that legal discourse leads to the belief they do not occur in the political-State sphere.

Feminist lawyers Chinkin and Gal affirm that the public/private dichotomy in the law has always been artificial, constructed through language and in the service of ideological purposes.[36] Chinkin believes this division has important consequences for international legislation, especially with regard to human rights, since it defines a State-centric vision of responsibility and attribution. She states that the demand for universal application of human rights assumes a largely unchallenged rationale that distinguishes between the conduct of State bodies and that of other bodies, the definition of which essentially depend on philosophical convictions that refer to the appropriate role of government and government intervention.[37]

According to the public/private division permeating human rights discourse, criminal activities occur in the criminal economy and do not constitute a social problem, with this being understood as the sphere of State policy. In Mexico, the public/private divide is no longer clear, and this serves to obscure the dynamics of power behind human rights violations, as indicated in the Bourbaki Report, which states that in the narcowar 'human fatalities' are not produced in 'the domain of torts' (criminal) and the 'domain of legal order' (agents of State power), but in a hybrid form.[38]

This intertwining of the State and the criminal is what scholars of mafias have named *intreccio*, which means 'more than reciprocity between the mafia and the State; it indicates a vast grey area in which it is impossible to determine where one ends and the other begins.'[39] Nevertheless, the dense intertwining of mafias and the State is not unitary,[40] and this generally implies a high level of internal inconsistency.[41] This is what Auyero has named the 'grey area of power', which implies a fusion of the violent activities of perpetrators and those who should prevent these. For Auyero, this grey area is both an empirical object and an analytical lens that directs attention to a murky area in which normative borders dissolve, enabling State actors and political elites to promote or tolerate and/or participate in the production of violence.[42] Human rights violations occur in this grey area and are not registered.

STRUCTURAL IMPUNITY

In Mexico, impunity is not the simple result of incompetence or the inability to investigate, but of the co-opted reconfiguration of the State, which occurs as a result of what has been called the 'capture' of the State, which is a form of institutional corruption in which business figures and State agents establish alliances for their own benefit, ignoring the rules of competition and with the explicit objective of establishing economic rules that benefit them personally and are not in the public interest.[43] In this way, corruption moves beyond bribes and becomes institutionalized. When those responsible for bribing are criminals rather than business figures, and when they take control of justice and public order institutions rather than economic institutions and rules, we are talking about a process of co-opted reconfiguration of the State since we are seeing a co-optation of those institutions 'responsible for enforcing the most essential normative provisions of the State'.[44]

Impunity resulting from the co-opted reconfiguration of the State is an important feature of the necropolitical governmentalization of the State. According to Mexican authorities,[45] more than half the country's municipalities (60–65 per cent) have been affected by organized crime. Drug cartels have infiltrated and used more than 1,500 cities as their operational bases for kidnappings, extortion and vehicle theft. For this reason, criminal gangs operate in 980 'impunity zones' without restriction. There are 'enclaves' in these impunity zones where criminal gangs exercise greater territorial control than the State. These enclaves are located in municipalities of the regions known as *Tierra Caliente* (Hot Lands – Michoacán, Guerrero, Colima and the Estado de México), *Triángulo Dorado* (Golden Triangle – Chihuahua, Durango and Sinaloa), and the Isthmus of Tehuantepec (Oaxaca), the Juárez Valley (Chihuahua), Tamaulipas, and the Mexico City metropolitan area.[46] According to the *Global Impunity Index México 2016*, analysing data from 2010 to 2012, only 4.46 per cent of crimes ended in a conviction, which represents an impunity index of 95 per cent. The 'unrecorded' crime rate would drive this figure up to 99 per cent.[47]

Impunity is also fundamental to ensure the dispossession of bodies. Even when the Global Index does not specifically report impunity with regard to gender-based crimes, it can be seen that those places where there is sexual and domestic violence, forced disappearances of women and feminicide, are located in states with margins that range from medium impunity (56–60 per cent), such as Mexico City, Chihuahua, Sonora and Chiapas; to high impunity (65–70 per cent), such as Jalisco, Puebla, Sinaloa, Tlaxcala, and very high impunity (70–76 per cent), such as the Estado de México, Nuevo León, Oaxaca, Tamaulipas, Coahuila and Guerrero.[48]

In addition, domestic violence is the most frequent crime in Chihuahua and San Luis Potosí, where the level of impunity is medium, which means that no more than half of cases are investigated. This crime is also among the five most common in Baja California Sur, Nuevo León, Puebla and Quintana Roo. Despite the fact Chihuahua is a state catalogued as medium impunity, this is where we find the highest rates of displacement, sexual and domestic violence and feminicide. Baja California Sur, Nuevo León and Quintana Roo have very high levels of impunity. Meanwhile, in Nuevo León, the domestic and sexual violence, forced disappearance and feminicide rates are among the highest in Mexico. In fact, the number of preliminary investigations for sexual crimes is highest in Nuevo León, Puebla and Baja California (2010–15).[49] The impunity index in Puebla is high and it appears on the list of states with the greatest number of feminicides. Also appearing on the list of states with the highest recurrence of the crime of failure to comply with family support is Chiapas, with high levels of feminicide, and Sonora, with a high rate of forced disappearances.

While the impunity index does not break down information on gender, the crimes of bodily injury and homicide may include sexual and domestic violence and forced disappearance, feminicide and forced displacement, and this allows us to cross-reference information concerning impunity with human rights violations involving women. On the one hand, the crime of bodily injury is among the five most common offences throughout Mexico, including the ten states with the highest rate of feminicide, the eight states with the greatest concentration of the forced disappearance of women, the nine states with the highest rate of domestic violence and the ten states with the highest number of mass forced displacements: Aguascalientes, Baja California, Baja California Sur, Chiapas, Chihuahua, Coahuila, Mexico City, Guerrero, Guanajuato, Hidalgo, Jalisco, Estado de México, Michoacán, Morelos, Nayarit, Nuevo León, Oaxaca, Puebla, Querétaro, Quintana Roo, San Luis Potosí, Sinaloa, Sonora, Tabasco, Tamaulipas, Tlaxcala, Veracruz, Yucatán and Zacatecas. On the other hand, homicide is among the five most recurrent crimes in Chiapas, Guerrero and Sinaloa, where impunity ranges from medium to very high and where feminicide is most prevalent.[50]

Forced disappearances, massacres and feminicide as technologies of death

As previously explained in the definition of necropolitical wars and their two primary characteristics, the battlefield, to put it in such terms, is semi-legal and characterized by the collapse of the public–private divide in the exercise of violence and the attribution of agents responsible for human rights violations. In such a scenario, we cannot expect the discussion to be of battlefields or front lines as such. Rather, there are three technologies of death that characterize necropolitical wars: forced disappearances, and massacres and feminicide.

FORCED DISAPPEARANCE

In the war for the necropolitical governmentalization of the State, the victims are military personnel and police as well as Indigenous peoples, racial others, activists, migrants and young people who engage in no political activity.

The forced disappearance of persons is sanctioned in the International Convention for the Protection of All Persons from Enforced Disappearance (ICPPED) and the Inter-American Convention on the Forced Disappearance of Persons, with the first establishing that:

> 'enforced disappearance' is considered to be the arrest, detention, abduction or any other form of deprivation of liberty by agents of the State or by persons or groups of persons acting with the authorization, support or acquiescence of the State, followed by a refusal to acknowledge the deprivation of liberty or by concealment of the fate or whereabouts of the disappeared person, which place such a person outside the protection of the law. (ICPPED, Article 2)

Forced disappearance is a crime that violates human rights when committed by an agent of the State or with the acquiescence of the State; it is a continuing offence since it begins with an extrajudicial detention that denies access to families but is not prescribed until such time as the person is discovered alive or dead. In human rights discourse, as in the case of persecution and torture, a disappearance is not considered forced if it occurs in the domestic sphere or the public sphere if committed by private agents.

What occurs in Mexico today challenges this definition since authorities of the State are not always directly involved, or at least not in an obvious or active way. In many cases, the degree of involvement of authorities is not known, or cannot be clearly established, since it may be through a network of corruption. It is this uncertainty that creates the grey area and related impunity, making forced disappearance a useful tool in the necropolitical governmentalization of the State, since the

State can easily distance itself from any responsibility when it appears to be the result of indiscriminate criminal violence that exonerates it from serious human rights violations. This is a strategy of necropower to create fear and avoid accountability with respect to the deaths of men and women. The disappearance that follows the abduction or illegal detention of migrants, activists, uncomfortable politicians, journalists, or the victims of crime by criminals and authorities allows authorities to evade responsibility.

With respect to women, as we know from the figures for deaths and the predominant place of women on search committees for the disappeared, in the war for control of the drugs market the rates of death and disappearance are higher for men. The effects on women are mostly indirect (mothers, sisters, wives, sisters-in-law, daughters-in-law and daughters). However, this does not mean that women are not murdered and disappeared. They are, but the violence associated with the war for the dispossession of women's bodies has another space-time dynamic formed by the non-securitized public sphere, the private or personal space, and a combination of the two, for the purpose of domination and sexual exploitation.

The non-securitized space is characterized by the invisibility of women in the category of enforced disappearances. In legal terms, if a woman is raped, murdered and disappeared by means of chemical degradation, disposal in deep waters, or clandestine burial, this does not constitute forced disappearance but is simply a disappearance. The exception to this configuration of the crime of forced disappearance is given in the Rome Statute of the International Criminal Court (ICC), which recognizes as forced disappearance the disappearance of a person in the context of crimes against humanity, which include 'rape, sexual slavery, forced prostitution, forced pregnancy, forced sterilization or other forms of sexual abuse of comparable gravity' when 'committed as part of a widespread or systematic attack directed against any civilian population, with knowledge of the attack' (CPI, 1998 Art. 7(1)(g)).

The justice system assumes the women reported as disappeared in reality 'are there with their boyfriends' or ended up this way 'due to their lifestyle', which connects them to spheres dominated by drug trafficking such as bars and brothels. The result is a convenient technology which is used to sell women's sexuality and enables a kind of patriarchy redux in the context of narcoviolence. For this reason, it is almost impossible to follow the trail of slavery and sexual and domestic violence in the public and private spheres.[51]

Studies of slavery for sexual exploitation have shown that traffickers 'hook' their victims by first becoming devoted boyfriends; or fathers, mothers and siblings use paralegal rules or appeal to tradition as a means to introduce them to prostitution, sell them, or make them personal sex slaves. These young women then simply 'disappear'. For example, according to a study of pimps in the Náhuatl communities of Tlaxcala, men have been prostituting women since 1960 and have established a 'school' where these pimps teach young men how to dress and speak in order to make young women from Oaxaca and Puebla, who work as carers or domestic workers in Mexico City, fall in love with them before forcing them into prostitution. As far as their families are concerned they simply 'disappeared', but in reality they are taken against their will and moved along a broad network of Tlaxcaltecan pimps in Mexico City, Guadalajara, Coatzacoalcos, Matamoros, Tampico, Tijuana, Tlaxcala and Apizaco, in Mexico; and New York, Chicago and Houston, in the United States.[52]

In order to dispossess women of their bodies, they make them their girlfriends, marry them and even have children with them to persuade them not to escape. To dominate them they brutally beat the women and their children, and even kill them, to keep them in slavery.[53] While this happens to the women, their families believe they simply disappeared since they never hear from them again. In the context of systematic forced disappearance in Mexico, families assume they were disappeared in the same way that men were disappeared, that is, in circumstances linked to drug trafficking rather than to sexual violence and trafficking.

MASSACRES AND FEMINICIDE

Killing the enemy, and even the indiscriminate killing of the civilian population, is not uncommon during war and is certainly common in these new wars and in necropolitical wars. As stated in the first part of this section, the number of deaths caused by the narcowar in Mexico now stands at 150,000, the majority of whom are men. But it is not only killing that distinguishes necropolitical wars. What differentiates them is the intensive use of massacres, which is the necropolitical technology par excellence. While in traditional wars, concentration camps were central to the administration of life and death; in necropolitics, the technologies are more mobile, such as massacres.[54] The target populations of massacres are suspected employees of rival cartels, relatives of people from rival cartels, and people who are direct objects of revenge. As mentioned above, those who are somehow involved in drug violence – *sicarios* and their relatives – are at the same time poor, urban, violent, misogynistic and disenfranchised males and their wives, children and other relatives.

In Mexico, from 2006 to 2015, there were at least 13 massacres recorded by the media, a count that does not exclude the possibility of others. In fact, the existence of 201 clandestine graves (2006–15) suggests that disappearances may be the result of various murders and massacres.[55] Among the known massacres are those perpetrated at La Marquesa, Estado de México (2008) where 24 bricklayers were abducted and murdered by suspected members of La Familia Michoacana; in Acapulco, Guerrero (2010) where an armed commando group abducted 22 tourists from Michoacán, 18 of whom were found dead days later; in Villas de Salvárcar, Ciudad Juárez, Chihuahua (2010) where suspected sicarios opened fire on 60 students aged 12 to 15, killing 16 and wounding 12; in Guadalajara, Jalisco (2011) where suspected narcos left the bodies of 26 people at the Arcos del Milenio monument just a few days after the Pan American Games had commenced in the city; in Allende, Coahuila (2011) where the army burst into homes in the town, setting fire to businesses and abducted 300 people who are still considered missing, and in San Fernando, Tamaulipas (2011) where 72 migrants were murdered by Los Zetas for refusing to work as *sicarios*.

Massacres were also perpetrated in Monterrey, Nuevo León (2011) where suspected members of Los Zetas burst into and set fire to a casino where they shot the owner for failing to pay protection and 52 people died in the fire; Cadereyta, Nuevo León (2014) where 49 torsos were dumped along a stretch of highway; Ayotzinapa, Guerrero (2014) where 43 students were abducted and disappeared by police and soldiers; Tlatlaya, Estado de México (2014) where the army executed 22 alleged criminals who had surrendered after being trapped; Tahuato, Michoacán (2015) where federal police also executed 42 alleged criminals who had already surrendered; Apatzingán, Michoacán (2015) where police and soldiers fired on self-defence groups, killing 16 and wounding 44; Zitlala, Guerrero (2015) where an armed commando group murdered seven people in this indigenous community; and Monterrey, Nuevo León (2016) where inmates at the Topo Chico prison clashed in a bloody brawl that left 49 dead.

Regarding feminicide, put simply it is 'the misogynistic murder of women by men; it is a form of sexual violence.'[56] However, what best defines feminicide, in an effort to explain the Mexican case, is the idea of systematic sexual feminicide as explained by Julia Monárrez. This idea 'includes or belongs to the totality of a system in which we find cultural, political, economic and religious elements that converge to create the conditions for feminicide'.[57] These elements include social class, 'skin colour, the hegemony of patriarchal violence, capitalist violence and illegalities'.[58]

Feminicide is used in the same way as extermination camps were used to implement the final solution to the Jewish question. Foucault stated that extermination camps were the most sophisticated biopolitical technologies used by the Nazis to leave to die and make die Jews who had no scientific use or function as a labour force: women, children and the old. In the war for the necropolitical dispossession of female bodies, the main technology is feminicide. As with massacres, the intention is not extermination; what the perpetrators do is make die or leave to die those women who are of no use, either because they resist sexual slavery for commercial purposes or due to the domination and self-affirmation of the Endriago.

This is due to the fact that Endriagos not only seek recognition and wealth, they also seek self-affirmation by imposing their control over their woman, their children and their home. The Endriago can murder their partner or children or pay someone to do it, if they discover they are straying from the private domain. They dominate through rape, the control of fertility, the control of sexuality and economic autonomy, and by abusing their children with impunity. There are women who accede to the terms of Endriagos to protect their lives and those of their children, or simply because they do not want to be alone because they have convinced they are worth so little that only he (the Endriago) could love them.[59]

Conclusion

Scholarly explanations of drug cartel violence tend to exclude examples of sexual and physical violence against women, dismissing these as problems confined to the private sphere.[60] However, New Wars literature considers women's bodies to be the target of competing political groups who use them as a means of revenge or as 'living parchment' for the exchange of deadly and brutal messages.[61] This chapter contended that while the first explanation, which excludes a focus on women, is androcentric, the second fails to grasp the gender continuities of criminal, and specifically drug-related, violence.

The idea of necropolitical wars was developed to indicate and name a kind of conflict that can simultaneously explain criminal violence and gender violence as part of a continuum of violence designed to ensure the continuation of the drug business and the commodification of women's bodies to affirm criminal markets. Since the narcowar and gender violence do not pursue the same objectives, a typology of necropolitical wars that divides them into two types was developed: the war for the necropolitical governmentalization of the State and the war for the dispossession of women's bodies. While one needs to co-opt and reconfigure the State, the other proposes the dispossession of women's bodies. However, they do share one characteristic: a dysfunctional socio-legal space, permanently corrupt and deliberately lethal, that ensures impunity for necropower's technologies of death: massacres, feminicide and forced disappearances.

Notes

1   M. Hernández Borbolla, 'Peña y Calderón suman 234 mil muertos y 2017 es oficialmente el año más violento en la historia reciente de México', *Huffpost. Mx Edition* (2017) [Online].

2   E. Reina, '¿Cuántos feminicidios más puede soportar México?', *El País* (2018) [Online].

3   Amnistía Internacional, *México 2017/2018* (Londres: Amnistía Internacional, 2018); INEGI, *Estadísticas a propósito del día internacional de la eliminación de la violencia contra la mujer (25 de noviembre). Datos nacionales*. México, 2017.

4   CMDPDH, *Episodios de Desplazamientyo Interno Forzado Masivo en México. Informe 2017*, Comisión Mexicana de Defensa y Promoción de los Derechos Humanos, 2018.

5   A. Estévez, *Administración de la vida y la muerte en América del Norte: Guerras Necropolíticas y Biopolítica de Asilo* (Mexico: UACM-CISAN, 2018).

6   D. Baum, 'Legalize it all: How to win the war on drugs', *Harper's Magazine*, April 2016.

7   Michel Foucault, 'El sujeto y el poder', *Revista Mexicana de Sociología* 50.3 (1988): 3–20.

8   Michel Foucault, 'Right of death and power over life', in *Biopolitics. A Reader* (London: Duke University Press, 2013), pp. 41–42.

9   Foucault, 'Right of death', p. 43.

10 Michel Foucault, *The Birth of Biopolitics* (New York: Picador-Palgrave Macmillan, 2004), pp. 216–237.

11 A. Mbembe, *Necropolítica* (España: Melusina, 2011).

12 A. Mbembe, 'Provisional notes on the postcolony', *Africa* 62.1 (1992): 3–37.

13 A. Mbembe, 'Figures of the subject in times of crisis' *Public Culture* 7 (1995): 323–352 (p. 327).

14 Mbembe, 'Figures of the subject', p. 324.

15 S. Valencia, *Capitalismo Gore* (España: Melusina: 2010).

16 Necropolitics in Valencia's Mexican interpretation of the politics of death is only part of a larger cultural and socioeconomic interpretative framework aimed at explaining the internal dynamics of violence in Northern Mexico, specifically in border cities. She calls this framework 'gore capitalism'. Valencia takes the term 'gore' from a cinema genre focusing on extreme and blunt violence so that she could describe the Third World's current stage of capitalism in which blood, corpses, mutilated bodies and captive lives are tools in capital reproduction. Gore capitalism builds on trans-feminism and the author's experience of living in a border city (Tijuana, Baja California), and informs globalization's 'B Side' – that is, the dark side of the global economy, the contradictory and out-of-control dimension of neoliberalism usually found in border cities. According to Valencia, this economy simultaneously destroys bodies and produces capital, the reproduction of which is based on the speculation of bodies as merchandises; and violence as investment. In Gore capitalism, murder becomes a transaction; violence a tool; and torture, empowerment (Valencia, *Capitalismo Gore*).

17 Valencia, *Capitalismo Gore*.

18 Valencia, *Capitalismo Gore*.

19 Valencia, *Capitalismo Gore*.

20 Paul Farmer, 'An anthropology of structural violence' *Current Anthropology* 45.3 (2004): 305–25 (pp. 307–308).

21 Bobby Banerjee, 'Necrocapitalism', *Organization Studies* 29.12 (2008): 15.

22 M. Kaldor, *New and Old Wars: Organized Violence in a Global Era*, second edn (Stanford, CA: Stanford University Press, 2006).

23 C. A. Flores, 'La lógica del botín: de la cooptación del estado y el estado "fallido"', *Arenas. Revista Sinaloense de Ciencias Sociales* 13.1 (2012): 11–44; C. A. Flores, *Historias de polvo y sangre: génesis y evolución del tráfico de drogas en el estado de Tamaulipas* (México: CIESAS, 2013).

24 M. Foucault, *The Essential Works of Michel Foucault: 1954–1984. Vol. I, Ethics: Subjectivity and Truth* (New York: The New Press, 1997), p. 67.

25 Foucault, *Essential Works*, p. 81.

26 R. J. Bunker, 'Criminal (cartel and gang) insurgencies in Mexico and the Americas: What you need to know, not what you want to hear', *Small Wars Journal*, 11 September 2011, http://archives.republicans.foreignaffairs.house.gov/112/bun091311.pdf [accessed 20 November 2018].

27 J. P. Sullivan, 'From drug wars to criminal insurgency: Mexican cartels, criminal enclaves and criminal insurgency in Mexico and Central America. Implications for global security'. *Fondation Maison des Sciences de L'homme – Le College d'Etudes Mondiales* 9 (2012), https://halshs.archives-ouvertes.fr/halshs-00694083/document [accessed 20 November 2018].

28 R. L. Segato, *La escritura en el cuerpo de las mujeres asesinadas en Ciudad Juárez. Territorio, soberanía y crímenes de segundo estado* (Buenos Aires: Tinta Limón, 2006); Rita Laura Segato, 'Las nuevas formas de la guerra y el cuerpo de las mujeres', *Sociedade e Estado* 29.2 (2014): 341–371.

29 Segato, 'Las nuevas formas de la guerra', p. 343.

30 Segato, 'Las nuevas formas de la guerra', p. 344.

31 Kaldor, *New and Old Wars*.

32 Segato, 'Las nuevas formas de la guerra'.

33 J. Butler and A. Athanasiou, *Dispossession: The Performative in the Political* (Cambridge: Polity Press, 2013).

34 D. Harvey, 'El "nuevo" imperialismo: acumulación por desposesión', *Socialist Register* 2004: 99–129.

35 Butler and Athanasiou, *Dispossession*, p. 5.

36 C. Chinkin, 'A critique of the public/private dimension', *European Journal of International Law* 10 (1999): 387–395; S. Gal, 'Language ideologies compared: Metaphors of public/private', *Journal of Linguistic Anthropology* 15.1 (2005): 23–37 (p. 25).

37 Chinkin, 'A critique of the public/private dimension'.

38 Equipo Bourbaki, *Reflexiones sobre la guerra en México. Un lector del Informe Bourbaki*, México, 2009, p. 9, https://issuu.com/mxlapazmx/docs/resumeninformebourbaki [accessed 20 November 2018]

39 J. Schneider and P. Schneider, *Reversible Destiny: Mafia, Antimafia, and the Struggle for Palermo* (Berkeley, CA: University of California Press, 2003), pp. 33–34.

40 Schneider and Schneider, *Reversible Destiny*, p. 31.

41 Schneider and Schneider, *Reversible Destiny*, pp. 33–34.

42 J. Auyero, *Routine Politics and Violence in Argentina: The Gray Zone of State Power*, Cambridge Studies in Contentious Politics (New York: Cambridge University Press, 2007), p. 32.

43 Flores, *Historias de polvo y sangre*.

44 Flores, *Historias de polvo y sangre*, p. 50.

45 Cited in Sullivan, *From Drug Wars to Criminal Insurgency*.

46 Sullivan, *From Drug Wars to Criminal Insurgency*, pp. 17, 20.

47 J. A. Le Clercq and G. Rodríguez Sánchez-Lara (eds), *IGI-MEX. Índice Global de impunidad México 2016* (Cholula, Puebla: Universidad de las Américas, Puebla, Consejo Ciudadano de Seguridad y Justicia de Puebla y Centro de Estudios sobre Impunidad y Justicia UDLAP, 2016).

48 Le Clercq and Rodríguez Sánchez-Lara, *IGI-MEX*.

49 Le Clercq and Rodríguez Sánchez-Lara, *IGI-MEX*; CEAV (Comisión Ejecutiva de Atención a Víctimas), *Resultados preliminares del Diagnóstico sobre la atención de la violencia sexual en México – resumen ejecutivo* (México: Comisión Ejecutiva de Atención a Víctimas, 2016), www.gob.mx/cms/uploads/attachment/file/118490/Resumen_Ejecutivo_diagn o_stico_violencia_Sexual_CEAV.pdf [accessed 20 November 2018]

50 Le Clercq and Rodríguez Sánchez-Lara, *IGI-MEX*.

51 J. L. Monárrez Fragoso, *Trama de una injusticia. Feminicidio sexual sistémico en Ciudad Juárez* (Tijuana: Estudios de Género, Colegio de la Frontera Norte, Porrúa, 2009).

52 O. Romero and A. Pech Matamoros, 'La violencia de los proxenetas en la prostitución de mujeres en la historia regional de los nahuas de la Malinche', in R. Romano, O. Romero and R. Jiménez (eds), *Escenarios, realidades, e imaginarios en tiempos violentos. Violencia, actores y enemigos del Estado* (Tlaxcala: Universidad Autónoma de Tlaxcala, 2014).

53 Romero and Pech Matamoros, 'La violencia de los proxenetas'.

54 Mbembe, *Necropolítica*.

55 Open Society Justice Initiative, *Atrocidades innegables. Confrontando crímenes de lesa humanidad en México* (New York: Open Society Foundations, 2016).

56 J. Radford, 'Introducción', in D. E. Russell and J. Radford (eds), *Feminicidio. La política del asesinato de las mujeres* (México: CEIICH-UNAM, Chamber of Deputies, 2006), p. 33.

57 Monárrez Fragoso, *Trama de una injusticia*, p. 12.
58 Monárrez Fragoso, *Trama de una injusticia*, p. 27.
59 L. Cacho, *Esclavas del poder: Un viaje al corazón de la trata sexual de mujeres y niñas en el mundo* (Madrid: Debate, 2010).
60 Sullivan, *From Drug Wars to Criminal Insurgency*; Bunker, 'Criminal (cartel and gang) insurgencies'.
61 Kaldor, *New and Old Wars*; Segato, *La escritura en el cuerpo de las mujeres*; Segato, 'Las nuevas formas de la guerra'.

5

The apotheosis of war in Colombia

Oscar Guardiola-Rivera and Kojo Koram

'Take my word for it kids. Whomever does not start from love will never know what war and peace are.'
Plato, by way of Ernesto Guevara and Alain Badiou

The war as dialectics at a standstill

It has been said that 'the image of happiness we cherish is thoroughly coloured by the time to which the course of our existence has assigned us … In other words, the idea of happiness is indissolubly bound with the idea of redemption and liberation. The same applies to the idea of the past.'[1] Indeed, the past carries with it a secret index. It is an *index veri* in the form of a fall (or throwing oneself, gratuitously and without reservation) on the side of everything that has been objectified and discounted – the side of all the lives that did not count in life, which were made disposable or disappear, and cannot be accounted for, because the record of law and the established institutions has failed them.

Nobody knows for certain how many have died, how many are missing, or who were erased by the War on Drugs and counterinsurgency in Colombia, which swiftly became one and the same. The Colombian National Centre of Historical Memory conservatively put the number at 220,000 throughout the conflict, with 5.7 million people forcibly displaced. In terms of further damage to the environment, 1 million hectares of native forest have been estimated to have been eliminated by policies of crop eradication and aerial fumigation that have been used to quash illicit drug production.[2]

This violence only expanded after Plan Colombia. So, we ask, what was Plan Colombia? In part, a security agreement between the United States of America and the Republic of Colombia, the two sovereign nations agreed to employ all the means at their disposal to save generations from the scourge of violence and the evil of drug addiction. By the

1990s, Colombia had become the world's largest cocaine supplier due to decades of neoliberal agricultural reforms which made it impossible for farmers and food producers to compete with subsidized American alternatives, thereby pushing vulnerable and impoverished populations out of legitimate crop production into illicit drug production.[3] In response, Plan Colombia was put together by the Clinton administration of the US and sold to unsuspecting Colombians as some sort of late twentieth-century Marshall Plan for the Americas. In part, it was also a project for the reformation of the state so comprehensive that in fact it amounted to a suspension of the 1991 Colombian Constitution and its substitution with a thanato-political apparatus. The latter is a global design, a cog in the planetary machinery of standardization and homogenization of the earth's space-time under the auspices of disaster capitalism by means of self-colonization. And thus it is also a narrative of stalled national progress, a local history of a failed state incapable of controlling its territory and exuberant natural resources as well as the excessive appetite of its semi-barbaric population, always at risk of becoming risks themselves. Ergo, in need of salvation, from themselves.

Plan Colombia was part Marshall Plan, part global design, and part a local history of chaos south of the border, read as a sign confirming the choice of the American people and its destiny as both saviour and reluctant giver and guardian of law and order in the Western Hemisphere – Manifest Destiny. With Colombia in the midst of a vicious civil war during this period, the drugs trade was equated with radical opposition groups such as FARC and ELN.[4] This only brought about a prophesied deterioration in relations between the US and Colombia over counter-narcotics policy, with the US refusing to certify Colombia as a cooperating agent in the 'War on Drugs' in 1996 and 1997. For the Americans, Colombian President Ernesto Samper Pizano was the quintessential corrupt South American leader with ties to the Cali Cartel. As is often the way, the child must seek to kill the father and thus Pizano's successor President Andrés Pastrana sought to re-establish ties with the US. In 1999, Pastrana secured the return of US certification before drawing up an aid plan for Colombia to provide sustainable economic support to cultivators. However, as Julia Buxton informs us, American prohibitionist directives redirected what had become 'Plan Colombia' from a peace plan into a battle plan, as 'nearly 80 per cent of the financing provided by the USA was ring-fenced for military assistance, with the entire funding package dependent on Colombian acceptance of an eradication strategy based on aerial fumigation.'[5] Whilst the promise of Plan Colombia was that it would combine an increase in enforcement capabilities with greater investment in development and social programmes, the scheme only exacerbated the militarization of drug enforcement, with the legal and security infrastructure of the country being strengthened so to be able to decimate other counterinsurgency initiatives.[6]

The War on Drugs in Colombia cannot be fully comprehended within the classic categories of post-war liberal international law, such as human rights or transitional justice. These categories deal with problems of law as episodes of moral failing, seeking to address this through attempting to identify who are the victims and who are the perpetrators, and asking whether punishment or forgiveness is the appropriate course of action. What the drug war in Colombia aimed for was a whole-scale restructuring of the political, social and ecological life of the country, a remaking of the order of the nation if you will. For if not this, then the War on Drugs in Colombia failed on its own terms. Plan Colombia's stated aim was to reduce the cultivation, processing and distribution of cocaine in Colombia by 50 per cent in six years.[7] However, even the architect of Plan Colombia, the United States, had to admit through its own Government Accountability Office (GAO) that coca cultivation and cocaine production in Colombia had increased by about 15 per cent and 4 per cent, respectively in the period 2000–06.[8] The illegal cocaine market in Colombia continued to expand despite the US State and Defense departments providing nearly $4.9 billion to the Colombian military and the National Police Force to fuel the violent drug enforcement which underpinned the apotheosis of war in Colombia.[9] Such numbers tell one story of the War on Drugs in Colombia: they map out an overview of the violence endured in this conflict, offer a glimpse of the incomparable scale of the pile of bodies upon bodies that are buried underneath this war. But statistics cannot transmit the feeling of living in a country that is the frontier of the War on Drugs. That is what we aim to offer in this chapter, a heady mix of memoir and study, synthesizing the details of what the drug war has done to Colombia with an illumination of life in this country on the Caribbean coast of South America as it is ravaged by panoramic military force. To be in Colombia over the final decades of the twentieth and the early decades of the twenty-first century is to be in the epicentre of a global conflict, where we find the world turning to see the Americas once again as its core around which its orbit spins, a fault and an opening, the zero-point where uttermost darkness coexists with hope or illumination – both in a relation of reciprocity and an altering, time-bending relation. Self-energizing. Dialectics at a standstill.

Atomic cannibalism, warfare and time

A recognition of the totalizing force of the violence of Plan Colombia invites questioning of the fear of drugs that invoked such a response. Underlying the paranoia of the 'evil' of drugs do we find the haunting spectre of rituals of ingestion and consumption, of the fear about alternative metaphysics and subjectivities? In the physics of the very small, the phenomenon of self-energizing is described as the emission of a virtual photon by an electron, which acts as a vehicle of electromagnetism, and is then swallowed by the same electron that produced it in the first place. It's a strange phenomenon, a sort of atomic cannibalism. It is also described in terms of self-referencing. Richard Feynman, the physicist who has done more than most to advance our understanding of the weirdness that is our incomplete, self-touching reality, refers to the observable phenomenon of self-energy as fundamentally perverse, not just weird, but a kind of ethical perversion by nature of its own rules. And yet, that phenomenon seems to be at the heart of the fabrication of space and time – the fabrication of the future.

To make matters even weirder, it is said that some Indigenous peoples in the Amazonian region between Brazil, Venezuela and Colombia have long practised ritual warfare or vengeance as a way to create one or several enemies and then, sometimes literally and other times metaphorically or metonymically, swallowing them. In this manner, their memory is circulated through their enemies so that it isn't really theirs, but the gift of others. Here lie the long roots that intertwine Amerindians and Indigenous people with transgressive or dangerous consumption, a link that extends to consumption of what Europeans who encounter it see as non-normative plant-life. This plant-life would eventually crystallize into the spectre of what we now term as 'drugs', European visitors being confused by the decoupling between consumption and accumulation practiced in these Indigenous societies.

Latter-day explorer, the anthropologist Michael Taussig, provides an immersive account of the devastation of the drug war being visited upon this region of Cali, Colombia through his field diary, later published as the book *Law in a Lawless Land*.[10] Subsuming himself into the communities of Amerindians and peasants who are the primary victims of Colombia's drug war violence, Taussig learns from these communities how the violence of the war which is legitimized plays from the perspective of those who experience it. Subtitling this book as the *Diary of a Limpieza in Colombia*, Taussig places the focus on the purifying impulse underlying the violence in Colombia, which was popularly described as a *limpieza* – a cleansing. As a word, *limpieza* contains two interwoven understandings in common usage in Colombia: the older meaning referring to a traditional practice of spiritual healing which cleanses the body of a sick person or a house after it has been infested by malevolent sorcery; however, in the wake of the rise in conflict within the country, *limpieza* took on an additional meaning as the description for the public acts of purifying violence.[11] This time concerned with cleansing the corrupting forces of a body politic rather than the body of a person, *limpieza* came to refer to the – often public – slaughter of 'undesirables' by paramilitary forces. Those determined to be delinquents or degenerates, a category that recycled familiar tropes of peoples involved in drugs or in league with the guerrillas, are purified from the social order through mass execution. Among those rendered most exposed to this violence are those known locally as '*vicioso*', meaning 'druggie'.[12] Drugs are awarded a transformative power here again, capable of turning a life into something sacrificial, serving as an agent of the contagion. The *limpieza* carries out the act of sacrifice, purifying the contagion but in the process fixing a structure of containing violence with violence.

Taussig's title captures the persistent presence of the law within this context of violence; the *limpieza* doesn't happen outside of the gaze of the law but again, often realizes itself through the law. It is a testament to lawfare. While the public executions may be carried out by paramilitaries, these killings are often state-sponsored or at least occur under the complicit gaze of the state. Disturbing the presumption that such violence happens in the absence of law, Taussig describes:

> The brazenness of the killing today takes your breath away, in broad daylight, in the street – the exact opposite of anonymity. This is not some remote hamlet where there are no police or law courts. This is a town just forty-five minutes by road from Cali, police, 5 judges, 3 district attorneys, a jail with 120 prisoners, and an elaborate judicial system.[13]

Whilst the ostensible targets of the *limpieza* are *narcotrafficantes* or guerrillas, the expansive scope of the violence and the impunity with which it is enacted allow the production of a constant fear and uncertainty amongst the population as 'one never really knows who next will be murdered, tortured, intimidated, or run-out-of-town.'[14] The entire region that Taussig visits, Valle del Cauca, in the Cali region of Colombia that is home to the infamous Cali drug cartel, could be said to exist in juridical theodicy that parallels Fanon's 'zone of non-being'.[15] The population exists within the scope of the law but in a condition of exclusion, allowing for violence enacted upon their being to not sufficiently disturb the order of the law. Drawing on both Benjamin's and Nietzsche's critique of legal violence, Taussig echoes these sentiments when describing how 'the violence of law is not only a question of guns, handcuffs, and gaols, but, far worse, what gives that violence its edge and its lip-smacking satisfaction is deceit in the service of justice … is it so surprising that the paras and the police are virtually the same?'[16] Of course, Taussig does recognize that the representatives of the law are not the only source of violence in the region, and he notes that the traffickers are not above employing paramilitaries to wield indiscriminate violence amongst target populations themselves.[17] However, despite their shared contributions to the culture of violence, one would be a fool to read any false equivalency between the traffickers and the state, for the violence from the state is infused with the claim to jurisdictional production. Describing the violence of drug traffickers as a response to the violence of the state, Taussig states that 'criminals become hardened by observing that they and the police use the same methods, except with the police, the methods are worse because the police excuse their actions in the name of justice.'[18] The impetus to enforce law and order gives the *limpieza* its cleansing quality, with drug laws a key element in this network of violence.

Warfare, for these indigenous peoples, would be a sort of time machine, a way to go from no-time to all-time or a different opening for time, a tool to fabricate the future as a different beginning – not at all unlike the self-energy phenomenon of cutting-edge physicists. Is the light of a star the light we must move towards, the proverbial light at the end of the tunnel? Or is it rather the explosion of a supernova, threatening to consume everything and lead us to ruin? We are not allowed to answer. For ours is not the view of the Angel of History suspended in mid-air, whose mouth and eyes, wide open, contemplate one single ruin. As we know, 'the Angel would like to stay, awaken the dead, and make whole what has been smashed. But a storm is blowing from Paradise and has caught him', unaware. This storm called progress 'drives him irresistibly into the future, to which his back is turned, while the pile of debris before him grows towards the sky.' We no longer have the luxury of that view. For we are the debris.[19]

Not the Angel, not even God, would bother coming here.

The apotheosis of war in Colombia

During the days of unending war, the city of Bogotá was lost. Turning its back, the city closed itself to eyes and ears. It surrounded me but never faced me. The solitude around imposed upon me a background of meaning: 'the city was human but cried like a caged animal'. It had become a black box. I was the cat within it. The city was Bogotá, but could have been any other city. Many years ago I was a kid in Colombia who spent long afternoons during summer break doing work at his Aunt Clara's shop, trying to get a little money to buy himself a bicycle. The shop sold colours, creams and slimming girdles made by the present-day incarnations of what once was IG Farben, once the most powerful and richest chemical and cosmetics maker in the world. Colours, creams and girdles promised unwary passersby all sorts of magical effects. In they came, dead city dwellers; out they went, made up, alive. It is true that in most cities reality is defined by whether you are dead or alive. Not in Bogotá. To begin with, it rains too much. The city turns grey and you cannot see, for it rains lead and heavy metals. Then there is the apotheosis of war, which appeared before our eyes as a pyramid of debris and buried coffins piled high like a colossus in the central square. There were no remains in those wooden boxes. It was more like an artwork of the future, only that in it the people are missing.[20]

Consider the artwork of the future in the age of unending war and digital reproduction – the time of the War on Drugs in Colombia. This period of Colombia's history resurrected the latent hostilities of the ten-year civil war that ravaged the country from 1948 to 1958, that we call 'La Violencia'. The War on Drugs in Colombia is but the latest war in a chronology of war. It can only be understood in relation to what we have called 'apotheosis'. The term 'apotheosis' has two meanings: first, deification, and second, quintessence. As regards the first, ever since violence and war have come to be the one and only true religion in the land of our childhood, it has become impossible to know with certainty whether to count ourselves among the living, for how long, or whether a life can be accounted for and even if it has any value. The entrapment of lost lives in what Fanon called the 'zone of non-being' becomes the very art of the Caribbean. In this sense, life and death have become matters of probability, not so much in the manner of a game of chance or a throw of the dice, but rather, in the aesthetic sense that fables invented by purely contingent means – in the same way collectors go about collecting and detectives solve their cases – provide us now with as much conviction as facts, statistics and historical examples.

The second meaning of apotheosis is quintessence. Verestchagin's 1871 painting *The Apotheosis of War* aptly manifests such meaning. The painting was dedicated to all conquerors, past, present, and to come. That image, more real than reality itself, evokes the quintessential underside of our reality, our sur-reality. As it is manifested in the painting, reality in the war-torn cities and countryside of our childhood soon began to look more and more like a bad B-list film or a zombie apocalypse. An art of the future, no doubt, but in it the people are missing.

Some may call this local history, the history of places like Colombia, a mess. We called it the funk. The funk is an affine of ritual warfare and organized hopeful pessimism, a kind of contingency that falls on the side of objects without reservation, and in doing so turns decisive: an index of truth, for it alone determines what goes into the notebook or the collection, and how to use it in order to solve irresolvable riddles.

Thus, for instance, a painting, a photograph, or a fragment of poor cinema might decide the direction of trade, war and global geopolitics, not the other way around. A decisive contingency. This is the ideology, or perhaps better described as the theology, behind the material struggle of a crisis such as the War on Drugs.

Focus on the funk

Let us call the subjective effect of a landscape torn apart by war and violence, such as that of the land of my childhood in Colombia during the apotheosis of the War on Drugs, an organization of dreams or a coup de funk. Let us do this all the while paying homage to Verestchagin's prophetic 1871 painting, to the late John Berger who invented the concept I have just referred to – a landscape's address – and to the artist and filmmaker Ken McMullen, as well as to the 1970s and '80s music and visual nostalgia recently recovered by Baz Luhrmann and the Duffer Brothers, which provided the soundtrack of our lives.

This concept of a landscape's address sums up very well my feeling of that summer in the upside down during the apotheosis of war in Colombia. I do not mean it in the sense of the current fashion for emotion and affect, supposedly previous to or untouched by reason, which nowadays predominates in the vacuum of academia. I mean something different, more akin to Raymond Williams's notion of a 'structure of feeling' (a structure that vanishes at the point where it touches a concrete singularity, a silenced voice, or a missing body) and, as said before, something much closer to what Berger had in mind when he coined his marvellous realistic, spacetime-bending notion (in reference to the 'torrid zones' of desert Spain).

The summer of the apotheosis of war in Colombia was a long lonely silent season. A mess. The funk. While on a hunting expedition to the back of the shop where I worked to make some money I found a pile of books similar to the pyramid of empty coffins piled up in the central square. Unsolvable crimes in the stories by Edgar Allan Poe rendered by Cortázar's unparalleled translation; Dashiell Hammett's The Maltese Falcon; Burroughs's Cities of the Red Night, which updated the cut-up technique invented first by the Négritude writers and a group of Chilean concrete poets; a compendium of mysteries penned by one Horacio Bustos Domecq; and that wonderful Parisian detective named Lemmy Caution. Surrounded by authors and philosophers who always already suspected that the very notion of human is racist and ethnocentric. That summer I played my funk mix-tape on and on, and read. The summer of solitude was saved by pulp fiction. Almost. Then, my cousin went missing.

Entanglement

Common sense dictates that a missing person is either alive or dead. Yet during our youth a word was invented for the singular status of such people in the Americas. It connotes the fact that they remain in a state of entanglement, like the famous cat in a box. As such, they are our fetish as well as the icon of our sadness in the realization that life can not matter: los desparecidos. There were thousands during the apotheosis of war in Colombia; my cousin Hugo was just one of them. His mother would come to the shop and tell me that on Sunday morning, when she was still in bed, a bird flew in. Mistaking a huge photograph of a forest for the real thing it circled the room, saw his error and flew back out the window past the orange trees to alight on a high-voltage wire. Were those the real trees or the photographed ones? My aunt didn't say, but she believed the bird was her boy. For her, Hugo was neither dead nor completely alive. For her, as for Emily Dickinson, hope became a thing with feathers. Others began to call these hopeful missing 'false positives', or the resistant dead. They are in fact, an accurate instance of superposition and entanglement.

'*Watch out, living person, man of a century, you vassal of an idea that comes from the earth. For this is madness, this is the grave: infinity, a phantom idea.*' *A phantom idea. A photon idea. Such is the message of the resistant dead and the hopeful missing, preserved by Victor Hugo's writing on the Isle of Jersey. It means that our sense of ground (our nation-state, the orb of empire and globalization, the roundness of the earth as a justification of colonialism and original title) is a phantom idea. It sprung from the illusion of a line of the horizon, out of which yet another illusion (that of power as mastery and uninterrupted progress, and we as its vassals) has grown to the point of bringing the Earth to its knees. This doublet, this illusion of an illusion, which Joseph Conrad termed 'a fascination of abomination', goes through a double twist, interrupted by a cosmic shudder.*

This cosmic shudder is induced by the experience of what we can neither see nor expect. The bird which appears flying through the window on a Sunday morning, in the zero-degree space between viewer and plane, the ghost beneath horizon's line, the multitude of the disappeared and the departed, the very real and traumatic core of the terror and the unending war that the inhabitants of a village or a country, in this case Colombia, can neither symbolize nor describe in narrative faithfulness to the facts.

In other words, we speak of the cosmic shudder induced by the fine line that blurs the space between crime and horror. Can we explain the emergence of the Shining Path or FARC? *We* must confront peasants who grow coca building political identities in the midst of this conflict, political subjectivities organized around a substance for ingesting. It is in such a narrow space that our world of market-states is lodged, in that zero-point of contact with the spirit world, the skies above, and the underground of the fallen and the dead below. At this level, between heaven and *inferi* or hell, between sea and seaport, always already at war, the different perceptions of a ground or a plan 'are simply two mutually exclusive attempts to cope with this traumatic' core and antagonism, 'to heal the wound with the imposition of a balanced symbolic structure' or a supposedly harmonious whole.[21] What is being waged in this war is a violence that serves in the production of a world order of markets, enslavement and plunder. It is a war against all that is non-human, which collapses the drug, the environment and the Indigenous or Afro-Colombian into one, in defence of a narrow conception of what is the human.

Rescuing truth and justice from the measured repetition of tragedy

Let us say it at once: at this level, truth and justice depend not solely, perhaps not even minimally, on the faithful representation or the measurement of facts. Can any set of data statistics capture the ecological impact of aerial fumigation policies across rural Colombia or the extent to which the War on Drugs married with climate change to expedite planetary catastrophe? The deification of war and law and order has been for us a farcical tragedy not dissimilar to the fall of Icarus, compulsively measured and repeated time and again. It challenges us in a radical way, for we face an existential quandary: what modernity? What progress? What law? What project? If law, country and commerce did not bring about the promised perpetual peace, and instead, together with the intellectuals, became pro-war as a class as well as an ideology, then how could it be trusted? Plan Colombia serves as a totemic example of what John Comaroff describes as 'lawfare', the use of law as weapon wielded by the hands of the colonial state in ensuring and reifying the ghost of the empire.[22] We see this in Plan Colombia: war masquerading as bilateral treaty.

In the case of Colombia, as with much of Latin America, the violence of the drug war cannot be decoupled from process of neoliberalization imposed on Latin America at the behest of the global economy, as the twentieth century came towards its resolution. We looked into art (Eisenstein, Epstein and Espinosa) isolating in the writings of the poets formal features comparable to knowing procedures and to the sculpting of time made possible by visual poetry, performance and the moving eye of the camera. We did not throw bombs; we organized dreams, made them into poems, plays and cinema. But the bombs kept exploding around us: Jarry's Ubu (today's Trump) and Jodorowsky's primitive pop parody. Oswaldo, Parra and Pessoa. Picasso's plays, sketches and dance curtains. Fanon and Fantômas.[23] We looked at the skies (with the city at our feet) for a constellation that included Apollinaire and those searching for clues in the empty boxes piled high in the central square and in the mass graves dotting the countryside. In the theatre programme written for a 1917 play in which Picasso's falling angel appears for the first time, Apollinaire coined the term for a realism beyond realism that suited us as we turned away from the fire this time. Some rejected reason altogether, others opted for unreason. We the few turned towards myth, but never in the sense of an epic. Rather, in the sense of making possible a science (a social and literary, yet no less natural science) that not only admits to the principle of determinant contingency but also runs with it. Such is the method we have invented against the method of the military, the market-state, and the paramilitary. It came with a totem of our own – part human, part animal, part intelligent machine – which was our positive response to the appropriation of Amerindian names and totems by the violence of law, market and the state in the Americas: an eagle against the serpent, a falling angel, the Angel of History and debris. It heralded our brand of practice, and we entered into an alliance with it. Call this anomalous alliance a kind of anti-poetry turned philosophy and practice. Such is our brand of revolutionary Reformation.

Corollary

If we consider war and peace as we believe we should consider them, as public rituals, then in accordance with the foregoing fragments (we call them Reformations) peace fails when the hand is left dangling. This happens when we fall for the fantasy that has always dreamed of fixing for all eternity the fleeting chance to keep everything for ourselves (the spoils of war, money, all women …) and to keep to ourselves, to enjoy without sharing. This idea of a world without others turns into a fantasy image of heaven, redemption, or the bliss of the hereafter, what is in fact an absolute tragedy for the women raped, the children disappeared, the sliced and diced bodies of men. So that war may continue, unending. Plan Colombia is a local history turned global design. Therefore, peace succeeds not when we are left alone, but on the contrary, when the random inevitability of the encounter between one hand and another takes place, when the hand that must extend for something to be handed is met by the hand that must receive in a way that changes in retrospect the conditions of its own possibility. If this ritual enactment brings into effect a change of state in the main actors as well as in the cosmology or the myth that frames their views and actions, by making real a world presumed as its precondition through a sequence in which effects posit their causes, which take shape only in retrospect, then peace succeeds.

Notes

1 Walter Benjamin, 'On History', in H. Eiland and M. W. Jennings (eds), *Selected Writings*, vol. 4, 1938–1940 (Cambridge, MA: Belknap Harvard, 2003), p. 389, II.

2 *Organization of American States, General Secretariat, 'The drug problem in the Americas'*, 2013, p. 8, www.oas.org/documents/eng/press/Introduction_and_Analytical_Report.pdf [accessed 21 July 2018].

3 For further on the relationship between the 'shadow drug economy' and neoliberalism in Colombia, see Oscar Guardiola-Rivera, *What if Latin America Ruled the World? How the South Will Take the North Through the 21st Century* (London: Bloomsbury, 2010), pp. 10–11.

4 William O. Walker III, "The limits of coercive diplomacy: U.S. drug policy and Colombian state stability 1978–1997', in Richard H. Friman and Peter Andreas (eds), *When Policies Collide; The Illicit Global Economy and State Power* (Lanham, MD: Rowman & Littlefield, 1999), pp. 143–173.

5 Julia Buxton, *The Political Economy Of Narcotics: Production, Consumption and Global Markets* (London: Zed Books, 2006), p. 180.

6 For a full engagement with the overriding military impulse of Plan Colombia, see Noam Chomsky, 'Plan Colombia', *Alternative Press Review* 6.1 (Spring 2001).

7 U.S. Government Accountability Office (GAO), *Plan Colombia: Drug Reduction Goals Were Not Fully Met, but Security Has Improved; U.S. Agencies Need More Detailed Plans for Reducing Assistance, GAO-09-71* (2008), Highlights, p. 1.

8 U.S. GAO, *Plan Colombia*, Highlights, p. 1.

9 U.S. GAO, *Plan Colombia*, Highlights.

10 Michael Taussig, *Law in a Lawless Land: Diary of a Limpieza in Colombia* (Chicago, IL: University of Chicago Press, 2003).

11 Taussig, *Law in a Lawless Land*, p. xiii.

12 Taussig, *Law in a Lawless Land*, pp. 44, 81.

13 Taussig, *Law in a Lawless Land*, p. 133.

14 Taussig, *Law in a Lawless Land*, p. 120.

15 Frantz Fanon, *Black Skins, White Masks*, trans. Charles Lam Markmann (New York: Grove Press, 1967), p. 2.

16 Taussig, *Law in a Lawless Land*, p. 49.

17 Taussig, *Law in a Lawless Land*, p. 199.

18 Taussig, *Law in a Lawless Land*, p. 47.

19 Benjamin, 'On History', p. 392, IX.

20 The texts in italics are the personal reflections of Oscar Guardiola-Rivera of his experience of living in Colombia during the time of conflict.

21 Slavoj Žižek, *Absolute Recoil: Towards a New Foundation of Dialectical Materialism* (London and New York: Verso, 2014), p. 104. Žižek's reconstruction of Diamat takes a 'Southern turn' here, as he elaborates on Lévi-Strauss's exemplary analysis of 'zero value' institutions in Amerindian cosmography. He quotes Claude Lévi-Strauss, 'Do dual organizations exist?', in *Structural Anthropology* (New York: Basic Books, 1963), pp. 131–163.

22 Jean Comaroff and John L. Comaroff, *Law and Disorder in the Postcolony* (Chicago, IL: University of Chicago Press, 2006).

23 See Julio Cortázar, *Fantomas contra los vampiros multinacionales* (México: Excelsior, 1975), trans. David Kurnick as *Fantomas Versus the Multinational Vampires: An Attainable Utopia* (Cambridge, MA: MIT Press, 2014). See also Frantz Fanon, *The Wretched of the Earth*, trans. C. Farrington (London: Penguin Classics, 2001 [1961]), pp. 75–84.

6

A people's history of police exchanges: settler colonialism, capitalism and the intersectionality of struggles

Ashley Bohrer and Andrés Fabián Henao Castro

Introduction

In the contemporary imaginary, police are a purely domestic institution. They operate, so we are told, within the confines of nation-state boundaries to enforce sovereign laws. They are the institution which holds the domestic monopoly on the legitimized deployment of violence. And yet policing is a global phenomenon, and police organizations operate broadly and constantly outside of their 'domestic' homes, linked together in an international web of capitalism, coloniality and violence. While this global dimension of policing has existed nearly as long as the institution of the police itself, in the past several decades, police have become not only more globally networked, but also increasingly coordinated and increasingly militarized. A deeper understanding of the global networks of international policing will clarify the true extent of the racial and colonial politics of contemporary policing.

While there are a variety of ways in which police operate beyond their borders, this chapter focuses on police exchanges in particular. In highlighting police exchanges in particular, we seek to challenge the imaginary of policing as a domestic institution; doing so will reveal crucial openings for contemporary social movements against policing, incarceration and colonization. We focus on international police exchanges both because of their frequency and because of the various effects of their operations; we do however recognize that other techniques of globalizing policing are also deeply important.

Tracing the technique of police exchanges is not only an empirical exercise. In our research, we found that the phenomenon of police exchanges raises several important theoretical questions, pressing for both academics and activists alike. In order to explore the fullest implications of these programmes, we mobilize resources from a variety of theoretical traditions:

1 A critical literature of policing that focuses on the policing function of capital and the capitalist function of policing;
2 A liberal literature that highlights the historical consistency and contemporary scale of global police exchanges, even as it overlooks the resultant injustice, violence and political consequences of such intervention;
3 A contemporary intersectional literature that exposes the ways in which gender, race, sexuality, nationality, class and other axes of oppression are irreducibly bound together, both under the contemporary organization of policing, but also far beyond it, and
4 The discourse of settler colonization, which illuminates one of the most fundamental axes of contemporary global geopolitics, both generally and specifically in relationship to global police exchanges.

As Alex Vitale explains, the concretion of the first 'modern' police force – that of the London Metropolitan Police in the 1820s – was inextricably linked to the rising dictates of capitalist work discipline. In the first place, 'despite their claims of political neutrality, [the main functions of the police] were to protect property, quell riots, and put down strikes and other industrial actions.'[1] Harring traces this function of class control even beyond these more obvious examples, highlighting how policing the emergent working classes expanded to control over recreational activities and especially over unemployed people as a further means of concreting global capital.[2] Moreover, this form of class control was precisely not limited to the boundaries of the nation-state but was almost immediately globalized: the London model 'was imported into Boston in 1838 and spread through Northern cities over the next few decades'.[3] Rusche and Kirschheimer emphasize how penal transportation and prison labour constituted significant axes of policing and incarceration that contributed to the concretion of the world under a schema of globally integrated policing.[4]

Unlike the liberal literature on the police, the critical literature (traceable back to Karl Marx's work, if not before) includes policing, along with 'conquest, enslavement, robbery, and murder'[5] among institutionalized forms of violence that were the structural and logical preconditions of capitalism's emergence and later global hegemony. The police, and the forms of violence they deploy, can be seen as an integral component not only in historical forms of 'primitive accumulation',[6] but also in the contemporary scheme of global capital in which workers continue to be expropriated, a process sometimes referred to as 'ongoing primitive accumulation'.

This thread of policing literature runs through the work of Michel Foucault as well. He understood the police as providing a bio-political and disciplinary force concerned with the 'adjustment of the phenomena of population to economic processes', and was thus 'an indispensable element in the development of capitalism'.[7] Foucault's analysis, unlike Marx's, had the benefit of including the police within a broader analysis of race, even if he may have done so inadequately and incompletely.[8]

However helpful this literature has been at unpacking some of the connections between capitalism and policing, its under-thematization (or even complete exclusion) of the elements of gender, race, sexuality, ability and immigration status has severely limited this literature's ability to understand capitalism in all of its differentiated and intersectional nuance. More recent critical works on policing and incarceration have started to unpack the intersectionality of these dynamics in helpful and exciting ways.[9] As these and other works emphasize, policing has since its inception been characterized by gendered, sexualized and racialized dynamics that must be centred if we are to give an adequate account of the institution. Many of these in particular highlight the ways in which the context of European colonization formed the background conditions of these dynamics. While these studies are incredibly helpful, they often sacrifice the global dimension of policing in order to furnish their case studies with analytical depth and located specificity.[10]

One of the consequences of this absence is that most of the current literature available on global policing gets written from a liberal perspective. That is the case, for instance, of works by those such as Nadelmann, Andreas and Nadelmann, Lemieux, and Bowling and Sheptycki, all of which are quite rich on their historical tracing of various forms of 'police cooperation' across borders, but all of which also de-politicize the analysis by extricating that history from the ongoing structures of race and gender that settler colonial capitalism continues to reproduce.[11] In these studies, international police collaboration is treated either a neutral fact to be studied with scientific objectivity, or as a positive programme that should be explored in order to make it more capacious.

The literature on settler colonialism provides an incredibly helpful framework for thinking about the structural conditions framing racialized and gendered capitalist expansion over the last several hundred years. However, when and where policing becomes an explicit object of analysis for settler colonial studies, it does so often exclusively in relation to the relation between colonizer and colonized, nearly universally neglecting other kinds of global connections, especially that between the various colonial policing forces with one another.

In light of these four strands of theorizing, we propose to integrate the critical insights of each of these traditions in order to think more critically about the structural role of police exchanges in the contemporary world. Inspired by works like Lisa Lowe's,[12] which have started to work out the material connections between the emergence of European liberalism, settler colonialism in the Americas, the transatlantic African slave trade, and the East Indies and China trades, in this chapter we claim that it is important to historically contextualize global policing and the racial and gender boundaries this institution contributes to reproduce, within those material connections. Those connections we trace back to the ongoing structural logics of capitalist accumulation that settler colonialism set in motion. And we argue, in this chapter, that it is by paying attention to those logics that we can give a better explanation to the current 'police cooperation' taking place between the US and Israel, which is our main case study. In these logics, we seek a better explanation for the ways in which the boundaries between the military (sovereignty) and the police (bio-politics) are blurred under contemporary conditions of neoliberalism. Though the US-Israel exchanges are by no means the only such circuits of international police cooperation, it is an exemplary one that brings into sharp relief the interpenetration of capital, colonization and police cooperation. In these logics we also seek to materially ground Angela Davis's call for an 'intersectionality of struggles', as the political basis for international solidarity with the Palestinian people.[13]

Settler colonial logics of capitalist accumulation and neoliberal policing

Though the London Metropolitan Police is frequently seen to be the first 'modern' police force, the urban Charleston City Guard and Watch in South Carolina was also uniformed, accountable to civilian officials, and connected to a modern criminal justice system by 1783. Unlike in London, however, the main targets of the Charleston City Guard and Watch were not worker's strikes, nor the behaviour of European immigrants. They, like most other nascent police forces in the US South, had rather other aims, 'rid[ing] onto private property to ensure that slaves were not harboring weapons or fugitives, conducting meetings, or learning to read or write. They also played a major role in preventing slaves from escaping to the North, through regular patrols on rural roads.'[14] In the settler colonial context, police emerge, not primarily as a force to discipline the working classes, but rather as an institution aimed at concreting a specifically racial logic of accumulation. In other words, settler colonial policing is a fundamental project of racial capitalism.

Settler colonial studies provides a helpful reminder about the multiplicity of positions that structure settler colonization. Rather than think about the colour line exclusively through a Black–White binary, settler colonial studies argues that the settler colonial colour line is constituted through a racial triangulation between settler, alien and native in ways that equally prioritize the expropriation of land and the exploitation of labour.[15] In these accounts, indigenous people are often most directly targeted for the former, where other racialized groups are subjected to the latter. What makes the structure of settler colonialism unique to other organizations of capitalism is the way in which land and labour form twin functions of differential racialization. Of course, each of these positions and techniques of accumulation can only be adequately explained if we attend to the specificities of gender, sex and sexuality.[16] Given this, the 'class control' function of policing that emerges so clearly from the critical literature on policing cannot be explained in the same way in the settler colonial context.

Through the settler colonial analysis, we can see how the military and the police emerge as twin institutions in the global history of policing. In order to control a hyper-exploited workforce, modes of 'policing' were deployed. In order to concrete and perpetuate ever more violent forms of land expropriation, on the other hand, indigenous peoples were often subjected to violent interactions with the military and other state agencies targeting the geographical borders and peripheries of its territory. Seeing these institutions through settler colonial studies allows us to see the ways in which the police and the military emerged as institutions with different responsibilities in maintaining the settler colonial colour lines in the context of capital accumulation. From this perspective, it becomes clear that the police have never, in the settler colonial context, been an institution restricted to 'domestic' functions, but rather that the police work alongside other violent state institutions in order to secure the settler colonial order of racial capitalism; these functions can and have been historically both domestic and international.

This insight has several implications for the reconfiguration of global policing. First, the anti-blackness that targeted Black people with domestic exclusion via systems that reproduced their condition of social death, inclusive of the prison-industrial complex, police brutality, and the new segregation regime articulated around the criminalization of blackness, no longer targets Black people exclusively.[17] Indigenous peoples, as well as Asian-Americans, Latinxs and Muslim-Americans, are also frequent targets of these apparatuses and institutions, even if Black people continue to be the primary objectives of domestic repression in the US. Such a racial diversification of the labour force that the settler colony is politically interested in excluding has meant an exponential increase in police forces and police funding. Second, the particular threat of indigenous people to a settler colonial order reveals the integration of police and military functions. While some of the contemporary literature on policing has referred to this as the increasing militarization of the police, we must localize this phenomenon in the historical and structural commitments of the settler colonial order to conquest, land dispossession and its forms of border control.[18] Indigenous people are not, however, the sole and perhaps not even the main targets of these military/police forms of repressive convergence. The material and discursive production of the 'terrorist', as a position in between the external 'enemy' and the internal 'criminal' first occupied by indigenous people, makes Muslims today more vulnerable to this mutually reinforced institutional form of state violence. Third, the characteristic capacity of neoliberalism to intensify exploitation by commodifying aspects of human life not previously conceived of in economic terms, have also resulted in the greater implication of policing with other social apparatuses of control.[19] The most often studied aspect of this integration in the US is the school-to-prison pipeline, but one could also refer to the development of domestic surveillance technology, among others. If policing has encroached in other spaces, the economic logic of capitalism has also encroached in policing, in the more classical understanding of neoliberalism as the intensification of commodified life. Hence, fourth, the increasing transformation of the police, as well as the military, the para-police and the paramilitary, into a larger global capitalist industry of its own, an industry that includes police unions, and the greater circulation of police agents through different repressive apparatuses of the state, or from state apparatuses to private corporations. Fifth, the neoliberal intensification of accumulation through the global circulation of capital have also intensified 'police cooperation' across borders in more than one way. 'Cooperation' should not be understood exclusively in the narrow sense of greater exchange of technology, information and training among police departments across the globe, an exchange undoubtedly facilitated by the development of new technologies with the ability to more successfully confine and monitor the racially and gender-differentiated movement of labour. Neoliberal cooperation also refers to the inclusion of non-police institutions and organizations in the actual infrastructure that facilitates that cooperation, like the training itself, and one that actually outsources forms of policing to agents that are not subordinated to the same legal protocols to which police departments are. Finally, neoliberalism's gesture towards inclusion have also meant the greater participation of racialized populations in the worse forms of policing, as a way of whitewashing the very racialized and gendered structures police forces are structurally committed to support. Excluded workers can only partially overcome the worse effects of such exclusion through their complicit participation in the settler order – that is, by performing the most violent forms of social control against members from their own communities. The inclusion of cops of colour into the police force serves, ideologically, to conceal the gendered and racialized forms of labour exploitation global policing is called to reproduce.

A people's history of global policing: on the US-Israel 'deadly exchanges'

Police cooperation across broad geographical regions has a long history. Take the case of police officer August Vollmer, often called 'the father of American law enforcement', who became chief of police in Berkeley, California, and later in Los Angeles, after serving in the Philippines. The legacy of his international 'training' has reverberating effects beyond the jurisdictions in which he held positions; he was the president of the International Association of Chiefs of Police (IACP) and he lives on in the places in which his approach to policing, systematized into the influential *The Police and Modern Society* (1936), was implemented.[20] This text has been called 'the most influential textbook of modern policing'.[21] In other words, this foundational text in the history and approach of US law enforcement is based in the experiences and ideas of a soldier on duty during an explicitly colonial venture; it is not hard to conclude that elements of colonial control were implemented in the new formation of US police 'science'.[22] Vollmer is by no means an exception; for just one other example among many, one could look to General Smedley Butler who, after having 'created the Haitian police and played a major role in the US occupation of Nicaragua, served as police chief of Philadelphia in 1924'.[23] Especially relevant to the question of global drugs policing, enforcing prohibition seems to have been his number one priority; in the first 48 hours after taking his post, he coordinated raids on 900 speakeasies in Philadelphia, and continued to make the elimination of bootlegging, drug trafficking and sex work central parts of his policing strategy.

In addition to these international and colonial elements in the biographical details of important figures, larger-scale police exchanges have come to constitute a central axis of globalizing settler colonial power. In order to explore this dynamic, we will focus on the contemporary police exchanges between the United States and Israel as a particularly poignant example.

We should first clarify that most of the critical literature characterizes the Israeli occupation of Palestine as an ongoing case of settler colonialism, as it is the elimination of the Palestinians, rather than the exploitation of their labour, that fuels the violence of the Israeli military.[24] As Leila Farsakh claims, Israel's decision 'to incorporate, rather than separate, the Palestinian economy' was done in order to 'facilitate maximum territorial incorporation of the land but without creating an Israeli dependency on Palestinian labor'.[25] The proliferation of settlements, consolidation of checkpoints, institutionalization of a legal system of segregation that subjects settlers to Israeli civil law and Palestinians to military law, and the continuous building of the Separation Wall, among many other tactics, unmistakably point towards the territorial logic of settler colonialism.

Let us return to the forms of cooperation in place between the two settler colonial orders. First of all, it is important to highlight that police cooperation has been popular with governments on both the right and the left in both countries.[26] This not only emerges in the form of state and military aid for policing and military expansion, but comes also in the form of technology sharing and reciprocal tactical training. In particular, these projects are perhaps most developed in facilitating the training of US police forces by the Israeli military, not wholly unlike the training that Vollmer and Butler received during their colonial campaigns in the Philippines, Haiti and Nicaragua. To give but one example, preceding the murder of Michael Brown, St. Louis County Police Chief Timothy Fitch received 'counter-terrorism' training in Israel; as Asha Bandele and Patrisse Cullors have evocatively documented in their memoir about the Black Lives Matter Movement, much of the militarized occupation of Black neighbourhoods and the justification for intensified repression against protesters is articulated through the discourse of terrorism – hence the title of their book *When They Call You a Terrorist*.[27] Much of the exchanges between US police officials and agents of the Israeli state come under the auspice of such 'counter-terrorism' training; in practice, the exchanged techniques of crowd control, profiling, surveillance and deployment of advanced tactical weapons is used in the US in a wide variety of ways, that include drugs policing, policing 'lifestyle' offences under 'broken windows' strategies, and policing young people (in schools, in 'anti-gang' initiatives, etc.), among others. In particular, there has been a significant rise in the deployment of these 'counter-terrorism' techniques not only in repressing social movements, but also in controlling the trade in criminalized substances.

Such a condition is well represented in the 'deadly exchanges' documented by grass-roots organizations. Their activist-scholarship traces more than a thousand exchanges between the highest-ranking police officials and law enforcement executives from the police, Immigration and Customs Enforcement (ICE), border patrol, Homeland Security, Criminal Investigators with the Navy, US Air Marshalls, and FBI agents in the US, with soldiers, police, border agents and other state agents from Israel. In programmes such as the Anti-Defamation League's National Counterterrorism Seminar (NCTS), or the Jewish Institute on National Security of America's Law Enforcement and Exchange Program (LEEP), the Jewish Voice for Peace documents:

[the] 'worst practices' are shared to promote and extend discriminatory and repressive policing practices that already exist in both countries, including extrajudicial executions, shoot-to-kill policies, police murders, racial profiling, massive spying and surveillance, deportation and detention, and attacks on human rights defenders.[28]

They also highlight that the infrastructure that supports those exchanges is irreducible to the police, that such exchanges are facilitated by conservative Jewish organizations like the Jewish Institute on National Security of America (JINSA), Jewish Federations, the Anti-Defamation League, AIPAC, the Jewish United Front, and Birthright. Fitch, in other words, is not alone. In 2018, the then US Homeland Security Director Kirjsten Nielsen visited the 'hi-tech' fences used to blockade Gaza in order to implement them in the border with Mexico, and James Walker, the director of the Department of Homeland Security in Alabama, enthusiastically affirmed after his participation in LEEP: 'You've obviously given us a lot to think about, a lot of best practices to go back and put into place. And I promise you that we'll incorporate some of the great things that you've done here in the state of Alabama.'[29]

Like Walker, Nielsen and numerous others, the case of Fitch reveals that the policing of *de jure* Black citizens in Ferguson, Missouri actually implements the militarized strategies developed in Israel to police a colonized population. But these strategies are also re-deployed in much more mundane ways, in ways that specifically end up being used in the course of drugs policing. In the context in which such a significant amount of US policing focuses on drugs,[30] police departments utilize the strategies of racial profiling, surveillance, neighbourhood control and more in the course of their daily work, which, since the 1980s, has been more and more directed at drugs policing. In this context, the true meaning of US-Israel police exchanges amounts to two settler colonial powers comparing notes on the subjugation of racialized populations, even if on the face of it, the Occupation of Gaza and drugs policing appear as significantly different structures.

There are important lessons to extract from the inscription of these 'deadly exchanges' in broader colonial histories. First, this clarifies that the ongoing reproduction of settler colonial forms of racialization and gender policing have always crossed the borders of the nation-state. Second, such forms of policing, although always linked to the reproduction of capital, as in Karl Marx's famous analysis of the persecution of vagrants, has racialized and gendered differentiated impacts on the working class. Third, policing is an integral function of a larger colonial project that involves the participation of various transnational corporations, and that integrates policing into the circuit of capital as a global industry on its own. Moreover, insofar as these exchanges create lines of communication and information sharing between the Israeli *military* and US *police*, we can see even more clearly the integration of policing and militarization in the settler colonial order. But perhaps most importantly, looking at these police exchanges allows us to see any particular practice of policing as integrated into a material network of practices, strategies and knowledges that link specific, local struggles into global structures of settler colonialism, capitalism and militarization. In other words, what police exchanges highlight are the ways in which the struggles against racist policing in the US and indigenous dispossession in Palestine are fundamentally connected; indeed, it raises the possibility that local struggles against police and military alike are, inextricably, global problems.

Intersectionality of struggles for international solidarities

In her work on Palestine and American anti-blackness, Angela Davis articulates a novel form of intersectionality, what she calls 'movement intersectionality'. She argues that 'the greatest challenge facing us as we attempt to forge international solidarities and connections across national borders is an understanding of what feminists often call "intersectionality … [not] so much intersectionality of identities, but intersectionality of struggles".'[31] While intersectionality is often thought of as a theory about identity, Davis reminds us that the real interconnection between different positions in the world means that our struggles are in fact connected. It is because systems of power are multifaceted that multiple struggles can and must be invested in each other. According to that lesson, international solidarity should not be grounded in aspirational principles of social justice but in the concrete materiality of common connections. 'If that [connection] is not created,' Davis adds, 'no matter how much you appeal to people, no matter how genuinely you invite them to join you, they will continue to see the activity as yours, not theirs.'[32]

The connection must be created, not in the sense that it must be fabricated out of thin air, but in the sense that the connection must be made visible, must be turned into a narrative, a strategy that is actionable. 'Making' the connection thus means that, in theory as well as in practice, we need to trace the complicated circuits of global capital, the multiple lines of relay, the multiplicity of abuses and repressions that emerge if one follows a global supply chain. If one follows the Israeli Occupation far enough, one finds oneself on the streets of Ferguson, or in Standing Rock. One finds oneself inside a decrepit, overcrowded cellblock in California, where the combination of 'new' police tactics and 'three strikes' laws have made certain drugs offences punishable by life sentences. Solidarity, too, and the struggle – they must also follow the global supply chain.

An exemplary form of 'making' that connection took place, as Davis recalls, when Palestinian activists tweeted advice to Ferguson protesters on how to deal with tear gas. Those tweets were grounded in the fact that the tear-gas canisters used in Ferguson had been produced by the same US company that had produced the ones previously used by the Israeli military to police Palestinians. And they knew, from previous experience, that police officers would not use gas without a significant distance between protesters and police. The multiple forms of cooperation structuring the policing of Palestinians in Israel and peoples of colour in the US makes these counter-hegemonic forms of international solidarity necessary in combating a global structure of dispossession and violence that flows far beyond nation-state boundaries.

This claim is different than the naïve assertions that 'We are all Palestine.' The fact that the same actors, the same logics, the same dictates of settler colonial capitalism enframe Palestinian dispossession and racialized mass incarceration in the United States does not mean that they are applied or enforced in the same ways. Linked fate does not mean a shared or flat position.

Such a claim is neither new, nor has been exclusively made by scholars. Since the enslavement of Africans and the occupation of indigenous lands by European empires in the Americas, trans-continental connections have been forged among variously oppressed peoples. The decolonization of Africa and Asia, and the end of apartheid in South Africa in the twentieth century represent more contemporary cases whose success depended on the international awareness, among the various social and political movements dispersed throughout the globe and involved in multiple BDS campaigns, to support the local and regional struggle of liberation movements. Such international campaigns made the policing of the colour line impossibly expensive for the colonial and apartheid regimes that they targeted.

Adopting a more global framework to think about policing allows us to see not only the power of these connections, but also the danger of *not* seeing them. As W. E. B. Du Bois demonstrated, US 'emancipation' was incredibly functional for the 're-enslavement' of labour in Africa, Asia and the Americas through the consolidation of the international and commercial imperialism that it fuelled (materially and ideologically).[33] As Lowe argues, this explains why Du Bois's call for a General Strike, not unlike Davis, included the courageous agency of Black slaves as 'one part of the struggle of a necessarily international working class of color'.[34] In other words, if activists and scholars ignore the global connection of struggles to one another, even those struggles that might at first glance seem quite different, there is a danger that local wins might re-inscribe systematic oppression and dispossession. It is through tracing interconnected forms of domination that global rather than partial solutions begin to appear.

In sum, the success of such a struggle depends on understanding the material connections that actually make Palestinian liberation into our struggle, rather than their struggle, as non-Palestinians. But it also depends on our intersectional awareness of the social position that we occupy in that struggle, as variously gendered natives, aliens, or reluctant settlers with different capabilities, knowledges and stakes in the interruption of that ongoing structure.[35] It depends, finally, on our ability to properly historicize the multiple repressive apparatuses that expropriate us from our labour and/or land differently, in global, and not just local, or regional contexts.

Notes

1   A. Vitale, *The End of Policing* (London: Verso, 2017), p. 36.
2   S. L. Harring, *Policing a Class Society: The Experience of American Cities 1865–1915* (Chicago, IL: Haymarket Books, 2017).
3   Vitale, *The End of Policing*, p. 35. The London Metropolitan Police was professionalized after the Peterloo Massacre of 1819.
4   G. Rusche and O. Kirschheimer, *Punishment and Social Structure* (New Brunswick, CT and London: Transaction Publishers, 2009).
5   K. Marx, *Capital, Vol. I.* (New York: Penguin, 1976), p. 874.
6   While the term 'primitive' in English is a thoroughly racialized term, this is an English translation of Marx's term '*ürsprungliche*', which is much better translated as 'original' or 'originary' and does not hold any of the racial and colonial connotations of the term 'primitive' in English. We retain the translated term here because it is the standard in the field, including its use by indigenous scholars who write extensively about capitalism; see, for example, G. S. Coulthard, *Red Skin, White Masks: Rejecting the Colonial Politics of Recognition* (Minneapolis, MN: University of Minnesota Press, 2014).
7   M. Foucault, *History of Sexuality Vol. I: An Introduction*, trans. Robert Hurley (New York: Vintage Books, 1990), pp. 140–141.
8   This critique was perhaps first raised by A. L. Stoler, *Race and Education of Desire: Foucault's History of Sexuality and the Colonial Order of Things* (Durham, NC: Duke University Press, 1995), and most recently restated by A. G. Weheliye, *Habeas Viscus: Racializing Assemblages, Biopolitics, and Black Feminist Theories of the Human* (Durham, NC: Duke University Press, 2014). For his most comprehensive analysis of the police, see M. Foucault, '*Omnes et Singulatim*': *Towards a Critique of Political Reason*, in P. Rabinow and N. Rose (eds), *The Essential Foucault* (New York: The New Press, 2003), pp. 180–201.
9   See in particular, B. E. Richie, *Arrested Justice: Black Women, Violence, and America's Prison Nation* (New York and London: New York University Press, 2012); L. Ben-Moshe, C. Chapman and A. Carey, *Disability Incarcerated: Imprisonment and Disability in the United States and Canada* (New York: Palgrave Macmillan, 2014); J. L. Mogul, A. J. Ritchie and K. Whitlock, *Queer (In)*

Justice: The Criminalization of LGBT People in the United States (Boston, MA: Beacon Press, 2011); E. A. Stanley and N. Smith (eds), *Captive Genders: Trans Embodiment and the Prison Industrial Complex*, second edn (Oakland, CA: AK Press, 2015), and D. Spade, *Normal Life: Administrative Violence, Critical Trans Politics, and the Limits of the Law* (Durham, NC: Duke University Press, 2011).

10 Thus, Ana Muñiz, to give one example, details the ways in which policing maintains racial boundaries in Los Angeles, and Cadillac-Corning more specifically, but does not explore the ways in which the reproduction of those racial boundaries is connected to global forms of policing, or the ways in which the very racial regimes police forces maintain are indebted to colonial logics of accumulation: A. Muñiz, *Police, Power, and the Production of Racial Boundaries* (New Brunswick, NJ: Rutgers University Press, 1984). And even critical works that adopt a more global approach, like Martha Huggins's analysis of political policing as it emerged through the neocolonial relations between the US and Latin America in the nineteenth and twentieth centuries, fail to establish broader historical and geopolitical connections: M. Huggins, *Political Policing: The US and Latin America* (Durham, NC: Duke University Press, 1998). This is not so much a critique of Muñiz's or Huggins's individual works, as both local and regionally documented analysis of policing are obviously necessary. This is an argument for the need to complement those studies, without subsuming them in an overarching collection, with analyses that address policing as it is globally constituted, as James does in an exemplary way: J. James, *Resisting State Violence: Radicalism, Gender, and Race in the U.S.* (Minneapolis, MN: University of Minnesota Press, 1996).

11 E. Nadelmann, *Cops Across Borders: The Internationalization of US Criminal Law Enforcement* (University Park, PA: Pennsylvania State University Press, 1993); P. Andreas and E. Nadelmann, *Policing the Globe: Criminalization and Crime Control in International Relations* (Oxford: Oxford University Press, 2006); F. Lemieux, *International Police Cooperation: Emerging Issues, Theory, and Practice* (Devon, UK: Williams Publishing, 2010), and B. Bowling and J. Sheptycki, *Global Policing* (London: SAGE Publications, 2012).

12 L. Lowe, *The Intimacies of Four Continents* (Durham, NC: Duke University Press, 2015).

13 A. Davis, *Freedom is a Constant Struggle* (Chicago, IL: Haymarket, 2016), p. 144.

14 Vitale, *The End of Policing*, p. 46.

15 P. Wolfe, 'Settler colonialism and the elimination of the native', *Journal of Genocide Research* 8.4 (2006): 387–409; J. Byrd, *The Transit of Empire: Indigenous Critiques of Colonialism* (Minneapolis, MN: University of Minnesota Press, 2001).

16 I. Day, *Alien Capital: Asian Racialization and the Logic of Settler Colonial Capitalism* (Durham, NC: Duke University Press, 2016).

17 On the concept of social death, see O. Patterson, *Slavery and Social Death* (Cambridge, MA: Harvard University Press, 1982), and L. M. Cacho, *Social Death: Racialized Rightlessness and the Criminalization of the Unprotected* (New York: New York University Press, 2013).

18 See S. Graham, *Cities Under Siege: The New Military Urbanism* (New York: Verso, 2011), and L. Wood, *Crisis and Control: The Militarization of Protest Policing* (London: Pluto Press, 2014).

19 It is this integration, more than anything else, what the literature on neoliberalism most often distinguishes as its characteristic aspect. See D. Harvey, *A Brief History of Neoliberalism* (Oxford: Oxford University Press, 2005), and

W. Brown, *Undoing the Demos: Neoliberalism's Stealth Revolution* (New York: Zone Books, 2015).

20 August Vollmer, *The Police and Modern Society* (Berkeley, CA: University of California Press, 1936).

21 Vitale, *The End of Policing*, p. 42.

22 Interestingly, Vollmer was pivotal in the formation of US police 'science' and the discipline of criminology. He was the first head of UC Berkeley's criminal justice programme, and there he was O. W. Wilson's professor, who later went on to found the first US Department of Police Science at what is now Wichita State University. One cannot help but be reminded of Foucault's insistence that the modern regime of policing and incarceration was also at the same time, a project of founding a new technique of knowledge production.

23 Vitale, *The End of Policing*, p. 42.

24 See G. Shafir, *Land, Labor, and the Origins of the Israeli-Palestinian Conflict, 1882–1914* (Cambridge: Cambridge University Press, 1989); Wolfe, 'Settler colonialism and the elimination of the native', and I. Pappé, 'Zionism as colonialism: A comparative view of diluted colonialism in Asia and Africa', *The South Atlantic Quarterly: Special Issue on Settler Colonialism* 107.4 (2008): 611–633.

25 L. Farsakh, 'The political economy of Israeli occupation: What is colonial about it?', *Electronic Journal of Middle Eastern Studies* 8.1–14 (2008): 8.

26 In the US, during the Obama administration, the Israeli occupation of Palestine was supported by $8.5 million a day in military aid by the US government, funding that has increased after the election of Donald Trump to $3 billion per year. That aid includes, for example, $145 million the US Department of Homeland Security awarded Elbit Systems in 2014, to deliver more radar and surveillance towers in the militarization of the US-Mexico border. In Israel, these programmes have flourished and expanded under governments headed by Kadima, Likud and Labour.

27 A. Bandele and P. Cullors, *When They Call You a Terrorist: A Black Lives Matter Memoir* (New York: St. Martin's Press, 2018).

28 Jewish Voice for Peace, 'About deadly exchange', 2018, https://deadlyexchange.org/about-deadly-exchange/ [accessed on 20 November 2018].

29 Jewish Voice for Peace, 'What do participants say?', 2018, https://deadlyexchange.org/what-do-participants-say/ [accessed on 20 November 2018].

30 M. Alexander, *The New Jim Crow: Mass Incarceration in the Age of Colorblindness* (New York: The New Press, 2013).

31 Davis, *Freedom is a Constant Struggle*, p. 144.

32 Davis, *Freedom is a Constant Struggle*, p. 20.

33 W. E. B. Du Bois, *Black Reconstruction in America, 1860–1880* (New York: Free Press, 1998), pp. 632–634.

34 Lowe, *The Intimacies of Four Continents*, p. 170

35 'Reluctant settler' is Wolfe's way of referring to his own positionality within the settler colonial structure of Australia, as one that simultaneously acknowledges being a 'beneficiary and a legatee of the dispossession and the continuing elimination of Aboriginal people in Australia', while at the same time registering his individual preference to 'not be existing on somebody else's stolen land', allying him with the struggle for the liberation of the native: P. Wolfe and J. Kehaulani Kauani, 'Settler colonialism then and now: A conversation between J. Kehaulani Kauani and Patrick Wolfe', *Politica & Società* 1.2 (2012): 235–258 (p. 237).

7

Perpetuating apartheid: South African drug policy

Shaun Shelly and Simon Howell

'*We do not hate the European because he is white. We hate him because he is an oppressor. And it is plain dishonesty to say I hate the sjambok[1] and not the one who wields it.*'

Robert Sobukwe, 1959

'*Sjambok anyone that you see selling nyaope or providing, together we can break the silence ... We can even make our own Sjamboks.*'

Press statement by the Congress of South African Students, 2016

Introduction

No chemical substance, irrespective of form, effect, or composition, is innately, immediately, or naturally a 'drug'. Rather, chemical substances *become* drugs through a process of invention – ranging across social, political, economic and legal spheres – that is driven by partisan interests and personal agendas. Indeed, in tracing the origins of the prohibition of individual substances now widely understood to be 'illegal drugs' to their foundations, there is little more than a decision that has no justification other than itself. In this chapter, we trace the narrative of the prohibition of 'illegal drugs' in South Africa, the aim of which is to a) reveal this narrative as a continuation of the logic of racial segregation, formerly constituted as the form of government known as apartheid, and b) highlight how despite South Africa's 'turn' to democracy in 1994, the treatment of those defined as drug users contemporarily not only resembles, but reconstitutes the systematic violence of apartheid premised on the artificial discrimination of individuals.

It is not without some irony that South Africa has become one of the last outposts of the traditionally defined 'war on drugs', having been one of the primary instigators of the process that led to the prohibition of cannabis and furthermore, when remembering that it is a land whose history is littered with conquest, domination and artificial segregation. Throughout South Africa's history, one simple tool has been employed by those tasked with implementing the segregation of individuals and groups – the 'sjambok'. The sjambok, a long whip originally devised for use by someone seated on a cart to drive cattle or bulls, was by the sides of the first Europeans to clamber off their ships at the Cape of Good Hope, with its use on humans as a tool of discipline or punishment being recorded from the outset. It has remained by the side of the dominating party, finding extensive use by a litany of mine bosses digging for the gold upon which Johannesburg was built, by the farmers in the sugar cane fields upon which Durban was built, and by the apartheid police tasked with en*forcing* the imagined differences upon which the system was built. One would hope that the advent of democracy would have relegated this tool to history; however, even the mythology of Mandela could not overcome the fear and loathing of illegal drugs and drug users. Despite being formally illegal now, the sjambok's use has once again resurfaced, justified by a rhetoric that once again promises to drive individuals away from deviance, and to discipline them for their digressions.

In this chapter, we explore both the history of drug legislation and drug prohibition before and after apartheid, using the sjambok as the central artefact by which to guide the chronology and as a means of framing the argument. Our aim is to not only highlight how contemporary drug regulation continues the racist divisions historically formulated through colonial and apartheid architectures of governance, but to show how this assemblage of laws, precepts and tasks are themselves riddled with contradiction. The primary contradiction, per example, is that despite the two-decades-old aim of South African law and policy to 'eliminate drugs and drug use' in society, the mechanisms used in this 'elimination', such as heavy-handed policing and a lack of treatment efforts, have served to contribute to a steady increase in drug prevalence and use. In showing this, we draw on and bring to the literature new data previously unavailable to researchers. Before turning to the historical antecedents of this reality, finally, it should be noted that our aim here is not to crack yet another sjambok at those – such as the police – who may find themselves structurally implicated in the offences of South African drug regulation policy, but rather to add in some way to the basis of critical reasoning advancing alternative regulatory frameworks.

Colonial roots and imperial justifications

At the beginning of the twentieth century, the United States, the European colonial powers and China – driven by a combination of economic interests as well as racist perceptions masquerading as moral beliefs – sought to control the production, distribution and use of a number of pharmacological substances, although their primary focus was opium and later, cocaine. While couched in a moral narrative concerned with the 'saving' of the colonial 'natives' who were imagined as the primary users, the principle concern was, however, economic. Britain readily went to war with China, for instance, between 1839 and 1860 over the distribution rights to the opium trade (and indeed, Chinese sovereignty), or as understood in a contemporary rubric, the right to be the sole cartel dealing in opium. Similarly, when Karl Koller and Sigmund Freud discovered the anaesthetic qualities of cocaine, it was heralded as a 'medical miracle', with demand consequently outstripping production for some time. But both were to be deemed illegitimate and eventually illegal as a result of their association with Black and Asian labourers, in which their use became a vehicle for the moral condemnation of individuals and populations seen as different and inferior. In relation to opium, this was to be the basis for the fear of the 'yellow peril' that was used as a means of narrating the existential crisis encountered at the onset of the decline of the legitimacy of the British empire-building project, while in reference to cocaine, the basis for the primordialization of the 'negro race' in the US and the assemblage of the architecture of racial division that only began to be dismantled in the 1960s and which is still visible at the time of writing.

As such, motivated mainly by the commercial interests of European nations, early agreements and resolutions focused on regulation. The opium trade needed controlling to protect the United Kingdom's financial interests in the trade. However, in North America, the commercial imperative to control the production, trade and use of drugs had a second motivating factor: the need to control those seen as 'other', most often expressed within the context of racial identity. The White American population believed that the use of opium by Chinese immigrants was a significant threat to stability, and the use of cocaine by former slaves in the South made them impervious to the effects of a well-aimed bullet, necessitating the need to supply police with larger-calibre weapons. Similarly, cannabis (marijuana) used by Mexican men, according to the press of the time, resulted in the rape of White women.

There were moreover so many incidents of authorities meeting out physical reprisals that the use of the whip as a legitimate state response to the drug-using 'other' entered into the English lexicon, for it was hoped that they might be 'whipped into shape'.

There is a remarkable consistency between the arguments used to justify the prohibition of cocaine, cannabis and opium in the United States and Canada, and cannabis and opium in South Africa. Although not indigenous to Africa, Africans have used cannabis for centuries. Cannabis was medicine, social lubricant and mediator of religious experience for many cultural groups. David Livingstone reported that the Sotho smoked cannabis before going into battle,[2] while others claim that cannabis fuelled the Zulu victory at the Battle of Blood River.[3] In 1870, the Natal Colony prohibited the smoking, sale, or trade in cannabis by Indian labourers and in 1891, the Cape Colony followed. Concerns that cannabis reduced the efficiency and obedience of workers motivated the prohibition. Cannabis use and cultivation by Black Africans and Indian slaves was a point of ongoing discussion among the colonial authorities. While some were adamant that cannabis was the cause of all manner of crime and social disorder, mine managers expressed an ambivalence to prohibiting the sale of cannabis to mineworkers; in direct contradiction to the accepted narrative, they claimed it made the labourers more productive. Even with the motivation of profit, by the early 1900s, the cannabis conversation was one of race and class, enhanced by fear of the 'Black Peril', and the mixing of races through the cannabis trade.

Indeed, running parallel to the move towards cannabis prohibition, the South African opium trade was walking the line between regulation and prohibition. In the paper 'The rise and fall of the opium trade in the Transvaal, 1904–1910', Waentje describes the complex relationship between the economic interests of the mines, the moral and prohibitionist agenda of religious groups, and the pragmatic view of some medical doctors.[4] From 1904 to 1909, the notorious Labour Importation Scheme brought over 63,000 Chinese men to South Africa to work in the mines. With the new labourers came opium, a part of the social fabric in China. This new opium market saw a variety of routes opening up, and a number of attempts by government, immigrants, local farmers and mines to make a profit. In 1905, after failed attempts to control the opium trade through punitive measures, the authorities passed the Opium Trade Regulation Ordinance, allowing for two pounds of opium per person per month. By 1909, more than 16,000 pounds of opium had been distributed – legally – under the regulation. However, once the Chinese labourers had largely returned to China, the 'mine medicine' lost value as a tool for productivity. Soon it was labelled a threat to the morality of all, and when it was reported to Jan Smuts that opium dens were full of undesirables of mixed races and 'bastard women lying with Chinese men', the Opium Ordinance was quickly phased out. Like in Canada and the US, the threat of the 'yellow peril' was the primary motivation for universal prohibition. The colonial imperative of keeping races separate – and the White race pure – motivated the early prohibition of drugs. The reported true 'evil' of drugs was that their trade and use brought the races into the same space, often as equals. In South Africa, Canada and the US, reports at the time repeatedly reference White women, when intoxicated, being in the presence of men of colour as an example of the depravity attributable to drugs. Paterson convincingly argues that the reasoning that informed cannabis prohibition in South Africa was almost identical to the development of the apartheid laws.[5] By 1922, South Africa was committed to the prohibition of cannabis (hemp). This was of such importance that in 1923 South Africa petitioned the League of Nations to include Indian hemp on the International List of Habit Forming Substances. Cannabis was included, alongside opium and cocaine, on the list of dependence-forming drugs in 1925, ending the need for South Africa to justify local prohibition.

After the Second World War, the only superpower to emerge without crippling financial debt was the United States. By using financial aid as a bargaining tool, American influence in the international sphere grew, and the prohibitionist agenda gained traction, culminating in the 1961 Single Convention on Narcotic Drugs, which states that 'addiction to narcotic drugs constitutes a serious evil for the individual and is fraught with social and economic danger to mankind.'[6] Nations have a 'duty to prevent and combat this evil' and since 'effective measures against abuse of narcotic drugs require co-ordinated and universal action', they mandate 'international co-operation guided by the same principles and aimed at common objectives'. The convention of 1961 thereby obliged sovereign nations to adopt the principles of prohibition and legitimized foreign influence in the development of local responses to drugs. The convention was strengthened in 1971[7] and again in 1988, when the Political Declaration and Action Plan on Global Drug Control set the goal of a 'drug free world'.[8] The linking of a moral framework with that of a regulatory framework is clear here, operating at first as a justificatory strategy whereas contemporarily the artificial nature of the association has become hidden – for many, the fact that drug use is couched in terms of morality requires no questioning or even acknowledgement. As natural as this may seem, it is an entirely artificial product. It is furthermore not simply by chance that the moral condemnation of drug use lends itself so easily to the moral condemnation implicit in racist categorizations. Both mask the arbitrariness of the distinctions on which they rely by making these distinctions monstrous, and thereby, justifying the scorn and violence which has characterized the regulation of illegal drugs and the structural racism seen in assemblages, such as apartheid.

There is increasing acknowledgement that the approach to drug control, as promoted by the United States, and summarized as the 'War on Drugs', impacts on marginalized communities and people of colour disproportionally. Michelle Alexander has called the mass incarceration of African Americans the 'New Jim Crow'.[9] In *Culture and Imperialism*,[10] Edward Said defines 'imperialism' as 'the practice, the theory, and the attitudes of a dominating metropolitan centre ruling a distant territory' and 'colonialism' as 'the implanting of settlements on distant territory'. The role of imperialism and colonialism in shaping the war on drugs to fit an agenda of self-interest should not be underestimated. One need only highlight the actions and efforts of Harry J. Anslinger in reference to cannabis control to reveal both the potent political capital that the condemnation of drugs may have, as well as demonstrate how prejudice and racial hatred can underpin a lifelong career. The maintenance of the status quo of inequity and further marginalization, through the application of drug policy, to the benefit of the colonizing powers, is well documented, not only in this volume, but in the wider literature. The United States, through economic power, has imposed the ideology that informs their domestic drug policy globally, on sovereign states, with few exceptions. This meets Said's criteria for imperialism. Through the deployment (or implanting) of military and paramilitary forces, such as the Drug Enforcement Agency (DEA), and the training of local law enforcement, these territories have, effectively, become colonized.

Apartheid and the fear of difference

Apartheid formalized and took to their logical conclusion many of the pre-existing tenets of colonial South Africa. The new laws introduced under the Nationalist government sought to divide racial groups and ensure that the interests of White South Africans remained protected at all costs. By creating broad groups of apparent homogeny through the legal system, education and media misinformation, the government sought to dehumanize those who were placed lower on an imagined ontological hierarchy. The government conjured up four racial groups in this hierarchy of South African society: 'white', 'coloured', 'Indian' and 'black'. Each was constructed as having implicit and innate qualities and characteristics, with whiteness being seen as more 'pure' and it was perceived to be 'natural' for a minority of the population to rule over the majority. In doing so, groups could be dehumanized, presented as a threat, and thus the way in which they were controlled became understandable and justifiable to the privileged class, in this case, White South Africans.

In order to maintain the position of the economically privileged, the ruling party kept the protesting underclasses subdued through various means of social control. People of colour needed permission to move through areas where White people lived – a passbook was required. Rights to education, work and political organization were restricted. Most revealing, however, was the assemblage of laws known as the 'Immorality Act'. Originally passed in 1927 (Act 5 of 1927), the act prohibited sexual relations between 'Europeans' and 'Natives' outside of marriage. In 1949, Act 55 prohibited marriages between 'Europeans' and 'Non-Europeans', and in 1950 (Act 21 of 1950), the Immorality Amendment Act was expanded to intercourse between 'Europeans' and 'Non-Europeans'. The effect was to criminalize any 'mixed' births that occurred, although these were rarely pursued by the authorities. The 'immorality' was derivative of a fear that the mixing of racialized bodies would dilute the purity of whiteness and muddle the ontological categories upon which governance was based. Drug use, understood as irrational, immoral and deviant, was thought to encourage such behaviour and was thus placed within and condemned as a function of this larger moral governmentality. However, it is important to note that it was not that drugs and drug use were 'naturally' immoral, but that they were strategically positioned to reflect a moral architecture, albeit usually through its negation.

In terms of legal rights, if there is a violation of a right, and there is no means of remedy, the right is meaningless. In apartheid South Africa, access to courts to remedy the violations of rights was difficult for Black South Africans.[11] Historians and legal experts commonly acknowledge that Black South Africans were unlikely to receive the same level of support, quality of representation, and access to legal aid as other South Africans. In order to address the inability of the courts to deal with the large number of people before them, a number of legal procedures were denied, and those meant to uphold the law became complicit in the violation of rights.[12]

The policing of apartheid was particularly problematic. Police had to enforce the unenforceable in a population excluded from the establishment of the laws that controlled them. This immediately put the police and the population at odds with each other, and the principles of ethical policing, as described by Peel,[13] were impossible to fulfil. Without the support of the population, and with 'crime' being of a *mala prohibitia* nature and against the will of the people, the first principle of Peelian Policing Principles became impossible, namely 'to prevent crime and disorder as an alternative to the repression of crime and disorder by military force and severity of legal punishment'. In order to police the unenforceable, police were militarized, granted excessive powers to apply physical and lethal force, and when they failed to maintain the ordered suppression of communities, the military provided reinforcement. Such a strategy of engagement has been iteratively reflected over time in South Africa, perhaps most recently in the calls for military operations in some communities of Cape Town to 'root out' drugs and gangs. The apartheid police were armed with both firearms and the sjambok, a symbolic appointment compared with the efficacy of a modern firearm. That the sjambok was still provisioned for is indicative of its place in the governance of the country – it was meant to whip into shape the population, of course – but it was also emblematic of a particular conception of power in which those who ruled did so through the cracking of a whip across the backs of a population classed primarily as a labour pool for the mining of wealth.

'Worse than apartheid'

Around the world, as repressive regimes are overthrown, when borders are opened and the freedom of movement is restored, new trade routes open, and economic opportunities expand, allowing for the predictable and unavoidable increase in the availability of drugs. Similarly, after the fall of apartheid and the first free elections in 1994, a rise in the availability of drugs in South Africa was inevitable. In addition, in South Africa, with the focus of the struggle for freedom all but gone, the purpose that unified oppressed and marginalized communities dissipated. Rather, the focus shifted towards individual needs and a race to claim a part of the redistribution of wealth. With the move from collective cause towards individual identity, and the corresponding rise of the free market economy, there comes an increasing sense of psychosocial dislocation. For the majority of South Africans, the hope of meaningful participation in a new South Africa has failed to materialize. Neoliberal policies have replaced more socialist-oriented proposals[14] and many communities still lack basic services. South Africa has a GINI index that positions the country as one of the most inequitable in the world.[15] Social exclusion, defined as the 'restriction of access to opportunities and a limited capacity to capitalise on these opportunities'[16], is a key factor in determining the level of dependent drug use in communities. Bruce Alexander has persuasively argued that this sense of psychosocial dislocation, in many cases, leads to the rise of addiction to anything perceived to resolve the feeling of exclusion.[17] Since drugs became more available, they became one way of satisfying this need.

If Alexander's model is correct, the group racially classified by the apartheid government as 'coloured' is at particular risk due to the high levels of dislocation experienced by this community. This ethnic group is heterogeneous and their ancestors were early colonizers, Khoisan, Xhosa, and slaves from India, Malaysia and Indonesia among others. This initially resulted in a lack of unified cultural identity and narrative history. However, a unique 'Cape Coloured' cultural identity began to develop in the early twentieth century, specifically on the outskirts of the city centre in the region of District 6. Just as the people of District 6 started to find an identity, the apartheid government forcibly relocated them to the Cape Flats, breaking up families and sub-communities and putting them into accommodation that resembled human Skinner boxes – that is, the small, enclosed box used by B. F. Skinner to study operant conditioning. This act of incredible cruelty disrupted the emerging sense of community and 'belonging', and arguably makes the Cape Flats community the most psychosocially dislocated population in South Africa. As Alexander's theory predicts, it is therefore not surprising that the Western Cape accounts for almost 40 per cent of the South Africa's drug-related crime.[18] The 'coloured' population makes up 8.8 per cent of the total national population, yet 18.2 per cent of the total prison population are classified as coloured.

While people across the entire spectrum of economic status may experiment with the use of drugs, those that are more susceptible to dependency and the habituated use of drugs tend to come from communities where there are few choices and opportunities to find meaning beyond the use of drugs. The impact of adverse childhood events on the probability of adult dependent drug use is well publicized.

People who score a six on the Adverse Childhood Event score are 46 times more likely to inject drugs than those who score a zero.[19] Untreated mental health issues are also linked to the dependent use of drugs. Further, the likelihood of arrest for drug possession and use increases in communities where there is little private space and a high police presence. Once arrested, an individual is far less likely to find economic integration. The common and accepted narrative is that drugs cause economic deprivation and lack of opportunity. While this may be true in certain circumstances, it is far more likely that economic deprivation and lack of opportunity motivate drug use, and the criminal justice response further impacts on the individual's ability to engage with the formal economy.

The use of drugs and their trade has rapidly become a proxy for many of the social ills faced by communities in South Africa. The presence of drugs and the use in communities is seen as the cause of many of the social and economic issues people face. Drugs have become a politically expedient target, distracting the voters from the government's failure to address the real issues of inequity, lack of opportunity, and poverty.

By labelling drug dependency as 'a serious evil for the individual [that] is fraught with social and economic danger to mankind',[20] the message that the use of drugs is the cause and not the symptom is clear. Apartheid was never labelled 'evil' by the United Nations. Therefore, according to some, for example, the Premier of the Western Cape, Helen Zille:

> Our crisis of substance abuse is harming another generation of young people worse than even what apartheid did to their forefathers ... We can't deal with this problem unless the police manage to track down the drug dealers, charge them and put them away for as long as it takes. In the meantime we have to deal with the tragic victims of substance abuse, ensure education, prevention, early detection rehabilitation and aftercare.[21]

To describe drug use and dependence as causing more harm than apartheid would seem insensitive, ill-informed and irresponsible – yet there was no backlash to this statement. There was a tacit agreement among politicians and the press that the 'scourge of drugs' is the biggest problem the country faces. The statement suggests three standard responses to drug use: (a) police action to stop the supply by targeting 'dealers', (b) an effective criminal justice system to ensure that the dealers are removed from the community, and finally (c) demand supply-side reduction through detection, rehabilitation and aftercare. Each of these reductionist conceptualizations is lacking.

First, relying on supply-side reduction through police action has been the principle approach for decades, and has made little or no impact on the supply of drugs. This approach fails to acknowledge the most basic of economic principles: where there is a demand, there will be a supply. No amount of policing can stop the supply of all drugs, and in cases where the supply of certain drugs is restricted, and there is a demand, the drugs are synthesized or sourced in different ways. This can lead to significant increases in risk – an example would be the move from heroin to homemade desomorphine (Krokodil) extracted from codeine pills in the Ukraine.

Second, Zille's suggestion that police track down 'dealers', charge them and put them away for 'as long as it takes', implies that people who sell drugs are not entitled to due process and proportional sentencing. She further fails to define just who is a 'dealer'. The reality is that in gang-controlled territories, by incarcerating community-level dealers, a void is created that is soon filled – often after a turf war accompanied by an increased level of violence. In many cases, people labelled as dealers are nothing more than people who use drugs (PWUD) trying to fund their own habit through the sales of drugs to a small circle of friends and acquaintances. Again, the arrest of these individuals makes no impact on the supply of drugs and carries significant harms for the individual.

Finally, Zille victimizes and pathologizes PWUD, saying that the use of drugs 'must be prevented, detected and those that use drugs must be rehabilitated'. This statement is devoid of the nuances and complexities that lead to habituated, dependent drug use, and makes no provision for PWUD without developing a dependency. Most people who use drugs, even those considered to be dependent users, do not need rehabilitation and aftercare. Yet, she paints them all as victims in need of curing, incapable of being employed or being part of the community.

Each of the above strategies is misguided, and contributes to the imperial and colonial agenda entrenched in the International Conventions on Narcotic Drugs. Recalling that the original goal of the prohibition of drugs was not to protect the whole of society from the dangers of drugs, but rather to protect the interests of the elite at the expense of the working class (usually people of colour), it is not surprising that the current drug control system uses many of the resources once used to police apartheid. Ironically, communities accept these responses in the belief that they are beneficial, yet they have become a more insidious form of de facto apartheid, in much the same way that drug policy has emerged as the new Jim Crow in the United States.

Perpetuating apartheid

There ought to be as little need to speak of the role of the police in our apartheid society as there is to speak of the role of weather forecasting in our political system. Although the police in any political system have the role of ultimately applying that system and of enforcing compliance with it, there is a general acceptance in enlightened Western countries that to some extent at least the police ought to keep their distance from the conflicts of ideology and political opinion which necessarily characterise all mature societies.

B. Van Niekerk, 'The police in apartheid society'[22]

If you don't want us to militarise, to take over your neighbourhoods, keep us out of areas that require us to solve your social problems. But because the police have the biggest footprint across the country we are being called on to solve problems for other departments which are weak or insufficiently organised. So we end up trying to control what we shouldn't be controlling.

Major General Jeremy Vearey

In South Africa, as in many other countries, the prevention of the use and supply of drugs lies firmly in the domain of the police. Placing the police at the forefront of the implementation of drug policy, compromises their role. As with apartheid, they are policing the impossible – the goal of a drug-free society is impossible and even undesirable. When expected to perform a task that is impossible, the police often resort to hard policing. This includes a significant show of force and the arbitrary application of stop-and-search policies. As with apartheid, when people would insert cash in their passbook to ensure their freedom of movement,[23] the freedom to move with impunity can be bought in the ganglands of Cape Town.[24] Mass raids, when entire suburbs are cordoned off at the dead of night and as many as fifty doors are kicked in by police with military support, are direct repeats of apartheid policing, and are not indicative of considered and investigative policing. Many of these raids are nothing more than a show of force, and those caught are seldom more than drug users or low-level dealers. Despite the failure to find any evidence, police justify their actions, as the following quote from a 2015 report in *Eye Witness News* suggests: 'Sergeant Jerome Vogt says one of their aims is to disrupt drug operations in the area. "Even if we don't find drugs at a specific house, it's important that we disrupt the activities because we know that in the area there is selling of drugs. Fast disruptive operations are very important."'[25]

The impact of policing drugs on the individual is significant, but it moves beyond the individual to the collective. Through militarization and the scatter-gun approach, entire communities are alienated. The possibility of applying Peelian principles is minimized and the police become a tool of the state rather than a trusted resource for the community. The benefit of a strong police presence and a show of force may be welcomed by some, but when violence escalates and frustration rises, a community will turn on the police, regarding them as persecutor rather than protector. The arbitrary searches of schools, where children as young as age 12 are searched by armed police, does not reduce the trauma of children; it either contributes to the trauma or hardens them, setting up the future dynamic of distrust. This focus on the police's role in the war on drugs provides a dual distraction: Either the dealers (usually in the form of foreign nationals from other African countries) are blamed, or the police are targeted for failing to perform. In an effort to prove their commitment and utility, police quote numbers of arrests and the press are invited to witness their vigour and commitment to the task. All of this contributes to the breakdown of human rights, a disregard for the rights of all South Africans, and the othering of a large portion of the population.

Statistics relating to drug arrests are released annually as a subset of the larger crime statistics. These statistics are, however, aggregated and generalized, and contain little information relating to the arrest process, conviction rates, and any specific details. Further information was, however, provided to one of the authors, the results of which not only reveal how futile the past and present policing strategy has been, but that the police are simply just not the answer to the problems reflected by illegal drug use. Nationally, drug arrests increased by 181.5 per cent between 2005 and 2015, translating into some 266,902 arrests in the last year. Over the same period, national treatment levels rose just 27.5 per cent, with a mere 10,197 people receiving treatment, or just 3.8 per cent of those arrested. Focusing solely on the Western Cape province, the raw statistics between 2005 and 2015 reveal the absolute failure of policing to produce any form of 'success', even by the very definition used by the police – 'to reduce and eliminate the production, distribution and use of drugs in South Africa'. Of the 9,093 arrests reported in just one year (2013), 8,972 were for suspected possession while just 118 were for suspected dealing. This is a ratio of 1.32 per cent. Even *within* the War on Drugs paradigm, it was recognized that it was of far greater utility to arrest drug dealers rather than drug users. As such, the question is why the South African police have continued to do the precise opposite. The answer, it seems, is that drug users represent an easy 'resource' by which to ensure that arrest statistics, integral to the performance management system, are met. As such, drug users are easy to arrest, the moral condemnation of their use prevents any questioning of the process, and their numbers allow for the meeting of statistics that define 'success' and thus help to ensure promotion and career development. Once more, the whip has been cracked, and the police have responded.

Such responses are, however, not only prejudicial in terms of drugs themselves, but draw on the deeply embedded ontological framework established by apartheid that continues to define the parameters of daily life in the country. Drawing on the same data set, but focusing on four discrete suburbs that are homogenous in terms of population size and economic variables, but disparate in terms of racial makeup, it was found that coloured men are disproportionately at risk of being arrested by a factor of some 2.48 – or in other words, nearly 2.5 – times more likely of being arrested on suspicion of drug possession or dealing than other racial groups. This is in comparison of a factor of 0.01 for White men and 0.17 for Black men above the standard deviation. The risk of arrest factor for White women was 0.0038 – translated contextually, White women are at higher risk of being bitten by a shark than they are of being arrested on suspicion of drug possession/dealing. The statistics bear witness to an ontological framework in which race has become the marker of suspicion, justified teleologically by an implicit hierarchy in which colour and deviance are intimately interwoven, the result of which is that the policing of drugs continues the logic and effects of apartheid by other means. Drugs, in short, are the mask behind which apartheid reasoning continues to manifest itself in South Africa.

Once arrested for drug possession, people lose many of their rights to due process. In 2017, the Cape Town Network of People Who Use Drugs attended a hundred cases at five magistrate courts in Cape Town. This was to inform the processes and protocol for a formal study in 2018. Of the hundred cases observed, 97 people were charged with possession and three with possession with intent to distribute. In 76 cases, the defendant pleaded guilty, received a warning and was allowed to leave. After pleading not guilty, seven were found guilty and sentenced to a week in prison, two received prison sentences of 30 days with the alternative of a fine, and 15 were remanded. Only one person applied for bail, which was refused. While this may sound like de facto de-penalization, it must be remembered that all one hundred people were either convicted and will have a criminal record, or went to prison.

Even when incarcerated for a short period, and then found innocent, the consequences can be dire. The Constitutional Court of South Africa's Cameron Report on Pollsmoor Correctional Centre,[26] described the conditions in the remand centre as unhygienic, without hot water, and filled to three times the recommended capacity; it was reported that inmates spend 24 hours a day in their cells. Medical care is virtually non-existent and sickness is rife. What the report does not account for is the level of gang activity and drug use. South African prison gangs are based on a mythology of numbers: the '26s', '27s' and '28s'. The gangs are infamous and the story of 'The Number' provides an alluring oral history and sense of belonging, while creating order in a chaotic world, offering the aspiration of rank, and importantly, a potential to participate economically in the drug trade once released. For someone who is living in abject poverty and has no hope of securing a job with a criminal conviction to their name, this is an immensely attractive alternative, especially when a reluctance to embrace 'The Number' will almost certainly result in physical and sexual assault while in remand. It is also noted in the Cameron Report that the many prisoners awaiting trial posed no risk to society, and many could simply not afford the bail needed which was as little as ZAR50 (US$3.50) in some cases. It is also necessary to have a fixed address in order to be released on bail. Many people who use drugs are reluctant to provide an address due to stigmatization or because they are living in informal accommodation arrangements.

Considering the prison conditions, it is not surprising that those appearing before the magistrate plead guilty to avoid the immediate threat of prison, despite the long-term consequences of a criminal record. What is even more concerning is the total lack of legal representation for PWUD. When the public prosecutor at the Cape Town Magistrates Court was asked about this, the researcher was told that Legal Aid lawyers are only available for people charged with dealing. There was a further perception among the accused that if legal representation was requested, this would be seen by the court as an attempt to delay and obstruct the court, and as such, the risk of incarceration was increased.

The consequences that the economically marginalized face are not typically what the more privileged classes face. School raids are limited to the poorer schools, the indiscriminate restriction of movement and kicking down of doors is not the modus operandi in the leafy suburbs of South Africa's middle class. Cannabis is smoked behind the walls of gated communities, far from the noses of patrolling police. If, through some accident of fate, a member of the elite is found in possession of drugs, they are more likely to be sent to rehab than prison.

As the opioid crisis in the United States spreads to the Mid-West and the white middle class, there has been a corresponding increase in proclaiming drug-dependent people as patients, not prisoners. The National Institute on Drug Abuse (NIDA) is the largest funder of research on drugs scheduled by the conventions. The predominant focus over the last two decades has been on the neuroscience of addiction, and in 1997 Alan Leshner,[27] then director of NIDA, proclaimed that 'addiction is a brain disease, and it matters.' Leshner's replacement, Nora Volkow, has repeatedly proclaimed that addiction is a disease of free will, that if left untreated, will probably result in death. Despite the fact that this idea is repeatedly exposed as false by robust population-wide data, it has become the accepted narrative, and similar to the imperial and colonial actions of the past, the move to treat addiction the American way is promoted by the joint agencies of Substance Abuse and Mental Health Services Administration (SAMHSA) and the Addiction Treatment Transfer Centre Network (ATTCN). SAMHSA's mission is to reduce the impact of substance abuse and mental illness on American communities, and is a repository for 'evidence-based interventions'. The vision of the ATTCN is to unify science, education, and service to transform lives through evidence-based and promising treatment and recovery practices in a recovery-oriented system of care. More recently, they have focused on the dissemination and implementation of services internationally.

To those who are seeking relief from the War on Drugs approach, the medical approach may seem like a reasoned alternative, but for the more cynical it could be said that there is more profit in making people patients rather than prisoners. It should be noted that many of the interventions proposed by SAMHSA are delivered in a manner more aligned with a form of social control than health care. For example, methadone can only be accessed in specialist programmes, where doses are delivered daily along with compulsory psychosocial services for extended periods of time. This precludes the necessary levels of freedom of movement and autonomy to engage in meaningful employment or other activities, as well as being stamped with the label of diseased and incapable of making a rational decision. Goffman, in his seminal explorations of stigma and identity, highlighted the labelling of people who are dependent on drugs as *'bad, dangerous'* or *'weak and out of control'*.[28] In the same way as civilized society was threatened by the 'black peril' or the 'yellow peril', we now face the threat of the peril of the drug addict. The conceptualization of the drug user as patient instead of prisoner is once again an attempt to colonize the poor in distant lands by treating people in a specific way that labels them as diseased for life, at risk for life, and always vulnerable to relapse and therefore in need of ongoing care and monitoring.

What all of these responses have in common is that they keep the poor in a cycle of economic exclusion, keep them 'othered', position them as a threat to their community, and encourage the exclusion and marginalization of those that use drugs. This in turn motivates the continued use of drugs and encourages the escalation of responses guided by the scientific approaches funded by foreign interests. Importantly, they distract from the real causes of broken communities – poverty, lack of hope, poor resource management and allocation – as well as the failure of politicians to meet the needs of the people. It further blinds communities from seeing the harms that the accepted responses to drugs have. In combination, the response to drugs uses apartheid resources to the same effect – the marginalization and exclusion of the masses – to protect the interests of the few. This time, however, it is our own hand that wields the sjambok.

Undue support and influence

Despite the similarities in both methods and outcomes, there are some significant differences between enforcing apartheid and drug prohibition; the main difference being the level of support for the actions taken.

At a community level, despite the obvious disruptions that are caused by indiscriminate policing and the shutting down of entire communities, members of the community often support these efforts in the name of fighting 'drugs and gangs'. According to the *Cape Times*, for example, when a raid by police cordoned off Mannenberg, preventing all people from going to work, residents supported the move, even calling for a military presence.[29]

Internationally, foreign countries have provided services and policy guidance to South Africa. The United States DEA, the paramilitary force with the mission of enforcing the controlled substances laws of the United States,[30] conducts ongoing training with South African law enforcement agencies. The DEA are presented as experts in drug law enforcement, despite their failure to make any notable reduction in the availability of drugs in the United States,[31] their complicity in numerous scandals,[32] poor record relating to human rights, and being involved in a number of civilian deaths. The DEA has an annual budget of US$3 billion.

As Jonny Steinberg aptly states when commenting on the transfer of skills from foreign police to South African police:

> These ideas bore a bloated conception of urban security which inadvertently stimulated, and thus helped to keep alive, a similarly bloated conception of security that lay at the heart of apartheid thinking. Dressed in the garb of crime prevention, a modified version of the paramilitary policing practices that flourished under apartheid returned to the streets of democratic South Africa.[33]

Once more, the police have been used as the whip that is cracked across the back of crime, so drawing attention away from the fact that the back is bare and Black because of the failure of the South African government to attend to the lingering socio-economic disparities that underwrite the democratic dispensation.

No critical thought

Despite the clear history of racism, the subjugation of colonized people, and the undermining of sovereign rights that is woven into the War on Drugs, despite the involvement of South African colonialists actively shaping the future of the international drug control regime, there has been no serious political challenge to the War on Drugs approach in the South African context. While countries such as Portugal, Uruguay, Colombia and Ghana are seeking new and domestic ways of dealing with drug use, in South Africa, if anything, there has been an embracing of this approach, and the rhetoric employed, instead of being challenged and refuted, has been amplified.

The belief that we have drug problems, that drugs need to be 'eradicated' through increased police actions, and that PWUD must be incarcerated or treated and/or rehabilitated, is almost universal. Politicians, together with community, business, academic and religious leaders, and much of the general population, seem united on this issue: drugs are the source of all manner of social ills. By restricting supply and eradicating the use of drugs, it is believed, the negative impacts attributed to the distribution, sale and 'abuse' of drugs, will fall away accordingly. In reality, the problems our communities face have less to do with drugs than with the failure of all to build inclusive, caring and responsive communities who see individual well-being as inseparable from community well-being.

It is time that we looked critically at the policies that are keeping South Africa in a de facto state of apartheid. We need to realize that drug policy is the perpetuation of the imperial and colonial, through the myth of the international consensus that the use of drugs is evil. Without such critical reflection, the evil of apartheid continues to permeate through the rhetoric of drugs, the result of which is that contemporary drug regulation is the proxy through which apartheid continues to manifest itself in South African society. It is only through such a critical engagement that the sjambok can finally be removed from the belt of South African policing.

Notes

1 Sjambok – a long leather whip used normally to drive oxen, but also used to beat labourers.

2 Lukasz Kamienki, *Shoot It Up: A Short History of Drugs and War* (New York: Oxford University Press, 2016).

3 Martin Chanock, *The Making of South African Legal Culture: 1902–1936 Fear Favour and Prejudice* (Cambridge: Cambridge University Press, 2001), p. 95.

4 T. Waetjen, 2017. 'The rise and fall of the opium trade in the Transvaal, 1904–1910', *Journal of Southern African Studies* 43.4 (2017): 733–751.

5 C. Paterson, 'Prohibition and resistance: A socio-political exploration of the changing dynamics of the Southern African cannabis trade'. Unpublished Master's thesis, Rhodes University, Grahamstown, 2009.

6 United Nations Office on Drugs and Crime, *The International Drug Control Conventions* (New York: United Nations Publications, 2010), p. 23.

7 United Nations Office on Drugs and Crime, *The International Drug Control Conventions*.

8 A/RES/S-20/2* UN General Assembly, *Resolution Adopted by the General Assembly [on the report of the Third Committee (A/52/636)] 52/92. International action to combat drug abuse and illicit production and trafficking*, 26 January 1998, www.refworld.org/docid/3b00f21b8.html [accessed 12 December 2018].

9 Michelle Alexander, *The New Jim Crow: Mass Incarceration in the Age of Colorblindness* (New York: The New Press, 2012).

10 Edward Said, *Culture and Imperialism* (New York: Vintage Books/Random House, 1993), p. 9.

11 W. Lane and A. P. F. Williamson, 'Difficulties facing black South Africans in exercising their legal rights' in SPRO-CAS Occasional Publication Number 9: *Law, Justice and Society* 1972.

12 By example, see P. Gready and L. Kgalema, L., 'Magistrates under apartheid: A case study of professional ethics and the politicisation of justice'. Occasional paper written for the Centre for the Study of Violence and Reconciliation, South Africa, 2000.

13 C. Emsley, *The English Police: A Political and Social History* (London: Routledge, 2014).

14 Sagie Narsiah, 'Neoliberalism and privatisation in South Africa', *GeoJournal*, 57.1–2 (2002): 3–13, http://link.springer.com/10.1023/A:1026022903276 [accessed July 2018].

15 H. Bhorat, Carlene van der Westhuizen and Toughedah Jacobs, 'Income and non-income inequality in post-apartheid South Africa: What are the drivers and possible policy interventions?', 2009, https://ssrn.com/abstract=1474271 or http://dx.doi.org/10.2139/ssrn.1474271 [accessed July 2018].

16 A. Hayes, M. Gray and B. Edwards, 'Social inclusion: Origins, concepts and key themes', Department of the Prime Minister and Cabinet, 2008, p. 6.

17 B. Alexander, *The Globalization of Addiction: A Study in Poverty of the Spirit* (Oxford: Oxford University Press, 2010).

18 Crime Stats (South Africa), www.crimestatssa.com/ [accessed 3 November 2018].

19 V. J. Felitti, 'Origins of addictive behavior: Evidence from a study of stressful childhood experiences', *Praxis der Kinderpsychologie und Kinderpsychiatrie* 52.8 (2003): 547–559.

20 United Nations Office on Drugs and Crime, *The International Drug Control Conventions*, p. 23.

21 Helen Zille, Premier of the Western Cape, 2013, www.westerncape.gov.za/gc-news/97/26408 [accessed 3 November 2018].

22 B. van Niekerk, 'The police in apartheid society', *Law Justice and Society* (1972).

23 Gareth Newham and Andrew Faull, 'Protector or predator? Tackling police corruption in South Africa', Institute for Security Studies Monographs, 182 (2011), p. 65, http://reference.sabinet.co.za/webx/access/electronic_journals/ismono/ismono_n182_a1.pdf [accessed July 2018].

24 Author's experience in Steenberg area of Cape Town.

25 Monique Mortlock and Shamiela Fisher, 'Cops raid drug hot spots in Mitchells Plain', *Eye Witness News*, 30 April 2015, http://ewn.co.za/2015/05/01/Cops-raid-drug-hot-spots-in-Mitchells-Plain [accessed July 2018].

26 Justice Edwin Cameron, 2016. *Cameron Report on Pollsmoor Correctional Centre: Department of Correctional Services progress report*, Parliamentary Monitoring Group, https://pmg.org.za/committee-meeting/23123/ [accessed 17 September 2018].

27 A. I. Leshner, 'Addiction is a brain disease, and it matters', *Science*, 278.5335 (1997): 45–47.

28 E. Goffman, *Stigma: Notes on the Management of Spoiled Identity* (New York: Simon & Schuster, 1986), p. 3.

29 African News Agency, 'Undercover operation nets teen with 16 grams of dagga', *Cape Times*, 9 February 2018, www.iol.co.za/capetimes/news/undercover-operation-nets-teen-with-16-grams-of-dagga-13197957 [accessed 3 November 2018].

30 United States Drug Enforcement Administration, 'DEA Mission statement', n.d., www.dea.gov/about/mission.shtml [accessed 3 November 2018].

31 Dan Werb, Thomas Kerr, Bodhan Nosyk, Steffanie Strathdee, Julio Montaner and Evan Wood, 'The temporal relationship between drug supply indicators: An audit of international government surveillance systems', *BMJ Open* 3 (2013), doi: 10.1136/bmjopen-2013-003077 [accessed 3 November 2018].

32 Drug Policy Alliance, 'The scandal-ridden DEA: Everything you need to know', April 2015, www.drugpolicy.org/sites/default/files/DEA_Scandals_Everything_ You_Need_to_Know_Drug_Policy_Alliance.pdf [accessed 3 November 2018].

33 Jonny Steinberg, 'Crime prevention goes abroad: Policy transfer and policing in post-apartheid South Africa', *Theoretical Criminology*, 15.4 (2011): 349–364, https://doi.org/10.1177/1362480611406168 [accessed 3 November 20180].

8

Racism and social injustice in War on Drugs narratives in Indonesia

Asmin Fransiska

Introduction

There has been a lack of literature produced on the history of Indonesian drug policy and the law. This absence does not occur without reasons. First, because drugs are constituted as a dangerous topic, sinful to be discussed and desperately hidden within the culture of Indonesia, they are largely absent in scientific Indonesian studies.[1] Second, talking about drugs will require talking about crime and the illicit market that keeps growing within the Indonesian economy, and this overshadows any discussion of the benefit that drugs may offer for health and scientific purposes, such as treatment for trauma or psychological issues.[2] Instead, drugs offences are recorded as 'extraordinary crimes' in Indonesia.[3] The current fear of drugs is connected to how much the characterization of drugs in Indonesia remains indebted to literature from the Dutch colonial era, where early ideas of the danger of drug cultivation, consumption and distribution for the 'native' population began to form. Even after Indonesian independence, the issue of drugs became a key topic alongside other national issues, such as forged currency and corruption,[4] and thus the Indonesian government decided to ratify the UN International Drug Conventions and a new era of prohibition began.[5] Since then, the International Drug Conventions have been driving the law and policy related to drugs in Indonesia since the 1970s, unfortunately limiting successive governments' ability to explore alternative drug laws and policies which focus on protecting the human rights, and health and wider cultural rights of the general population.[6] The debate on the access to treatment for people who use drugs only began in Indonesia in 2009, when a new drug law provided the infrastructure for drug dependency rehabilitation;[7] however, the deployment of this treatment is limited since the regulation for the law's implementation only became active in 2011, and furthermore only acted upon as a compulsory treatment.[8] This example illustrates the extent to which draconian prohibitionist polices have overshadowed any attempt at a more humanitarian drug policy within Indonesia.

In order to understand this situation, we must unpack the relationship between the laws on drugs in Indonesia, which have been developed over the past few decades and the production and consumption of the drugs themselves, which have been present in Indonesia for many centuries. Indonesian drug-use history has its origins long before colonization, beginning in the early age of the so-called *Nusantara* (the Indonesian archipelago), before Indonesia as a country was established.[9] Marijuana and opium were the main drugs in use at that time, originally for food and beverages.[10] However, during the Dutch Colonial period in Indonesia (1820–1950), opium production and consumption became increasingly popular for recreational use amongst both the 'native' and colonial populations.[11] The Dutch Colonial government designed a regulated drug market policy in what was then called the Dutch East Indies and allowed production and distribution through retail shops and consumption in several places which were frequented by Europeans as well as locals.[12]

The structure of the legal drug market of that era brought the Dutch Colonial government a significant amount of revenue from opium, coca and other substances that are now perceived to be 'evil' drugs. Wealth was acquired through a model of monopolizing opium and coca production into colonial hands and distributing the drugs for both local users and a wider global market.[13] A modern, industrialized approach to drug production and trade, particularly for opium, was firmly established during the Dutch era.[14] Even after the Dutch Colonial-era ended in Indonesia, Japanese colonization ensured that natives were unable to develop their own laws and policies.[15]

The use, consumption and also production of drugs during the colonial era developed in line with wider ideas of racism in Indonesia. During the period 1630–1800, the multinational trading empire (*Vereenigde Oost-Indische Compagnie*/VOC) established itself in Indonesia and created the alliance with the elites to take control over the region's resources. However, the VOC declined into bankruptcy by the end of the 1700s and was replaced by the Dutch government, which placed its possessions in the East Indies under increasing colonial rule over the course of the nineteenth century. Racism was used by the Dutch regime in order to maintain power in the colony, while prejudice and stigmatization of marginalized groups was used to divide and conquer.[16] The Indonesian population at the time was divided into three groups: the European group (all Dutch citizens, and people originally from Europe and Japan),[17] the Far Eastern group (those who were not included as European or 'Pribumi' Indonesian origin, mostly Indian, Pakistan, Chinese, Arab, etc.),[18] and the members of the lowest group were of Indonesian origin ('Pribumi').[19]

Each of the groups had to comply with a different set of laws and policies. This differentiated legal system bestowed privilege and benefits upon the Europeans and stripped rights and protections from the lowest Indonesian-origin groups, creating division between the 'native' populations and the Far Eastern group as well. This division resulted in the intended consequence of pitting the group of Far East origin (especially the Chinese population)[20] against the Pribumi group, effectively isolating the groups from each other and eliminating the opportunity of any alliance between them. Racism was therefore concretized in legal form in the colonial era and resulted in the disproportionate application of harsh sanctions such as long periods of imprisonment and the death penalty on the native population.[21]

The colonial practice of societal division through racist laws and policies drove the development of drug policy as well. Although the drug laws of the colonial era may appear 'progressive' by today's standards – in terms of having a non-prohibitionist approach to drugs compared to today's draconian prohibitionist policy in Indonesia – the aim of the colonial-era drug policy was for the drug trade's economic and financial benefits to accrue only to the colonialists and leave the Indonesian population with limited access to the economic wealth of the nation's resources.[22] The law's underlying racism contributed to increased prejudice and stigmatization, leading to race riots. The 1740 Batavia Massacre was one of the worst atrocities from that period. The massacre, conducted by Dutch Colonial forces and some militia gangs, led to the deaths of 1,789 Chinese people, as the violence spread from Batavia (now Jakarta) to other cities.[23] The riots only fuelled colonial racial hostilities, leading to subsequent further outbreaks of violence, mostly between those of Indonesian origin (Javanese most frequently) and those of Chinese or Arab origin.[24] Thus the era of Dutch colonization, informed by an underlying racial structuring of society, brought the legacy of European racism into Indonesia in a way that still reverberates through the country's contemporary social structure of racialized neoliberalization and exploitation.[25]

During the era of colonization, Europeans and wealthy Indonesians, mostly of Chinese or prestigious Indonesian origin, could buy drugs without any worries from the authorities. However, a limit was set for the maximum quantity that could be bought in the sale areas.[26] Furthermore, research from this era suggests that although the majority of those who were drug dependent were Javanese, the number reduces dramatically once the category of tobacco use is removed, and the data presents a picture of opium consumption as dominated by the Chinese population,[27] which gives an indication of how drugs became reflective of the segregation in Indonesian society.

Nowadays, alongside drug policy, the application of the death penalty offers another example of how racial segregation in Indonesia maintains the legacy of colonization. The current prohibitionist impulse drives the inability of the Indonesian government to find alternative solutions for controlling the illicit market of drugs that is growing in Indonesia. During the colonial era, the death penalty was employed by Dutch colonial government in order to repress the indigenous population. The death penalty was usually imposed for rebellion by supporters of Indonesian independence movements, or by others unhappy with the social order.[28] Today, the death penalty is imposed for drug offences, with this draconian stance based on the commitment of successive Indonesian governments to pursuing a 'War on Drugs'. In 2017, there were 165 convicted people on death row, 75 of them sentenced for drug offences.[29] The total number of executions for drug offences for the period 2015–17 stood at 18.[30]

It is my argument in this chapter that it is important to describe how racism informs not only a policy of segregation of people based on race or colour, but also persists within new forms of social identity in contemporary Indonesia (for example, people who use drugs, who engage in drug-related crimes, or who are perceived as 'decadent' and 'subversive'). W. E. B Du Bois famously described racism as a 'colour line', but this understanding has been expanded by subsequent post-colonial and critical race scholarship, which has gradually developed a language for understanding the plethora of ways for dividing and separating people because of their race, ethnicity, or religion.[31] Racism also relates to the injustice of drug policy and law, for when the poorest communities in societies use drugs, they are treated as less than human, unable to access medical care, or receive a fair trial. The stigma of drug use leads to an exacerbation of the poverty and social-health issues of those most vulnerable in society,[32] betraying how the language of sub-humanity developed by European racism has subsequently evolved to be applied to new categories of peoples, such as drug users.

Another phenomenon to be noted is how the narrative of the War on Drugs has become a powerful tool for government to ignore their duty to protect, fulfil and promote human rights regardless of the social status, gender, colour, nationality and other identity claims of the subject. This concept of fighting 'evil drug use' successfully establishes the negative conversation about drugs. The War on Drugs narrative is a scapegoat used to mask the state's inability to control illicit drugs, borders and corrupt bureaucrats, as well as the failure of the criminal justice system to address the issues of drug dependency, mental health and the over-representation of foreign nationals in the criminal justice system (mostly Chinese and African as targeted groups).[33]

The draconian narrative of the War on Drugs illustrates how the process of demonizing racialized communities is a social construction. The Ontario Human Rights Commission defines racial profiling as 'any action undertaken for reasons of safety, security or public protection, that relies on stereotypes about race, colour, ethnicity, ancestry, religion, or place of origin, or a combination of these, rather than on a reasonable suspicion, to single out an individual for greater scrutiny or different treatment'.[34] In the United States, great racial disparities exist in sentencing for nonviolent crimes, especially property crimes and drug offences.[35] In addition to that, the American Civil Liberties Union (ACLU) adds that there are staggering racial disparities in life-without-parole sentencing for nonviolent offences.[36] In Indonesia, racial profiling in the policing of people who use and sell drugs is used on a regular basis. This method targets the people who use and sell drugs on the basis that they share certain characteristics, such as being an African migrant, which is often enough to be profiled as a criminal and subjected to search and arrest by the police.[37]

At the international level, it can be argued that the racism of drug laws and policies began over a century ago, when the early League of Nations opium treaties tried to classify and prohibit certain drugs based on prejudice towards certain groups of people. This underlying racism continues to create racial disparities in the application of 'objective' drug laws, for instance, the racialized sentencing for cocaine possession in the US.[38] Similar to Indonesia, the US Anti-Drug Abuse Act of 1986 has ignored empirical, scientific evidence and is instead committed to an inaccurate perception of differences in the harmfulness and danger of crack and powder cocaine, therefore offering unbalanced sentences for offences involving possession of the same amount of crack cocaine and powder cocaine.[39]

From drug control to drug prohibition: the impact of colonization and international drug control on Indonesian drug policy and laws

The War on Drugs was established and legitimized through international legal treaties. The international community, or at least certain countries, began to negotiate a 'consensus' on drug control in Shanghai in 1909 at the first major international meeting to control drugs and other substances.[40] The conference focused on restricting opium consumption, production and distribution, with little regard shown to the cultural, social and economic history of countries where opium had traditionally been used. When the Opium Commission organized the Hague Opium Conference in 1912, the first treaty was signed and used to establish a legal prohibitionist framework on drugs.[41] Drug prohibition became the norm, as the rest of the twentieth century saw increasing developments regarding prohibitionist drug laws and policies throughout the world, especially for opium, which would be controlled by the League of Nations following the 1912 treaty.[42]

The international drug control regimes established through the International Drug Control Conventions on Narcotics[43] and the International Convention on Psychotropic Substances in 1971[44] are legally binding for their signatories, which include most member states of the United Nations. The international drug control regimes successfully defined the restrictions of using and accessing drugs only for medical and scientific reasons.[45] The negative implications of the international prohibitionist regime impacted upon Indonesia. As a member state of the UN and the international drug control regime, Indonesia limits the use of drugs to medical and scientific purposes by only allowing limited prescriptions from doctors to justify the use of psychoactive substances, and the state will imprison those who fail to prove themselves as innocent on account of having obtained this medical exemption.[46] The authoritarian laws that were enacted from the Law on Narcotics 1976 until the Drug Law 1997 established new drug offences in Indonesian law, with the focus being placed on *papaver* (the opium poppy), cocaine, morphine, cannabis and their derivatives, regulating the cultivation of these substances, as well as other chemical substances such as Ekgonia.[47] The Narcotics Law contained criminal sanctions related to the cultivation and possession of certain types of drugs, such as *papaver*, coca, and marijuana.[48] The Drug Law clearly acknowledged and implemented the prohibitionist approach with a set of strict punishments established for drug offences, ranging from incarceration to the death penalty. These laws not only focus on drug users and/or drug traffickers, but also on their families, such as the guardian or parents who know (or are judged that they *should* know) about the drug activities of those under their responsibility. A failure to report any drug activities undertaken by family members to the authorities is a punishable offence.[49]

In 2002, the then President Megawati declared a renewed national 'War on Drugs',[50] promising to eradicate drug abuse and drug trafficking.[51] The establishment of the National Narcotic Board (BNN) in March 2002 offered a clear message on the national anti-drug policy. She also ensured that there would be harsher penalties for drug crimes by stating that 'Major offenders, like producers and dealers, should be punished by death. For me, it is better to have a person suffer capital punishment that to see the whole community become addicted to drugs'.[52]

In Indonesia, foreigners became a key target of this national policy of a War on Drugs, particularly Chinese or African immigrants. The BNN described the Chinese as a source of drug precursor chemicals used to produce synthetic drugs, and West Africans, such as Nigerians, as being at the centre of heroin and cocaine smuggling networks into Indonesia through criminal enterprises.[53]

Continuing with the War on Drugs rhetoric offered by the international community, in 2008, President Susilo Bambang Yudhoyono declared the War on Drugs in Indonesia should aim at producing a 'drug-free Indonesian society'.[54] This populist euphoria at invoking the dream of a drug-free world[55] continues today and fuels the escalation of the war, with prohibitionists ignoring the current de facto moratorium of the death penalty and pushing eagerly for the death penalty for drug offenders under the current President Joko Widodo.

Therefore, despite the differences between drug law and policy during the Colonial era and the current government's approach, with the Colonial era allowing a regulated market through a monopolist system and the current approach insisting on authoritarian prohibition enforced through penalties and forced rehabilitation, there are also similarities between the two. During the Colonial era, the markets were focused on ensuring that the economic benefits incurred from the drugs trade remained primarily with the colonialists; the rest of the country lacked the healthcare system to supervise and manage drug users in order to ensure their safety. In the current government's approach, drugs issues come under the security section of national policy and therefore drug policies must prioritize the support given to security forces like the BNN, the judiciary and the police, in a system that seeks to stamp out drug consumption and possession. This contributes to people who use drugs being neglected and abused by the security forces. For example, the majority of people in prisons who use drugs are given very limited access to the health care and treatment they need; moreover, prison can in fact serve as the centre of an illicit market for drugs distribution throughout Indonesia.[56]

There is also a failure to consider proportionality in the application of penalties for drug consumption, possession and trafficking. Proportionality can be used as an approach to scrutinize the aim of the law and policy on drugs. Moreover, the proportionality test can be used to evaluate and analyse the implementation of drug law and policy, since it is a principle of the rule of law that can turn attention away from an automatic presumption of punishment to a concern with fairness and justice. Proportionality could be a tool to drive the protection of human rights within the criminal justice system, as well as ensure that the economic and social situations of those who are trapped in the complex system of criminal justice are considered. Indonesian law should be able to answer the question of whether the law and policy on drugs has legitimacy, if it achieves the wider aims of reducing the fundamental rights for those who are within criminal justice system. If the legitimate aim of drug laws is to control the substances that may injure the health and welfare of the community, then the standard of proportionality should be based on this concern with health.[57] The Universal Declaration of Human Rights (UDHR) states

in the exercise of his rights and freedoms, everyone shall be subject only to such limitation as are determined by the law solely for the purpose of securing due recognition and respect for the rights and freedoms of others and of meeting the just requirements of morality, public order and the general welfare in a democratic society.[58]

Moreover, the committee of the International Covenant of Civil and Political Rights (ICCPR) urges states to 'demonstrate their necessity and only take such measures as are proportionate to the pursuance of legitimate aims in order to ensure continuous and effective protection of Covenant rights'.[59] However, the current Indonesian administration fails to apply the proportionality principle, instead claiming that drug crimes are extraordinary crimes and constitute a national security threat.[60] The result of this claim is that sentencing for drug crimes lacks sufficient checks and balances, and therefore allows for bias against foreigners, ethnic minorities, or those with undiagnosed medical reasons for using drugs. Indonesian drug law in its current form struggles to be able to distinguish between people who possess drugs for personal use or for trafficking purposes, as well as people who might be using drugs for a medical condition that remains undiagnosed.[61] The inability to differentiate between people who need treatment or not leads to forced treatment, since it is not necessarily based on the patients' needs.[62] Under Indonesian regulation, forced treatment applies to the person who is by law not convicted as a drug offender because even if she/he is found not guilty of drug possession, as long as that person's urine test is positive for drug use at some point in the past, that individual is required to attend rehabilitation.[63] This kind of forced treatment can increase the possibility of the victim being subjected to torture.[64]

The War on Drugs in its present form

As described above, the War on Drugs continues to discriminate against people through many forms. Aside from the failure to apply proportionality in drug sentencing, which means marginalized or vulnerable groups face human rights violations, the War on Drugs also puts people who use drugs at greater risk of violence from the drug kingpins whose wealth flourishes in the illegal market. Many people in the criminal justice system are from the ethnic minorities, are mentally or physically ill, are women trapped in the illicit drug market, or are street children. The Berkeley Foundation found that, given the ways in which drug law enforcement has hindered access to HIV prevention and care services, the drug laws are disproportionately and negatively impacting people living with HIV. In countries across the world, the supply-side focus of law enforcement has driven drug policy and has been allowed to overshadow the socioeconomic root causes of problematic drug use and involvement in drug-related crime. A key element of the right to non-discrimination, however, is the positive obligation to identify those groups and individuals in need of special care and assistance to ensure that their rights are guaranteed.[65]

In Indonesia, the numbers of drug offences increased rapidly after the new drug laws in 2009 were implemented. In December 2010, 3,183 drug offences were recorded in total. The arrest and imprisonment rate for people who use drugs and minor drugs traffickers increased by 2,847 per cent (that is, 90,616 drug offences) within seven years.[66] Despite the increase of punishments, the aim of reducing drug consumption is failing: prior to the new law being implemented, it was estimated that 3.6 million people used drugs in 2014, a figure that has grown to around 5.1 million people. This increased number is an indication of how the harsh prohibitionist and law enforcement approach with regard to tackling drugs issues fails to limit the use of prohibited substances. Furthermore, most cases for drug offences use the possession threshold in Indonesian law, rather than drug dependence thresholds. Therefore, it is unsurprising to find that law enforcement sentences 90 per cent of drug offenders to imprisonment rather than rehabilitation, regardless of the medical records and the needs of the offenders.

As has been seen across the globe, the War on Drugs has fuelled an escalation in Indonesia's prison population. In their 2017 report, the Ministry of Law and Human Rights stated that 40 per cent of Indonesia's prison population are incarcerated due to drug offences. In the Riau Prison, of a total of 4,426 prisoners, 1,935 are imprisoned for drug offences (43.71 peer cent). In Sulawesi Province, 60 per cent of 7,500 prisoners are classified as drug offenders.[67] Between 2014 and 2017, there was a 27 per cent increase in cases involving drugs. Unsurprisingly, due to the escalation of the War on Drugs narrative, prisons are suffering from overcrowding. Prisons in Indonesia are currently estimated to be 123.248 per cent over capacity,[68] which impacts negatively upon access to health care for people who use drugs. In 2009, the Ministry of Law and Human Rights stated that out of 140,423 drug-offence prisoners, at least 89 people have died due to HIV/AIDS-related diseases.[69] In 2004, the Social Ministry stated that there are 105 social rehabilitation centres.[70] However, as there are 943,000 people who use drugs in urgent need of treatment, the capacity of those centres is so limited that they are only able to provide social rehabilitation for 1,725 people.[71]

The War on Drugs also leads to the most vulnerable and impoverished members of Indonesian society facing the criminal justice system with no knowledge of law, as well as foreign nationals who may not speak the language. Again, we see a legal system that protects different members of society to different degrees, just as when there were separate legal systems applied to different groups in the Colonial period. Access to lawyers or legal representatives has remained restricted for marginalized and vulnerable populations. LBH Masyarakat in its research found that in the capital DKI Jakarta, among 388 respondents, there were 204 people (52 per cent) who did not have access to a legal representative.[72] Based on that data, the question we must ask is how the law and policy on drugs has managed to satisfy the state's obligations to protect the human rights of its citizens. The implications are serious, resulting in human rights violations and the return of racial/ethnic division. The International Convention on the Elimination of Racism Discrimination defines racial discrimination as:

> any distinction, exclusion, restriction or preference based on race, colour, or national or ethnic origin which has the purpose or effect of nullifying or impairing the recognition, enjoyment or exercise, on an equal footing of human rights and fundamental freedoms in the political, economic, social, cultural or any other field of public life.[73]

Any discrimination based on national origin and ethnicity that creates inequality against drug offenders before and under the law, therefore can be seen to deprive them of their human rights. The non-discrimination principle is violated when the people who use drugs, who are drug dependent, or who possess drugs, are denied health care, social rights, access to employment or access to a lawyer to assist them in the criminal justice system.[74]

As mentioned above, one of the negative consequences of Indonesia's drugs law and policy is profiling people who use drugs, or even more racial profiling which is used for delivering sentences for people who have committed drugs crimes. Racial profiling violates human rights and as a method it leads to ineffective law enforcement efforts.[75] In many cases, racial profiling of drug users has lead to unfair judgments and disproportionate sentencing by the criminal justice system. This is caused by the stereotyping of drug use within certain racialized communities, or seeing those racialized communities as being the cause of drug crime. 'Racialized communities' is a social construct to view persons or groups who share (or are perceived to share) a given ancestry as different and unequal in ways that matter to economic, political and social life; this view is not based in reality.[76] Those who are targeted based on racial profiling suffer a violation against their liberty. In many countries, including in Indonesia, they will face being stop-and-searched, arrested, subjected to unwarranted force, detained in custody and in the most extreme cases, shot, tortured, or killed.

Behavioural science research has documented that prosecutors also harbour unconscious racial biases.[77] The findings illustrate how 'these unconscious biases play a role whenever prosecutors exercise their broad discretion, such as in choosing what crimes to charge and when negotiating plea bargains.'[78] Race, ethnicity, religion, language and nationality should be omitted from criminal proceedings, since these are irrelevant to the merits of a criminal prosecution.[79] True justice is at high risk when the criminal proceeding values these irrelevant backgrounds.

The unconscious bias affects the application of drug laws in Indonesia, such as the Narcotics Law of 2009. For example, with an inherent association of foreigners, particularly West Africans, as being drug traffickers, we can see how there is a presumption towards administering the steepest possible punishment of foreigners caught with drugs. In Indonesia, even drug mules, who may have had little knowledge of the drugs they were carrying or lack the power to refuse the trafficker, are usually prosecuted as heavily as possible. They will generally not be recommended for rehabilitation or for health treatment; they will be prosecuted as having committed a serious crime, especially if the amount they were caught with reaches the drug quantities threshold. Indonesia's drug laws in application tend not to differentiate on legal grounds between the drug trafficker and drug mule, the degree of punishment being the same. The judges, prosecutors, or even lawyers are unlikely to explore the characteristic differences between drug mules and drug traffickers, not taking into consideration that fact that a drug trafficker carries drugs that they have paid for and are willing to risk prison for because they have the intention to gain economic benefit from their sale.[80]

In Indonesia, many death-penalty cases involve drug mules, while the drug 'kingpins' remain invisible and untouched by the law. Most drug offenders facing execution are lowly drug mules, with particular stigma and prejudice being applied against people who come from the Black community and Chinese immigrant population. Mary Jane, a domestic worker from the Philippines, Rodrigo Gularte, a person with mental illness from Brazil, Humphrey E. Jefferson from Nigeria,[81] as well as Zainal Abidin from Indonesia[82] are people who face execution without proper investigation, their mental health issues overlooked and the important issue of racism unexplored, as in the case of Humphrey Jefferson. Judges mete out punishments based on the War on Drugs sentiment. Recently, very disturbing cases of extrajudicial killings have been recorded in Indonesia, carried out by clandestine forces; the targets are again often the minor drug dealers, often foreigners, mostly of African descent. At least 92 people involved in drug offences were killed in 2017, 60 of them simply people who use drugs or drug dependent.[83] The current president, Joko Widodo has not only promised to reject all clemency requests related to drug offences, he intends to reinforce his hard message on the War on Drugs by encouraging law enforcement and clandestine security forces to 'shoot on the spot the foreign national drug traffickers with no mercy if they resist'.[84] Apparently, the failure of the War on Drugs that has been acknowledged by many countries continues to have been ignored by the Indonesian government. This draconian approach will lead Indonesia nowhere besides ensuring continuing failure for some years to come.

Such a simplistic policy approach unsurprisingly leads to errors being made. The death penalties that have been imposed upon unaware drug mules or wholly wrongly convicted persons are easy to be found. The deterrence effect, as a primary reason to impose the death penalty for drug offences, has proven to be a myth. The BNN in its research in 2014 mentioned that there are 397 drug cases, with 583 drug offenders. However, in 2015 while Indonesia implemented the death penalty, there were 664 drug cases, with 1,024 people arrested for drug offences.

The risk to the general community is also greater when Indonesia's drugs law and policy proclaims the 'War on Drugs' as a mantra to eliminate drugs and the illicit drugs market. Women are also negatively impacted by Indonesian drug policy. In Indonesia, 11 per cent of drug users inject drugs and among that percentage, 57 per cent of them are women.[85] Forty-five per cent of the people who will face the criminal justice system are women and among them, at least 93 per cent of them are arrested, searched and punished based on drug offences. Furthermore, at least 87 per cent of those women are the victims of bribery, sexual violence and mental and physical abuse from the law enforcers.[86] Furthermore, vulnerable children also face horrific issues. The data shows that in 2011 among those age 15–21, 12 per cent were injecting drug users.[87]

Conclusion: no future in the War On Drugs

Racism emerges easily in an unequal society and is rooted in a historic imbalance in the implementation of the law. Although Indonesia's War on Drugs started when the country decided upon and strictly implemented the drug control convention treaties, the root of the War on Drugs can be found in the period of colonization. Unfortunately, a reflection of the division and racism produced under the Dutch Colonial era can be seen as reflected within Indonesian law and policy towards communities which have been marginalized as 'decadent' and sub-human at the present time, despite the Dutch having encouraged drug production and trade for economic profit. The death penalty, for example, was a punishment earlier used to punish marginalized groups because of the independence movement; now it is applied against foreign drug mules or low-level criminals perceived as weakening the country. In most judicial decisions, the War on Drugs is driven by a commitment to impose as harsh a punishment as possible on a person in possession of or using drugs.

One of the criteria to differentiate between someone who is drug dependent and someone who is a drug trafficker is through the threshold quantities of drugs. However, this is not the sole solution to achieving proportionality in drug law and a clear distinction between types of drug cases are also needed. People who use drugs, are drug dependent and/or are drug mules are currently filling the prisons whilst suffering neglect and having their human rights violated. They lack access to legal assistance due to their poverty, and leading to some of them being executed. The narrative of the War on Drugs remains rooted in the law, and the policy of law enforcement. The death penalty and recent extrajudicial killings against minor drug dealers and people who use drugs, have become the tools through which the government can show off 'success' in the War on Drugs in Indonesia.

The broader spectrum of national debate currently remains concerned with how to expand the role of law enforcement to be able to tackle the supply of drugs into Indonesia. We forget that the control of the drug supply will never be achievable until the wider socioeconomic issues that underpin the harm of the illicit drug market are understood and steps are made to supply proper health provisions for those who need them and ensuring the social justice for the vulnerable groups of society.

I would argue that the international drug laws probably will be changed in the coming years, moving away from incarceration towards more harm reduction and rehabilitative methods but we must ensure that the failure of the War on Drugs does not carry over into this new epoch. In places like Indonesia, we have already seen how forced rehabilitation can work hand in hand with the empowerment of the law enforcement to do more harm than good in the campaign against drug trafficking. This is because of the failure to unpack the history of stigmatization and discrimination that has underpinned drug prohibition. For as long as we place the notion of drug use as a crime, and drug users as criminal at the centre of our drug policy, both domestically and internationally, we will be likely to create another disproportionately applied law which impacts heavily on marginalized and vulnerable communities.

Notes

1 Dr Irwanto et al., 'Evidence-informed response to illicit drugs in Indonesia', *The Lancet* 385 (2015): 2249–2250.
2 See ASEAN Narcotic Cooperation Center (ASEAN-NARCO), *Report of Indonesia in ASEAN Drug Monitoring*, 2015, pp. 12–13.
3 Indonesia House of Representatives Minute of Meeting in 2009 when the Parliament discussed about the draft new Law on Narcotic Year 2009 to replace Narcotic Law No. 22 Year 1997.
4 Presidential Instruction No. 6, Year 1971, on Establishing State Intelligence Coordinating Board.
5 Indonesia ratified the Single Convention on Narcotic 1961 through Law No. 8 of 1976. The Indonesian House of Representatives agreed to ratify the Single Convention on Narcotic, together with its Protocol.
6 Law No. 9, Year 1976 on Narcotic tried to establish the foundation of rehabilitation for drug dependence; however, until the new Drug Law in 2009, there was no mechanism on how to implement the policy regarding access to treatment for drug dependence, or people who use drugs.
7 Law No. 35, Year 2009 on Narcotic provides rehabilitation for drug dependence through article 54; however, the process and place of rehabilitation did not exist until the new guidelines for compulsory rehabilitation were issued in 2011.
8 Governmental Regulation No. 25, Year 2011 on Compulsory Rehabilitation.
9 Tyas Suci, Asmin Fransiska and Lamtiur Tampubolon, *Long and Winding Road: Jalan Panjang Pemulihan Narkotika* (Jakarta: Gramedia, 2015), pp. 18–32.
10 Diana Putri and Tom Blickman, 'Cannabis in Indonesia: Patterns in consumption, production, and policies', Transnational Institute, Drug Policy Briefing 44, January 2016.
11 James R. Rush, *Opium to Java: Revenue Farming and Chinese Enterprise in Colonial Indonesia 1860–1910* (Jakarta: Equinox Publishing, 2007); see also J. F. Scheltema, (1907) 'The opium trade in the Dutch East Indies. II', *American Journal of Sociology* 13.2 (September 1907): 224–251.
12 Rush, *Opium to Java*.
13 Rush, *Opium to Java*; see also James R. Rush, 'Social control and influence in nineteenth century Indonesia: Opium farms and the Chinese of Java', *Indonesia* (Cornell Southeast Asia), 35 (April 1983): 53–64.
14 Rush, *Opium to Java*.
15 Asmin Fransiska, *Decriminalisation Approach to Drug Use from a Human Rights Perspective* (Lambert Academic Publishing, 2017), pp. 47–51.
16 In many literatures, Dutch scientists proclaimed that Indonesian origin of '*Pribumi*' means a mistrusted group, giving false witness, or belief in flawed or incorrect information; for details see J. E. Sahetapy, *Ancaman Pidana Mati terhadap pembunuhan Berencana* (ALUMNI Bandung, 1979).

17 Article 163 (2) IS (*Indische Staats Regeling*).

18 Article 163 (4) IS (*Indische Staats Regeling*).

19 Article 163 (3) IS (*Indische Staats Regeling*).

20 There are many laws that governed limited access for those of Chinese origin to economic, political and socio-cultural opportunities. See Ananta Toer, *Hokiau di Indonesia* (Jakarta: Garda Budaya, 1998), pp. 124–126. Those of Chinese origin were forced to live in the '*Wijen*' or '*ghetto-stelsel*' and they could not freely conduct businesses or run farms. Chinese groups also had no freedom of movement, since the Dutch Colonial government applied the *passenstelsel*, that obliged everyone to possess a pass card; most Chinese people could not obtain the card unless they paid an extortionate price and/or bribed the authorities.

21 Institute for Criminal Justice Reform, *Politik Kebijakan Hukuman Mati di Indonesia Dari Masa Ke Masa* (ICJR Publishing, 2017), pp. 47–60.

22 R. Wiseman, 'Assimilation out: Europeans, Indo-Europeans and Indonesian sugar 1800s to the 1950s', ASAA 2000 Conference, University of Melbourne, 3–5 July 2000; Session: Colonial Southeast Asia, p. 3.

23 Thomas Stamford Raffles, *The History of Java* (London: Black, 1830).

24 In 1998, race riots occurred in various Indonesian cities during 13–15 May. The national report stated that the riots targeted Chinese people, including the rape of Chinese women. See Komisi National Penghapusan Kekerasan terhadap Perempuan (National Commission on Violence against Women), *Seri Dokumen Kunci: Temuan Tim Gabungan Pencari Fakta Peristiwa Kerusuhan Mei 1998* (Publikasi Komnas Perempuan, 2006). See also Jemma Purdey, 'Anti-Chinese violence and transition in Indonesia June 1998–October 1999', in Tim Linsey and Helen Pausacker (eds), *Chinese Indonesians: Remembering, Distorting, Forgetting* (Singapore: Institute of Southeast Asian Studies, ISEAS Publication, 2005), pp. 14–35.

25 Melissa F. Weiner, 'The ideologically colonialized metropole: Dutch racism and racist denial', *Sociology Compass* 8.6 (June 2014): 731–744.

26 James R. Rush, 'Opium farms in nineteenth century Central Java: Institutional continuity and change in a colonial society 1860–1910'. PhD dissertation, Yale University, 1977, pp. 142–143.

27 James R. Rush, 'Opium in Java: A sinister friend', *Journal of Asian Studies* 44.3 (1985): 549–560.

28 See ICJR, *Politik Kebijakan Hukuman Mati di Indonesia Dari Masa Ke Masa*.

29 Gen Sander, 'The death penalty for drug offences: Global overview 2017', *Harm Reduction International* (March 2018): 30.

30 Amnesty International, 'Death sentence and execution 2016', *Amnesty International* (April 2017).

31 Yusuf Bangura and Rudolfo Stavenhagen, 'Introduction: Racism, citizenship and social justice', in Y. Bangura and R. Stavenhagen (eds), *Racism and Public Policy* (London: Palgrave Macmillan, 2005), pp. 1–21.

32 Lembaga Bantuan Hukum Masyarakat (LBHM), *Di Ujung Palu Hakim: Dokumentasi Vonis Rehabilitasi di Jabodetabek Tahun 2014* (Jakarta: LBHM, 2016).

33 Asmin Fransiska and Ricky Gunawan, 'Jokowi should halt execution under Indonesia's corrupt judicial system', *The Conversation* (16 February 2016); Prashanth Parameswaran, 'Who will Indonesia execute next in its war on drugs?', *The Diplomat* (15 July 2016); Prashanth Parameswaran, 'Indonesia to

execute 10 foreigners in War on Drugs', *The Diplomat* (12 May 2016).

34 Ontario Human Rights Commission, 'Paying the price: The human cost of racial profiling', December 2003, www.ohr.on.ca/en/resources/discussion_consultation/RacialProfileReportEN/pdf [accessed 10 November 2018].

35 The Sentencing Project, 'Racial disparities in sentencing: A review of literature', 2005, www.sentencingproject.org/doc/publications/rd_sentencing_review.pdf [accessed 23 August 2018].

36 American Civil Liberties Union (ACLU), 'Racial disparities in sentencing: Hearing on the report of racism in the justice system of the United States', submitted to the Inter-American Commission on Human Rights, 153rd Session, 27 October 2014.

37 Asmin Fransiska, 'Kesewenang-wenangan Penegak Hukum dan Stagnanya Reformasi Kebijakan Napza', *Jurnal Kajian Putusan Pengadilan: Dictum*, I (October 2012 – Leip 2012): 4–28.

38 ACLU, 'Racial disparities in sentencing', p. 5.

39 ACLU, 'Racial disparities in sentencing'.

40 Richard Lines, *Drug Control and Human Rights in International Law* (Cambridge: Cambridge University Press, 2017), pp. 1–3; William C. Plouffe Jr., '1909 Shanghai Conference', in Mark A. R. Kleiman and James E. Hawdon (eds), *Encyclopedia of Drug Policy* (Thousand Oaks, CA: SAGE Publications, Inc., 2011).

41 The 1912 Hague International Opium Convention (League of Nations, entered into force 28 June 1919), 8 UNTS 187. This was the first Convention on drugs which issued a declaration of the dangers of smoking opium and the non-medical trade in opium and other drugs. It also elaborated issues on relation to morphine, cocaine and heroin.

42 David Bewley-Taylor and Martin Jelsma, 'Fifty years of the 1961 Single Convention on Narcotic Drugs: A reinterpretation', *Transnational Institute, Series on Legislative Reform of Drug Policies*, 12 (March 2011).

43 The Single Convention on Narcotic Drug 1961, as amended by the 1972 Protocol (adopted by the Economic and Social Council of the United Nations Resolution 689 J (XXXVI) of 28 July 1958, entered into force 16 May 1967), 976 UNTS 3.

44 The Convention on Psychotropic Substances 1971 (adopted by the Economic and Social Council of the United Nations of the UNGA Resolution 366 (IV) of 3 December 1949, entered into force 16 August 1976), 1091 UNTS 175.

45 See the Preamble of the Single Convention on Narcotic Drug 1961.

46 Narcotic Law No. 35, Year 2009, art. 8.

47 Narcotic Law No. 35, Year 2009, art. 1.

48 Narcotic Law No. 35, Year 2009, art. 23.

49 Narcotic Law No. 35, Year 2009, art. 32.

50 Jun Honna, 'Orchestrating transnational crime: Security sector politics as a Trojan horse for anti-reformists', in Edward Aspinall and Gerry van Klinken (eds), *The State and Illegality in Indonesia* (Leiden: KITLV Press, 2011), p. 267.

51 The Presidential Instruction *(Inpres-Instruksi Presiden)* 2002 Number 3, on Eradication on Counter Measure of Drug Abuse and Illicit Drug Trafficking.

52 Fabiola Desy Unidjaja, 'Megawati gets tough on drug dealers', *Jakarta Post*, 20 October 2001.

53 Honna, 'Orchestrating transnational crime', p. 268.

54 Preamble to President Instruction 2011 Number 12, on the Policy Implementation and National Strategy on Prevention and Eradication of Drug

Abuse and Illicit Drug Trafficking (P4GN).

55 'Drug-Free World – We can do this!', report of the United Nations Office on Drug and Crime (UNODC), 1998. It drives the international policy on drugs issue for encouraging abstinence and focusing on security. However, the UNODC acknowledged later that the drug-free world campaign has failed by publishing the analysis that global drug-control efforts have had dramatic unintended consequences which has resulted in a criminal black market of staggering proportions.

56 Fuzi Narindrani, 'Sistem Hukum Pencegahan Peredaran Narkotika Di Lembaga Permasyarakatan Studi Kasus Di Lembaga Pemasyarakatan Cipinang', *Jurnal Rechts Vinding*, 6.1 (April 2017).

57 Gloria Lai, 'Drugs, crime and punishment', *Transnational Institute, Series on Legislative Reform of Drugs Policies*, 20 (June 2012).

58 Universal Declaration of Human Rights (adopted 10 December 1948), UNGA Res. 217 A(III) (UDHR) art. 29(2).

59 Human Rights Committee (2004), General Comment No. 31 on the nature of the general legal obligation imposed on the state parties to the Covenant, UN Doc. CCPR/C/21/Rev/1/Add.13.

60 Indonesia Parliament Report, para 2.

61 Indonesia Narcotic Law 2009, No. 35, art. 4 (b).

62 Manfred Nowak, 'Treated with cruelty', *Open Society Foundation* (June 2011): 3.

63 Article 4 (2) of The Regulation No. 01/PB/MA/III/2014 on The Measurement of Drug Dependence and Victims of Drug Abuse in Rehabilitation Centres.

64 Nowak, 'Treated with cruelty'.

65 The Berkeley Foundation, 'Recalibrating the regime: The need for a human rights-based approach to international drug policy', Report 13, March 2008, p. 7.

66 From the report of the Ministry of Law and Human Rights, 'Kasus Narkotika Salah Satu Penyumbang Besar Overkapasitas pada Rutan dan Lapas', in *Focus Group Discussion for Drafting new Narcotic Law*, January 2018.

67 Ministry of Law and Human Rights, 'Kasus Narkotika Salah Satu …'.

68 Ministry of Law and Human Rights, 'Kasus Narkotika Salah Satu …'.

69 Ministry of Law and Human Rights, 'Kasus Narkotika Salah Satu …'.

70 Aghnia Adzkia, 'BNN: 943 Ribu Pengguna Narkotika Kronis Harus Direhabilitasi 2015', www.cnnindonesia.com/nasional/20150909221424-12-77758/bnn-943-ribu-pengguna-narkotika-kronis-harus-direhabilitasi [accessed 20 August 2018].

71 Adzkia, 'BNN: 943 Ribu Pengguna Narkotika …'.

72 Ricky Gunawan et al., *Membongkar Praktik Pelanggaran Hak tersangka di tingkat Penyidikan: studi Kasus terhadap tersangka Kasus Narkotika di Jakarta* (Jakarta: LBH Masyarakat, 2013), pp. 128–130.

73 Article 1 of the International Convention on the Elimination of Racial Discrimination.

74 Canadian HIV/AIDS Legal Network, 'Legislating on health and human rights: Model Law on Drug Use and HIV/AIDS Module 7: Stigma and discrimination' (Toronto: Canadian Legal Network, 2006).

75 Reem Bahdi, Olanyi Parson and Tom Sandborn, 'Racial profiling', Position Paper, BC Civil Liberties Association, 2009, p. 2, https://bccla.org/wp-content/uploads/2014/02/2009-Report-Racial-Profiling.pdf [accessed 23 August 2018].

76 Bahdi, Parson and Sandborn, 'Racial profiling'.

77 Sunita Sah, Christopher T. Robertson and Shima B. Baughman, 'Blinding prosecutors to defendants' race: A policy proposal to reduce unconscious bias

in the criminal justice system', *Behavioral Science & Policy* 1.2 (2015): 69–76.

78 Sah, Robertson and Baughman, 'Blinding prosecutors to defendants' race'.

79 Sah, Robertson and Baughman, 'Blinding prosecutors to defendants' race'.

80 Jennifer Fleetwood, 'Penalties and practice in the international cocaine trade', *British Journal of Criminology* 51 (2001): 375–393.

81 In July 2017, the Indonesia Ombudsman Commission declared that the District Court has been conducting discrimination against the case of Humphrey E. Jefferson because the District Court did not deliver Mr Jefferson's case to the Supreme Court without clear and transparent legal reasoning, when the District Court had delivered another similar case to the Supreme Court.

82 In 2015, the District Court acknowledged the maladministration process by being unable to deliver the case review to the Supreme Court although Zainal Abidin had requested the Supreme Court to review his case since 2005. The District Court finally delivered his case to the Supreme Court on 8 April 2017; it was under review by the Supreme Court on 21 April 2015 and the decision was released to reject his request on 27 April 2015. On 29 April 2015, he was executed.

83 Deutsche Welle, 'Darah Narkoba di Tangan Jokowi', 24 November 2017, www.dw.com/id/darah-narkoba-di-tangan-jokowi/a-41514334 [accessed 10 November 2018]. See also Deutsche Welle, "Perintah Tembak di Tempat Jokowi Menelan Puluhan Korban Jiwa', www.dw.com/id/perintah-tembak-di-tempat-jokowi-telan-puluhan-korban-jiwa/a-40115527 [accessed 20 August 2018].

84 Deutsche Welle, 'Darah Narkoba di Tangan Jokowi'.

85 Perempuan Bersuara, 'Memahami Perempuan Pengguna NAPZA suntik di Indonesia', presented in a workshop on Women Drug Offenders in 12 February 2018 (Jakarta: Lembaga Bantuan Hukum Masyarakat, 2018).

86 Bersuara, 'Memahami Perempuan Pengguna NAPZA Suntik di Indonesia': this is a collaborative research project between Persaudaraan Korban NAPZA Indonesia (PKNI) with Oxford University (Jakarta: PKNI, 2016), pp. 16–17.

87 UNICEF, *Young Drug Users and Their Access to Harm Reduction Services* (Jakarta: UNICEF, 2012).

9

Colonial roots of the global pandemic of untreated pain

Katherine Pettus

The dominant power is the one that manages to impose and, thus, to legitimate, indeed to legalize (for it is always a question of law) on a national or world stage, the terminology and thus the interpretation that best suits it in a given situation.

Jacques Derrida, 2003[1]

Law is politics ... The distinction between law and politics is only a part-truth. Law is made by political actors, through political procedures, for political ends. The law that emerges is the result of political forces; the influences of law on state behaviour are also determined by political forces.

Louis Henkin, 1989[2]

Introduction

This chapter is an exercise in legal hermeneutics: it analyses the deep historical roots of the Single Convention on Narcotic Drugs (1961) (hereinafter SC) in an effort to shed light on the symbiotic relationship between the colonial origins of this particular instrument of international law and the contemporary global pandemic of untreated (cancer) pain.[3] My argument is premised on two historical facts that rarely figure in analyses of the SC and the extant international narcotics control regime: first, that all the countries now identified as low- and middle-income countries (LMICs)[4] – the epicentre of the global pandemic – were once colonies either of the European empires or of the former Soviet Union. Second, that the narratives and institutions of contemporary international law were constituted and (self-) legitimated by means of many iterations throughout the (long) modern imperial era, which began in the sixteenth century.[5] In my reading, the SC, which imposes stringent, punitive narcotics control obligations on all signatory Parties,[6] is a multilateral twentieth-century iteration of all the previous (imperial era) drug control treaties enacted by the (former) 'Great Powers'. As such, it encoded and continues to reproduce the asymmetric imperial power relations and structural vulnerabilities constituted during the colonial era. Since this legal instrument, via the International Narcotics Control Board, is the official global gatekeeper of the 'licit' flow of *all medical opioids on the planet*, my theoretical argument centres on a genealogy that reveals the lineaments of the pandemic and, importantly, sites for intervention and effective transformation.

The analysis that follows reflects on how post-/neocolonial power masquerades as normatively neutral (positivist) yet ideologically charged international law that deepens intentionally produced structural vulnerabilities and causes global, human suffering. For instance, the origin of the modern concept and language of 'addiction' lies in the colonial era's industrialization of opium for the profit of British mercantilists, and the subsequent expansion of the British Empire. The stakes of the analysis are practical: they concern how parties most harmed by the operation of the (post-colonial) SC might select effective strategies to remedy that harm within the confines of the current legal framework.

While I am influenced by the fine-grained historical and empirical work done by the scholars of the international drug control regime,[7] that body of scholarship largely accepts at face value the relevant treaty texts and narratives that constructed the international framework. Taking Jacques Derrida at his word that 'deconstruction is justice'[8] – and I would add 'mercy' – this work interprets deconstruction as a project that

hold[s] the constructedness of the law plainly and constantly in view so as to subject [it] to relentless analysis, revision, and repeal, to rewriting and judicial review, in the light of the unconditional demand of justice ... Deconstructing the law means to hold the law in question, to solicit the law, to hire a radical solicitor who will make the law tremble, while always letting oneself be solicited and troubled by the event of justice that is trapped inside.[9]

My perspective is informed by liberation theology, with its 'preferential option for the poor', the historical sociology of path dependence,[10] and critical international law and international relations theory. These latter two claim that 'International law remains oblivious to its imperial structures even when continuing to reproduce them, which is why the traditional history of international law regards imperialism as a thing of the past',[11] and that 'the world order continues to be determined largely by imperialism, including neocolonial political forms, and ... the assumptions, concepts, and language of enquiry in IR remain infused with imperial and colonial reasoning.'[12] Liberation theology and philosophy provide the essential critical perspective from the global South to deconstruct the legal texts of the international narcotics control regime and in Basque/Salvadoran theologian Jon Sobrino's words, 'take the crucified people from the cross':

> Simply from a human viewpoint, changing a heart of stone into a heart of flesh – conversion – is a fundamental problem for the First World. And this is what the Third World offers as a possibility. Above all, the Third World portrays in its own flesh the existence of an immense sin that brings slow and violent death to innocent human beings. To express it in inescapable terms, it holds the power for conversion. In another way, if entire crucified continents do not have the strength to convert hearts of stone into hearts of flesh, we must ask ourselves, what can? And if nothing can, we must ask what kind of future awaits a First World built, consciously or unconsciously, on the corpses of the human family. There can be no reason for living if we live this way.[13]

This critical, rather than clinical, perspective on the global pandemic of untreated pain emerges from reading the history and social science literature on the international narcotics control regime 'against the grain', upside down and inside out, from the lived experience of palliative care physicians, and from the bedsides of patients. It is the perspective of those who are systematically, iatrogenically damaged by current drug policy practices rather than the legal positivist view 'from nowhere', or the fantasy objective social science view 'from everywhere'. It is the perspective of the patient dying in pain that her family and physician (if she is lucky enough to have one) are helpless to relieve because pain medicines containing 'narcotic drugs' are unavailable for a multitude of ultimately unjustifiable (and very well-documented) reasons. It is the perspective of individuals and communities marginalized, stigmatized, punished and sickened by the physical and emotional torment of 'illegal' dependence on narcotic drugs and the collective failure of their governments to constructively address the harm and pain generated by that illegality. Even the now-mainstream view that the War on Drugs has been a 'failure', once only fashionable in critical and drug policy reform circles, dangerously misses the mark, because from the standpoint of those who originally devised and continue to refine and prosecute it, both internationally and domestically, the strategy of using narcotics law as a mechanism of social control always was, and still is, successful.[14]

Imperial roots of the Single Convention on Narcotic Drugs 1961

Before the US- and Chinese-led opium suppression campaigns at the beginning of the twentieth century, opium was the *legal* and extremely profitable coin of the realm – literally – of the European empires[15] 'Without the drug', according to economic historian Carl Trocki, 'there probably would have been no British Empire.'[16] And before it was industrialized by the imperial powers to fund their own development, it was cultivated and grown for traditional medicinal and ceremonial purposes by indigenous cultures whose internal social mechanisms contained use that could result in dependence and broader social harms.[17]

The nineteenth-century opium trade not only destroyed the integrity of traditional social and political structures in China and South East Asia, it also helped to build and finance the creation of new and alternative structures. In South East Asia, these were the colonial states, most of which were supported by opium revenues.[18] Trocki's central thesis is that the colonial drug economies were central to the production of modern states, stepping stones to the capitalist political economy, whose forces of production entwine synergistically with the grammar of modern (positivist) international law and the lineage of the theory of state sovereignty.[19]

American diplomatic attempts to control the global opium trade, at the behest of the Chinese government as well as in response to the agitation of British and American (Protestant) missionaries in China and the Philippines, began in Shanghai in 1909.[20] Although US merchants had been significant players in the Chinese opium trade during the latter part of the nineteenth and early twentieth centuries, the US was interested in gaining a foothold in the lucrative Chinese consumer goods market, an aspiration that meant respecting Chinese demands to curb opium imports. The US had inherited the Philippines as spoils of the Spanish-American War at the turn of the twentieth century, making the new colony, which had a significant Chinese opium-smoking population, one of the first feathers in the US's imperial cap.[21] The Episcopal Bishop of the Philippines, Bishop Charles H. Brent, appointed by President Theodore Roosevelt in 1902, was the ecclesial powerhouse behind the nascent US narcotics control regime, which legitimated itself in terms of the narrative of the Protestant missionary movement.[22] As historian Julia Buxton puts it:

> Two important principles [were] set out by the influential missionary groups. Firstly, that the use of intoxicating substances was morally wrong and injurious and that national governments had the responsibility to step in to prevent people from doing harm to themselves. Secondly, that this could only be achieved by reducing the supply of narcotic substances from cultivator and producer countries. This prohibitionist, supply-side focused thrust shaped the structure and orientation of the international control regime that was to emerge.[23]

The colonial powers enacted six multilateral drug control agreements between 1909 and the Second World War. These were reasonably successful in curbing the *licit* global production and supply of opium and very successful in producing the ideology that demonized and continues to stigmatize people who use drugs. Since the legal and diplomatic pre-history of the Single Convention which took shape during the European imperial and Mandate periods is the subject of excellent contemporary scholarship,[24] it serves no purpose to replicate the details here. The point is that by 1958, when the United Nation's Economic and Social Council was instructed to consolidate all the prior drug control agreements into a single treaty, the colonial lineaments and zero-sum narrative of the Single Convention were already fixed both in international relations and in international law.

The post-Second World War, Cold War decades definitively transformed the imperial power and property relationships that had configured the global metropolis/periphery since the Spanish conquest of the 'Americas'. Although most of the Latin American colonies had won their independence during the early nineteenth century, and the Ottoman Empire and German colonies had been placed under the Mandate system after the First World War,[25] the newly independent British, French, Belgian and Dutch colonies were 'étatised'[26] – reinvented as 'new' (sovereign) states in what is known as the Westphalian system – after the Second World War.[27] As colonies, by definition the subordinated areas, had no control over the disposition of their raw materials, which were systematically extracted and marketed by the European colonists for their own benefit. As 'new' states entering a world governed by international law, though, the colonies' legal status changed: now technically 'sovereign' under the Westphalian system, they had the right to control their own natural resources.[28]

This meant the former colonial powers, and particularly the US, in the context of the Cold War, had to act quickly to prevent those natural resources from becoming the extraordinarily valuable *legal* coin of the realm of the new states and emerging non-aligned movement, a source of wealth and power that would allow them to establish themselves on the world scene as a power or collective power bloc to be reckoned with. This was no abstract speculation on the part of US foreign policy insiders and observers of the nascent Non-Aligned Movement coalescing between the new leaders of the former colonies.[29] As noted above, the great 'saltwater' colonial empires – the British, French and Dutch empires in particular – had been built on, and ran on, wealth produced by the (then legal) opium economy.[30] Under no circumstances could the newly decolonized, newly 'non-aligned' bloc be allowed to control such a potent source of wealth and power that had always 'belonged' to the European countries by dint of (legal) conquest.

By persuading the new states to relinquish sovereignty over their natural resources that were the raw materials for the pharmaceutical industry, the US, through the SC, succeeded in snatching control, under international law, of this game-changing source of wealth and power. Many political elites in the newly sovereign nations went willingly into the camp of supply control and prohibition, identifying with the colonial narrative of drugs as 'native', and adopting dominant elite habits of consuming alcohol and tobacco.[31]

The endgame of the Single Convention, which ostensibly consolidated earlier treaties dating back to 1912, but in fact was much greater than the sum of its parts, was to 'enclose' the (worldwide) commons[32] of the natural resources that are the raw materials for the production of 'narcotic drugs' for medicinal use.[33] Because the focus of the SC and its precursor treaties was on controlling *supply* rather than consumption, the cultivation, manufacture and distribution of narcotic drugs that was *not* legally 'enclosed' – officially designated as 'licit' for minutely documented scientific and medicinal use – became instantly 'illicit' and subject to criminal sanction. At the stroke of a pen (several strokes actually, since representatives of 63 countries originally signed the

Convention), the delegates in New York transferred control of all actual and potential property in opium poppies, coca bushes and cannabis plants from their customary and legal status as privately or nationally owned to objects of legitimate surveillance and military intervention under international law. Thus, once again, a 'great power' used international law to 'extract' their raw materials, but this time from ostensibly sovereign nations. This meets Ghanaian president and philosopher Kwame Nkrumah's definition of 'neo-colonialism': 'As [Nkrumah] puts it, any outside attempt to "thwart, balk, corrupt or otherwise pervert" the true independence of a sovereign people is neo-colonialist. It is neo-colonialist because it seeks, notwithstanding the acknowledged sovereignty of a people, to subordinate their interests to those of a foreign power.'[34]

Moreover, under the SC, all the *people* involved in the (licit *and* illicit) cultivation, manufacture, distribution, consumption, etc. of narcotics became the objects of surveillance of both (their own) domestic and international law. The 'inconceivable amounts of violence and distress' this has caused, in the words of Colombian President Juan Manuel Santos,[35] can be traced to the legal and political command language of the Preamble and key sections of the Single Convention, the colonial Rosetta Stone of the contemporary international narcotics control regime.

Constitutional preambles express what legal theorist Carl Schmitt called 'fundamental political decisions' of the constituting parties.[36] American political decisions during the late 1950s and early 1960s were taken in the global context of the Cold War (including the escalating nuclear arms race), rapid African and Asian decolonization, the Vietnam War, the consolidation of communist China, and the US civil rights movement. Malcolm X once referred to this period as a 'tidal wave of color'.[37] Public narratives of that period reflect and legitimate binary ideological coding and the drift toward 'trilateralism'.[38] The UN representatives from Europe and the US were well aware of the power conferred by opium in the history of political economy. The full weight of the UN and the new Bretton Woods Institutions had to be brought to bear on the new states that controlled the raw material for narcotic drugs.[39]

By delineating the 'licit' centres of production, manufacture, distribution, etc. of narcotic drugs 'for medical and scientific purposes', and setting out the administrative apparatus whereby the system was to be regulated, the SC simultaneously delineated the reciprocally 'illegal' peripheries, thereby guaranteeing the local incubation and eventual flourishing of the black market cultivation, manufacture, trafficking, etc. that afflicts producer and transit countries today.[40] By obliging Parties to conform their domestic criminal law to mandate punishment for non-compliance, the emerging drug control regime was 'groundbreaking as it led to the introduction of uniform penal sanctions across countries and established principles of criminal law on an international basis'.[41]

Unsurprisingly, therefore, reproducing a meta-ethic of punishment grounded in the Protestant missionary morality of the early opium eradication campaigns in China and the Philippines, the Preamble of the SC, like the multiple colonial documents concerning drug policy that preceded it, is studded with the words 'evil', 'abuse' and 'addiction'. In my reading, the Preamble reflects the former colonial powers' reflexive need to re-assert disciplinary control over newly decolonized 'Others'. This abusive language, which encodes and projects the arrogance, fear, cultural stereotyping, racism and bunker mentality of mid-twentieth-century realpolitik diplomacy still governs the public policy of many countries in the global South and the (private) lives (of those with 'dependence disorders') and deaths (without appropriate analgesia) of billions of people. It also functions as a transmitter of meaning for the inextricably intertwined historical legacies of colonialism and domination created by the opium trade with all its associated pain and trauma for subjugated populations. It is no wonder, seen from this perspective, that multiple barriers exist in the LMICs (former European and Soviet colonies) to palliative care and the use of medical opioids for the treatment of pain.

The imperial genesis and colonial rationality of international law[42]

This section briefly introduces the basic concepts of critical international law, to lay the foundation for my claims about the colonial rationality of the Single Convention. The concept of 'rationality' in philosophy and economics refers, most basically, to consistency between means and ends.[43] 'Rational actors' pursue the most efficacious means to attain identified ends that they perceive to be beneficial. By 'colonial rationality', I mean the socially and historically specific logic of colonialism, which (again at its most basic) as Edward Said pointed out in *Orientalism*, relies on the construction of an inferior Other 'against which flattering and legitimating images of the metropolitan Self were defined'.[44] According to Peter Fitzpatrick, 'The supreme justification of imperial rule was that it brought order to chaos, reined in "archaic instincts," and all this aptly enough through subjection to "laws".'[45] The 'great powers' saw themselves as bearers of a common civilization and believed the violence of imperialism to be legitimate because it brought 'progress' to 'the native'.[46] The key point for the purpose of this chapter is that this cultural attitude of superiority, translated into commercial activity and organized violence, was inscribed in, and legitimated by means of, international law produced (first) in Europe and (later) the United States for the benefit of elites on both continents. It is not only radical post-colonial legal and international relations theorists who expose the ideological bones of international law. The great 'realist' theorist Hans Morgenthau regarded international law as an ideological disguise for political policy, used by States whose power interests were served by retention of the status quo.[47] In the case of the Single Convention on Narcotic Drugs, the former colonial powers' interests were served by consolidating the status quo inscribed in the earlier series of drug control treaties they had collaborated on prior to the Second World War, treaties that gave them absolute power over cultivation and movement of all the raw materials necessary for their pharmaceutical industries.

According to international legal theorist Anthony Anghie, the ideological legitimation of international law began during the Spanish conquest of what is now known as the Americas: 'The vocabulary of international law, far from being neutral, or abstract, is mired in this history of subordinating and extinguishing cultures.'[48] Anghie analysed the work of the sixteenth-century theologian and legal scholar Francisco de Vitoria, who justified the Spanish conquest by applying the 'logic' of European norms to trump the natural rights of the indigenous inhabitants of the lands the Spanish desired to possess, claiming that these norms were neutral and rational.[49] This elision of European-ness and sovereignty with universality and neutrality is woven into the history and texture of modern international law to the point that its imperial register is now normative and invisible from the perspective of those who are 'inside' the metropolis of lawgivers.[50] The Westphalian world, constituted by equal, sovereign (European) nation-states is the foundation of the international legal system and as such its legitimation is tautological. From the perspective of the post-colonial periphery, however, the pathologies of the Westphalian system's so-called 'rationality' are and always have been brutally evident and iatrogenic.[51] Although the 'global pandemic of untreated pain', which maps seamlessly onto the cartography of colonialism, can be stipulated as undeniable evidence of this claim, until only recently its victims were consigned to total invisibility in the world of international public health. The given-ness and sheer scale of the pandemic simultaneously contradicts and bares the fault lines in the universal rationality narrative of international law, exemplified in this particular case by the Single Convention. The imperial gaze, confident of its superiority, is repelled by critique from the periphery, which depicts the negative externalities of metropolis rationality, its excrescence, its collective shadow.[52] That shadow holds the pain and humiliation of 'the losers' in the game of global power, those 'private subjects' with whom international law need not concern itself.[53]

Yet it is precisely this point that must be challenged. The practical issue – the stakes of the analysis – concerns not simply how to disrupt or delegitimize the self-congratulatory narrative of the metropolis, but how to lure the imperial gaze to the/its damaged periphery in order to enlist its (dare I say) solidarity and resources[54] in an inclusive participatory project of reconstruction.[55] The key is to posit an ecological rationality and praxis that is epistemologically more evolved than the historically prior, zero-sum logic that must be superseded.[56] It must be, because the distorted/distorting binary logic of colonialism is dangerous/lethal both to those who are (have been) the direct victims of colonialism and to its perpetrators in the global institutions that are its contemporary instantiation. As Anne McClintock puts it so poetically:

> a proliferation of historically nuanced theories and strategies is called for, which may enable us to engage more effectively in the politics of affiliation, and the currently calamitous dispensations of power. Without a renewed will to intervene in the unacceptable, we face being becalmed in an historically empty space in which our sole direction is found by gazing back, spellbound, at the epoch behind us.[57]

The epistemological self-satisfaction of contemporary international law derives from the false assumption of universality, an assumption that seems self-evident when august international bodies such as the United Nations produce multilateral treaties with near-universal adherence, such as the Single Convention on Narcotic Drugs. I engage this assumption with a strategy of genealogical analysis that challenges the law's own structures of argumentation and rationality – immanent critique, in other words – in order to reveal its non-universality and epistemological vulnerability. As Foucault taught, scholars can use genealogy as a diagnostic tool to discern what is dangerous, and to whom.[58]

Martiniquan poet, essayist and activist Aimé Césaire testified to the cumulative danger of imperialism to Europeans when he identified the link between colonialism and the Shoah:

> what [the very distinguished, very humanistic, very Christian bourgeois of the twentieth century] cannot forgive Hitler for is not the crime in itself, the crime against man, it is not the humiliation of man as such, it is the crime against the white man, the humiliation of the white man, and the fact that he applied to Europe colonialist procedures which until then had been reserved exclusively for the Arabs of Algeria, the 'coolies' of India, and the 'niggers' of Africa.[59]

And as Mignolo comments: 'We should add the Indigenous, Native, Fourth Nations, Aboriginals of Americas from Chile to Canada, Australia and New Zealand.'[60] Césaire explains how the blowback mechanism from colonialism damages the colonizing countries: colonialism 'decivilize(s) the colonizer, brutalize(s) him in the true sense of the word ... at the end of all the racial pride that has been encouraged, all the boastfulness that has been displayed, a poison has been distilled in the veins of Europe and, slowly but surely, the continent proceeds towards savagery.'[61] And indeed, such was the case with the Shoah. Although philosophers, theologians and scholars of many disciplines have analysed and reflected on the Shoah and continue to do so in part because they hope to understand how to prevent organized violence on such a scale from happening again to any population, the fact that the multi-century imperial genocides perpetrated by Europeans in the global South are not analysed from a similar perspective because they have been consigned to the dustbin of history, is a red flag.[62] Not because the former colonial subjects need or are owed their proverbial pound of flesh – that is an entirely separate discussion – but because to repress the awareness of complicity, however innocently, in such legitimated institutionalized violence, is to nurture its potential (random) reappearance in the heart of the metropolis itself.

Theodor Adorno was a twentieth-century German philosopher who drew attention to the importance of not resorting to the use of universals to gloss over particular historical experiences of extreme suffering under modernity: 'Enlightenment about what happened in the past must work, above all, against a forgetfulness that too easily goes along with and justifies what is forgotten':[63]

> For Adorno, truth-telling is crucial if humanity is to learn about itself, and what it is capable of, and seek to do things differently. Against rationalisation and denial, he pushes for remembrance and reflection, arguing that what is repressed or unconscious will do much more damage than that which is made conscious. He argues that effective remembrance is extraordinarily difficult; it does not begin and end with reproach, but requires one to '[endure] the horror through a certain strength that comprehends even the incomprehensible.'[64]

While effective remembrance for Europeans has been about the Shoah, for the global South it has always been about conquest/colonialism. And yet now that the stakes are ecological and planetary, the work of resisting forgetting must be collaborative, not just European, not just African or Asian or American. Adorno saw the process of 'working through' as one that can never be complete because trauma can never fully be worked through or fully mended. The historically seeded ongoing harm has metastasized beyond the inter-human institutionalized violence of imperialism and has, predictably, spilled over into ecological damage that affects everyone living now, as well as future generations. So now some form of global 'truth telling' about the legacy of colonialism, the spiritual and psychological damage to *all* parties, and its inscription in global institutions and international law is essential to efforts to prevent further human and ecological damage. Adorno saw that failure, unwillingness, to engage one's own and others' pain, in critical individual and national self-reflection results in coldness, indifference towards pain, and indifference towards others, what is biblically known as 'hardness of heart' (Mark 3:5):

> Coldness, a profound indifference toward all except those with whom they have close (often self-interested) ties, is another psychological characteristic that is prevalent under modernity. The reigning principle of the *status quo* is to look out for one's own interests first and foremost; this was put to the test again and again by the Nazi regime and it rarely failed.[65]

An entirely disruptive disciplinary perspective, the ecofeminist analysis, clearly connects coldness to the dominant culture's marginalization of Others, which is rooted in culturally induced cognitive disconnection from the natural world, and now with ecological crisis.[66] What binds us all – metropolis and periphery alike – is what our separate identities have in common: the prospect of losing the biological foundations of our very lives and well-being on this planet. Coldness produced by our failure to understand our embeddedness in and dependency on nature distorts our perceptions in ways that make us insensitive to human and non-human limits, dependencies and interconnections. According to physicist Werner Heisenberg, this failure was a reflection of the modern scientific paradigm:

> The human attitude toward nature changed from a contemplative one to a pragmatic one. One was not so much interested in nature as it is, one rather asked what one could do with it. Therefore, natural science turned into technical science; every advancement of knowledge was connected with the question as to what practical use could be derived from it. This was true not only in physics; in chemistry and biology the attitude was essentially the same, and the success of the new methods in medicine or in agriculture contributed essentially to the propagation of the new tendencies … in this way, finally, the 19th century developed an extremely rigid frame for natural science which formed not only science but also the general outlook of great masses of people … matter was the primary reality. The progress of science was pictured as a crusade of conquest into the material world. Utility was the watchword of the time.[67]

The global palliative care movement contains within itself the evolutionary potential to embrace and transcend 'coldness', and disrupt the sclerotic binary rationality of imperial international law, to give a voice to suffering, the condition of all truth, in Adorno's words.[68] With its multiple synergistic dimensions of participation and accompaniment, palliative care represents a pragmatic progressive alternative to 'the ontology of dichotomization [that, like the War on Drugs itself] generates an ontology of domination, over nature and people'.[69]

Notes

1 J. Derrida, in Jürgen Habermas, *Philosophy in a Time of Terror: Dialogues with Jürgen Habermas and Jacques Derrida* (Chicago, IL: University of Chicago Press, 2003).

2 L. Henkin, *International Law: Politics, Values and Functions: General Course on Public International Law* (Leiden and Boston, MA: M. Nijhoff, 1989), p. 4.

3 '5.5 billion people (83% of the world's population) live in countries with low

to nonexistent access [to pain management], 250 million (4%) have moderate access, and only 460 million people (7%) have adequate access. Insufficient data are available for 430 million (7%)': M.-J. Seya et al., 'A first comparison between the consumption of and the need for opioid analgesics at country, regional, and global levels', *Journal of Pain and Palliative Care, Pharmacotherapy* 25 (2011): 6–18.

4 This is the World Bank criteria for classifying economies: gross national income (GNI) per capita for operational and analytical purposes. See https://blogs. worldbank.org/opendata/new-country-classifications-income-level-2018-2019 [accessed 4 December 2018].

5 See A. Anghie, 1996: 'Francisco de Vitoria and the colonial origins of international law', *Social and Legal Studies* 5.3 (1996): 321–336; A. Anghie, *Imperialism, Sovereignty and the Making of International Law*, Cambridge Studies in International and International Law, Vol. 37 (Cambridge: Cambridge University Press, 2007); J. M. Hobson, *The Eurocentric Conception of World Politics: Western International Theory, 1760–2010* (Cambridge: Cambridge University Press, 2012); B. G. Jones (ed.), *Decolonizing International Relations* (Lanham, MD: Rowman & Littlefield, 1996); T. Kayaoglu, 'Westphalian Eurocentrism in international relations theory', *International Studies Review* 12.2 (2010): 193–217, and A. Orford (ed.), *International Law and Its Others* (Cambridge University Press, Cambridge, 2006).

6 Neil Boister, an expert on the penal provisions of the Conventions, notes: 'While the substance of the drug control conventions is complex, their function is simple. They provide the legal structure for an international system of drug control by defining control measures to be maintained within each state party to these conventions and by prescribing rules to be obeyed by these Parties in their relations with each other. These rules can be categorized by two principal methods of achieving drug control. These are commodity control (the definition and regulation of the licit production, supply and consumption of drugs) and penal control (the suppression through criminal law of illicit production, supply and consumption': N. Boister, *Penal Aspects of the UN Drug Conventions* (The Hague and London: Kluwer Law International, 2001), pp. 1–4.

7 See inter alia: D. Bewley-Taylor, 'The 2009 Commission on Narcotic Drugs and its High-Level Segment: More cracks in the Vienna Consensus', *Drugs and Alcohol Today* 9.2 (2009): 7; D. Bewley-Taylor, 'Towards revision of the UN drug control conventions: Harnessing like-minded-ness', *International Journal of Drug Policy* 24.1 (2013): 60–68; J. Buxton, 'The historical foundations of the Narcotic Drug Control Regime', World Bank Policy Research Working Paper 4553 (Washington, DC: World Bank Publications, 2008); J. Buxton, 'A history of drug control', in P. Keefer and N. Loayza (eds), *Innocent Bystanders* (Washington, DC: World Bank Publications, 2010); J. Buxton, 'Opportunity lost: alternative development in drug control', in J. G. Tokatian (ed.), *Old Wars, New Thinking* (Buenos Aires: Libros Zorzal, 2010); H. Derks, *History of the Opium Problem: The Assault on the East, ca. 1600–1950* (Leiden: Brill, 2012); D. T. Courtwright, *Forces of Habit* (Cambridge, MA: Harvard University Press, 2002); W. B. McAllister, *Drug Diplomacy in the Twentieth Century* (London: Routledge, 1999), and D. F. Musto, *The Quest for Drug Control: Politics and Federal Policy in a Period of Increasing Substance Abuse 1960–1980* (New Haven, CT: Yale University Press, 2002).

8 Jacques Derrida, 'Force of law: The mystical foundation of authority', in Drucilla Cornell and Michael Rosenfeld (eds), *Deconstruction and the Possibility of Justice* (New York: Routledge, 1992), pp. 14–15.

9 J. D. Caputo, *The Weakness of God: A Theology of the Event*: (Bloomington, IN: Indiana University Press, 2006).

10 '... path dependence characterizes specifically those historical sequences in which contingent events set into motion institutional patterns or event chains that have deterministic properties': J. Mahoney, 'Path dependency in historical sociology', *Theory and Society* 29.4 (2000): 507–548.

11 Anghie, *Imperialism, Sovereignty and the Making of International Law*, p. 312.

12 J. Saurin, 'International relations as the imperial illusion; or, the need to decolonize IR', in B. Gruffydd Jones (ed.), *Decolonizing International Relations* (Lanham, MD: Rowan and Littlefield, 2006).

13 J. Sobrino, *The Principle of Mercy: Taking the Crucified People from the Cross* (Ossining, NY: Orbis, 1994).

14 L. Wacquant, *Punishing the Poor: The Neoliberal Government of Social Insecurity* (Durham, NC: Duke University Press, 2009).

15 C. A. Trocki, *Opium, Empire and the Global Political Economy: A Study of the Asian Opium Trade 1750–1950* (London: Routledge, 1999); Buxton, 'The historical foundations of the Narcotic Drug Control Regime', and Derks, *History of the Opium Problem*.

16 Trocki, *Opium, Empire and the Global Political Economy*, p. xiii.

17 S. C. Dwarakanath, 1965: 'Use of opium and cannabis in the traditional systems of medicine in India', 1965, www.unodc.org/unodc/en/data-and-analysis/bulletin/bulletin_1965-01-01_1_page004.html [accessed 10 November 2018]; T. Szasz, *Ceremonial Chemistry: The Ritual Persecution of Drugs, Addicts, and Pushers* (Garden City, NY: Doubleday/Anchor, 1975), and M. Booth, *Opium: A History* (New York: St Martin's Griffin, 1999).

18 Trocki called the British Empire 'a global drug cartel ... [that] enslaved and destroyed millions and enriched only a few': Trocki, *Opium, Empire and the Global Political Economy*, p. 160. For a theory of institutionalism, see also Max Weber, *The Theory of Social and Economic Organization*, trans. A. M. Henderson and Talcott Parsons (Glencoe, IL: Free Press, 1947).

19 'Once the initial determination had been made and accepted that the colonial world was not sovereign, the discipline could then create for itself, and present as inevitable and natural, the grand redeeming project of bringing the marginalized into the realm of sovereignty, civilizing the uncivilized and developing the juridical techniques and institutions necessary for this great mission. Within this framework, the history of the colonial world would consist simply of the history of the civilizing mission': Anghie, *Imperialism, Sovereignty and the Making of International Law*, p. 3. See also Max Weber, *The Protestant Ethic and Spirit of Capitalism* (New York: Routledge, 2001 [1904]).

20 'Missionaries also realised the opium trade hampered their primary goal of converting Chinese ... Attitudes toward opium also changed over time. For example, the great Evangelical leader William Wilberforce who spearheaded the British abolitionist movement and the movement to allow missionaries in British colonies was a regular opium user. Negative attitudes towards opium developed partially in connection with the temperance movement also initiated by Evangelicals'; see R. D. Woodberry, 'The shadow of Empire: Christian missions, colonial policy and democracy in postcolonial societies', Doctoral

thesis submitted to the Department of Sociology, University of North Carolina, 2004, for an exhaustive analysis of the British missionary campaign against opium and the tensions between missionaries and the empire.

21 For analysis of US opium policy in the Philippines, see A. Taylor, 'American confrontation with opium traffic in the Philippines', *Pacific Historical Review* 36.3 (1967): 307–324, doi:10.2307/3637153, and Anne L. Foster, 'Prohibiting opium in the Philippines and United States: Creation of an interventionist state', in A. W. McCoy and F. Scarano (eds), *Colonial Crucible: Empire in the Making of the Modern American State* (Madison, WI: University of Wisconsin Press, 2009).

22 The word 'moral' appears 37 times in the first report from Shanghai on opium and the word 'evil' forty times. See Edward Champe Carter, Charles Henry Brent and José Albert, *Report of the committee appointed by the Philippine Commission to investigate the use of opium and the traffic therein and the rules, ordinances and laws regulating such use and traffic in Japan, Formosa, Shanghai, Hongkong, Saigon, Singapore, Burmah, Java, and the Philippine Islands* … (Washington, DC: US Government Printing Office, 1905). This language found its way into the Single Convention on Narcotic Drugs (1961, 1972) which is still in force today in 2018. The word 'moral' also appears 17 times in The International Opium Commission Part 2 Government Action since the publication of the 'Philippines Report, The International Opium Commission and Hamilton Wright', *American Journal of International Law* 3.4 (October 1909): 828–868, www.jstor.org/stable/2186415 [accessed 25 January 2013].

23 Buxton, 'The historical foundations of the Narcotic Drug Control Regime', p. 11.

24 McAllister, *Drug Diplomacy in the Twentieth Century*; D. F. Musto, *The American Disease: Origins of Narcotic Control* (Oxford: Oxford University Press, 1999 [1973]); Boister, *Penal Aspects of the UN Drug Conventions*, pp. 1–4, and D. Bewley-Taylor, 'Challenging the UN drug control conventions: Problems and possibilities', *International Journal of Drug Policy* 14.2 (2003): 171–179.

25 Re: the legal structure of the League of Nations Mandate system: Article 22 of League Covenant reads 'To those colonies and territories which as a consequence of the late war have ceased to be under the sovereignty of the States which formerly governed them and which are inhabited by peoples not yet able to stand by themselves under the strenuous conditions of the modern world, there should be applied the principle that the wellbeing and development of such peoples form a sacred trust of civilisation and that securities for the performance of this trust should be embodied in this Covenant. The best method of giving practical effect to this principle is that the tutelage of such peoples should be entrusted to the advanced nations who, by reason of their resources …', etc.

26 See C. Focarelli, *International Law as Social Construct: The Struggle for Global Justice* (Oxford: Oxford University Press, 2012), p. 156, on étatization and the justice of the statist model, and B. Rajagopal, *International Law from Below: Development, Social Movements and Third World Resistance* (Cambridge: Cambridge University Press, 2003), pp. 9, 231.

27 Revisionist scholars who critique the Westphalian narrative first developed by nineteenth-century imperial international jurists claim that 'Western states produce norms, principles, and institutions of international society and non-Western states lack these until they are socialized into the norms, principles,

and institutions of international society. In this perspective, international society is a normative hierarchy assumed to reflect the natural division of labor in international relations ... [The] Westphalian narrative distorts the emergence of the modern international system and leads to misdiagnoses of major problems of contemporary international relations': Kayaoglu, 'Westphalian Eurocentrism in international relations theory', pp. 193–194.

28 'The manner in which sovereignty is brought into being, the complex political and economic forces which finally shape the appearance of an equal and sovereign state, is ... suppressed [by the doctrine of acquired rights]. As with nineteenth century positivist jurisprudence, the real work of sovereignty doctrine occurs at a level which is based on a question of how order is maintained among "sovereign states." The presumption that states are sovereign and equal prevents an examination of the processes by which sovereignty is shaped in such a way as to preclude scrutiny of its historical engagement in the colonial encounter ... The West relied on the relationships of power and inequality that had been created by the colonial past to maintain its economic and political superiority, which it then attempted to entrench through an ostensibly neutral international law': Anghie, *Imperialism, Sovereignty and the Making of International Law*, p. 215.

29 The history of the Non-Aligned Movement (NAM or G-77) is usually traced to a 1955 meeting in Bandung, Indonesia. The meeting included some of the people who were to be the leading statesmen of what came to be called the 'Third World', including Nehru, Chou en Lai, Nasser and Sukharno. 'On paper the Third World gleamed. As the project met governance it began to tarnish rapidly. One of the reasons for this is that the Third World failed to seriously undermine the deep roots of the landed and financial gentry in the social and political worlds that had been governed from above by imperial powers and their satraps': V. Prashad, *The Darker Nations: A People's History of the Third World* (New York: The New Press, 2008), pp. 22 and vii, for discussion of the unrepresentative nature of new political elites in the NAM. I would add that much of that governing from above was done by selectively apportioning opium monopolies and revenues. See Trocki, *Opium, Empire and the Global Political Economy*, and Derks, *History of the Opium Problem*, for the details, particularly how this worked in the Dutch colony of Indonesia.

30 Trocki, *Opium, Empire and the Global Political Economy*; A. W. McCoy, 'From free trade to prohibition: A critical history of the modern Asian opium trade', *Fordham University Law Journal* 28 (2000): 307, and Derks, *History of the Opium Problem*.

31 Szasz, *Ceremonial Chemistry*.

32 The debate over PSNR (Permanent Sovereignty over Natural Resources). General Assembly resolution 1803 (1962) came too late for the countries that had signed the Convention in 1961.

33 George Orwell on the enclosure movement: 'Stop to consider how the so-called owners of the land got hold of it. They simply seized it by force, afterwards hiring lawyers to provide them with title-deeds. In the case of the enclosure of the common lands, which was going on from about 1600 to 1850, the land-grabbers did not even have the excuse of being foreign conquerors; they were quite frankly taking the heritage of their own countrymen, upon no sort of pretext except that they had the power to do so': George Orwell, 'As I please',

Tribune, 18 August 1944. See also E. P. Thompson, *The Making of the English Working Class* (Harmondsworth: Penguin, 1991), and Karl Polanyi, *The Great Transformation* (Boston, MA: Beacon Press, 1991 [1944]).

34 R. P. Barnidge, 'Some (preliminary) thoughts on neocolonialism and international law', *Indian Society of International Law* 2009: 115–21, http://ssrn.com/abstract=1344202 or http://dx.doi.org/10.2139/ssrn.1344202 [accessed 10 November 2018].

35 A. Moloney, 'Outgoing Colombian president calls for end to mounting violence against activists', *Reuters*, 9 July 2018, www.reuters.com/article/us-colombia-rights-murders/outgoing-colombian-president-calls-for-end-to-mounting-violence-against-activists-idUSKBN1JZ2TK [accessed 16 August 2018].

36 C. Schmitt, *Constitutional Theory* (Durham, NC: Duke University Press, 2008).

37 Cited in Robin D. G. Kelly, 'A poetics of anti-colonialism', *Monthly Review*, 1 November 1999.

38 H. Sklar, *Trilateralism: The Trilateral Commission and Elite Planning for World Management* (New York: South End Press, 1980).

39 'In strictly legal terms, the Mandate System was succeeded by the Trusteeship System. But in terms of technologies of management, it is the international financial institutions (IFIs), the World Bank and the IMF that are the contemporary successors of the Mandate System. Indeed, whereas the Mandate System was confined in its application to the few specified territories, the IFIs have in effect universalized the Mandate System to virtually all developing states and, more recently, to the transition states of Eastern Europe, as all these states are in one respect or another subject to policies prescribed by these institutions': Anghie, *Imperialism, Sovereignty and the Making of International Law*; S. V. Scott, 'International law as ideology: Theorizing the relationship between international law and international politics', *European Journal of International Law* 5 (1994): 263.

40 See notes 44, 46, 52, 53 on how the US has used this parallel economy for its own foreign policy purposes.

41 Buxton, 'The historical foundations of the Narcotic Drug Control Regime'.

42 For an excellent theoretical analysis of colonial rationality, see G.. Wilder, 'Colonial ethnology and political rationality in French West Africa', *History and Anthropology* 14.3 (2003): 219–252.

43 From the Latin *ratio* 'reckoning, calculation, business affair, procedure'.

44 E. Said, *Orientalism* (New York: Pantheon Books, 1978).

45 P. Fitzpatrick, 'Terminal legality: Imperialism and the (de) composition of law', in D. Kirkby and C. Colebourne (eds), *Law, History, Colonialism: The Reach of Empire* (Manchester: Manchester University Press, 2001), p. 19.

46 A. Nandy, *The Intimate Enemy: Loss and Recovery of Self Under Colonialism* (Oxford: Oxford University Press, 1983), p. 69.

47 H. J. Morgenthau, *Politics Among Nations: The Struggle For Power and Peace* (New York: Alfred Knopf, 1948).

48 Anghie, 'Francisco de Vitoria and the colonial origins of international law'.

49 By violating the Spanish right to 'travel and sojourn' in colonial territories, the Indian transgressed universal norms. The structure of deficiency is at the base of Vitoria's notions of sovereignty: the Indian was clearly not sovereign because by definition a sovereign is bound by international law. Given this, the European sovereign was justified in waging war against the non-

sovereign Indian violator: Anghie, *Imperialism, Sovereignty and the Making of International Law*, pp. 10–11.

50 On international law as ideology, see Scott, 'International law as ideology', p. 313.

51 'Vitoria's real importance lies in his developing a set of concepts and constructing a set of arguments which have been continuously used by western powers in their suppression of the non-western world and which are still regularly employed in contemporary international relations in the supposedly post-imperial world. In particular, we see in Vitoria's work the enactment of a formidable series of manoeuvres by which European practices are posited as universally applicable norms with which the colonial peoples must conform if they are to avoid sanctions and achieve full membership': Anghie, 'Francisco de Vitoria and the colonial origins of international law', p. 332.

52 For an argument that makes this point in rich analytical detail, see U. Mattei and L. Nader, *Plunder: When the Rule of Law is Illegal* (Oxford: Blackwell, 2008), p. 5, on the dark side of the law: 'We argue that the rule of law has a bright and dark side, with the latter progressively conquering new terrain when the former is not empowered by a political soul. In the absence of such political life the rule of law becomes a cold technology, and the dark side can cover the whole picture as law yields to the embrace of brute violence.'

53 Another false dichotomy in legal and political theory, exposed first by feminist scholars, is that between public and private. Because 'sovereign states' are the (public) 'subjects' of international law, private individuals, no matter how viscerally impacted by the direct effects or negative externalities of law, are of no concern to the Parties. See Focarelli, *International Law as Social Construct*, pp. 223–240, on 'legal personality' in international law, and L. E. Wolcher, 'The ethics of the unsaid in the sphere of human rights', *Notre Dame Journal of Law Ethics and Public Policy* 26.2 (2012): 533–547: 'The enemy of justice, and the source of all injustice, is the will to deny the particular.'

54 As much of the current wealth of the advanced democracies, including narcotics for pain management, originated in their former colonies, a restorative justice approach – an underdeveloped international conceptual framework – might be an appropriate point of departure.

55 And in fact there is a plethora of formal and informal, privately funded and volunteer transnational solidarity work going on at the level of global civil society.

56 Just one of many possible examples of this zero sum logic: 'The savage ... was denied participative legal personality. It was solely the colonist who was to provide civil and civilized order. There were no rights for the savages in this scheme apart from 'rights' to have things done to them so as to bring them within the ambit of civilization': Fitzpatrick, 'Terminal legality', p. 20.

57 A. McClintock, 'The angel of progress: Pitfalls of the term "post-colonialism"', *Social Text* 31/32 (1992): 84–98.

58 'In a late interview Foucault says he was concerned with claiming not that "x is false" or "x is bad," but rather that "x is dangerous." The dangerous is what we must *preeminently* concentrate attention upon, what we must *before all else* take care to consider ... Genealogy as pursued by Foucault ... is a way of concentrating attention on a given situation in the context of an imminent danger. The discrimination of what is more dangerous from what

is less demands detailed historical presentation of the specific case': R. Geuss, *Outside Ethics* (Princeton, NJ: Princeton University Press, 2005), p. 159; original emphasis.

59 A. Césaire, *Discourse on Colonialism* (New York: Monthly Review Press, 2000 [1972]), p. 36.

60 A. Mignolo, 'Dispensable and bare lives: Coloniality and the hidden political/economic agenda of modernity', *Human Architecture: Journal of the Sociology of Self-Knowledge* 7.2 (2009): 7, https://scholarworks.umb.edu/humanarchitecture/vol7/iss2/7/ [accessed 10 November 2018].

61 Césaire, *Discourse on Colonialism*, pp. 36–37; original emphasis.

62 The total death toll from colonialism is estimated to be 50,000,000. See R. J. Rummel, *Statistics of Democide: Genocide and Mass Murder Since 1900* (Charlottesville, VA: Center for National Security Law, School of Law, University of Virginia, 1997).

63 T. W. Adorno, 'What does coming to terms with the past mean? The memory of offense', in G. Hartman (ed.), *Bitburg in Moral and Political Perspective* (New York: John Wiley and Sons, 1986).

64 K. Shick, 'To lend a voice to suffering is a condition for all truth: Adorno and international political thought', *Journal of International Political Theory* 5.2 (2009): 148–149.

65 Shick, 'To lend a voice to suffering', pp. 151–152.

66 'Where mind is taken as coincident with the human, hyperseparation is expressed in denying both the mind-like aspects of nature and the nature-like aspects of the human: for example, human immersion in and dependency on an ecological world. When we hyperseparate ourselves from nature and reduce it conceptually, we not only lose the ability to empathise and to see the non-human sphere in ethical terms, but also get a false sense of our own character and location that includes an illusory sense of agency and autonomy. So human-centred conceptual frameworks are a direct hazard to non-humans, but are also an indirect prudential hazard to Self, to humans, especially in a situation where we press limits': V. Plumwood, 'Nature in an active voice', in R. Irwin (ed.), *Climate Change and Philosophy: Transformational Possibilities* (London: Continuum International, 2010).

67 W. Heisenberg, *Physics and Philosophy: The Revolution in Modern Science* (New York: Harper & Row, 1958), http://dx.doi.org/10.1063/1.3062735 [accessed 10 November 2018].

68 T. W. Adorno and E. B. Ashton, *Negative Dialectics*, trans. E. B. Ashton (New York: Continuum, 1973), pp. 17–18.

69 V. Shiva, *Staying Alive: Women, Ecology, and Development* (Berkeley, CA: North Atlantic Books, 2016), and K. Pettus, 'Ecofeminist citizenship', *Hypatia* 12.4 (1997): 132–155.

Notes on contributors

Dr Ashley Bohrer is an Assistant Professor of Philosophy at Hamilton College, New York. Her work focuses on the intersections of capitalism, colonialism, racism and hetero/sexism in the early modern period and the contemporary world. Her recent interests include the philosophy of incarceration. She has also been a committed activist who has organized extensively in Palestine.

Dr Andrés Fabián Henao Castro is Assistant Professor of Political Science at the University of Massachusetts Boston. Before joining UMB, he was the Karl Lowenstein Fellow at Amherst College, and currently holds a post-doctoral fellowship at the Academy of Global Humanities and Critical Theory at the University of Bologna. His research deals with the relationships between ancient and contemporary political theory, via the prisms of decolonial theory, performance philosophy, and post-structuralism. His current book manuscript criticizes the theoretical reception of Sophocles' tragedy, *Antigone*, in democratic theory, queer theory, and the theory of biopolitics by foregrounding the settler colonial logics of capitalist accumulation by which subject-positions are aesthetically distributed in the play and its theoretical reception. His research has been published in *Theory & Event*, *La Deleuziana*, *Theatre Survey*, *Contemporary Political Theory* and *Hypatia: A Journal of Feminist Philosophy*, among other journals. He is also a member of the international research network Performance Philosophy and a columnist for the online journal of political analysis, *Palabras al Margen* (Words at the Margins), in which he has published extensively on the relationship between politics and aesthetics.

Dr Tanzil Chowdhury is a Lecturer in Public Law at Queen Mary University of London (QMUL) and co-founder of the Northern Police Monitoring Project (npmp.co.uk). His current research focuses on UK war powers, colonial wars and contemporary military interventions as well as looking at British Overseas Territories constitutionalism through post-colonial theory. He has also written on human rights, decolonization, and policing.

Dr Evandro Piza Duarte is Professor of Criminal Procedural Law and Criminology at the Faculty of Law of the University of Brasília (UnB), and Doctor of Law at UnB. He is the author of *Criminology and Racism* (2017) and *Criminology of Prejudice: Racism and Homophobia in Criminal Sciences* (2017); Professor at the Brazilian Chair on Race Relations (CAPES) at the National University of Colombia (2014); Coordinator of the Center for Studies on Inequality and Discrimination (CEDD/FD/UnB), the Center for Marine Studies on Juridical Culture and Black Atlantic, the Corpolítica Project: Dialogues on Race, Gender and Sexuality, and the Justice, Racism and Sexism Project: Dimensions of Inequality in Justice Systems (CAPES, Abdias do Nascimento). He is also a member of the IDCARÁN/UNAL/CO Group.

Dr Ariadna Estévez has a PhD in Human Rights from the University of Sussex, UK, an MA in Political Sociology from City University, UK, and a first degree in Journalism and Mass Media from the National Autonomous University of Mexico (UNAM). She currently works as a full-time researcher (tenured professor) at the Centre for Research on North America at UNAM. She is a member of Mexico's National Researchers System (Level 2), the International Studies Association, and the *Biopolitica* Network. She is joint coordinator of: UNAM's Migration Studies Seminar (SUEM); the Situated Biopolitics and Necropolitics Seminar (UNAM-UACM), and the Human Rights Multidisciplinary Study Seminar. She teaches human rights and forced migration at UNAM's Faculty of Political and Social Sciences, and critical perspectives of human rights at *Instituto de Estudios Críticos*. Her current research interests include: the biopolitics of asylum in the US and Canada; forced migration and violence; the critique of forced migration studies; necropolitical and biopolitical nomospheres; necropolitical wars and women's rights; the construction of a socio-political theory of human rights, and the socio-legal study of films and TV series.

Dr Asmin Fransiska is a lecturer at the School of Law, Atma Jaya Catholic University of Indonesia (AJCUI). Her teaching and scholarship focus on human rights and drug policy, particularly in the right to health, children and women protection. She is also the Director of Research and Social Engagement Institute of AJCUI. She holds a PhD in International Public Law from Justus Liebig University – Giessen, Germany and a masters in International Human Rights Law from Northwestern University – Chicago, USA. Her PhD dissertation appeared as a book, *Decriminalisation Approach to Drug Use from a Human Rights Perspective: The Counter War on Drugs in Indonesia* with Lambert Academic Publishing in 2017 and contributed in a chapter, 'Between Diego and Mario: Children, Families, and the Drug War in Indonesia' in a book *Children of the Drug War* (IDEBATE Press, 2011).

Felipe da Silva Freitas is a PhD student and Master of Laws at the University of Brasília where he is developing a study on police and racial relations in Brazil. He is co-author of the book *Black Discourses: Penal Legislation, Criminal Policy and Racism* (Brasília: Brado Negro, 2015). Between 2012 and 2105, he worked at the Secretariat for Policies for the Promotion of Racial Equality of the Presidency of the Republic, where he coordinated the National Plan for the Prevention of Violence against Black Youth, and between 2016 and 2017 he was a consultant for the United Nations Program for Development for the preparation of the National Training Matrix of Professionals in the Criminal Services Area in the National Penitentiary Department (DEPEN). Member of the Criminology Research Group of Feira de Santana State University and a fellow of the Coordination of Improvement of Higher Education Personnel (CAPES).

Dr Oscar Guardiola-Rivera joined Birkbeck College, University of London in 2005. He is now Reader in Law and Assistant Dean of the School of Law. He is the writer of the award-winning *What If Latin America Ruled the World?* (London: Bloomsbury, 2010), chosen as one of the best non-fiction books that year by the *Financial Times* and reviewed in the *Washington Post*, the *Sunday Times*, the *Guardian*, BBC Radio 4's *Start the Week, with Andrew Marr*, Al-Jazeera's *The Riz Khan Show*, *Folha de São Paulo*, and other major newspapers and media around the world. His work has been published in *Granta*, and he is a weekly columnist of *El Espectador* (Colombia), and a frequent contributor to the BBC World Service's *Nightwaves*, *The Stream*, *Monocle Radio 24*, *NTN 24*, and *Al-Jazeera*, among others. He has been invited to take part in the Hay Festivals (Wales, Colombia, Lebanon and Mexico), and contributed as a curator and speaker with the Serpentine Gallery, Southbank Centre, Intelligence Squared, Tate Modern and PEN International. Born in Colombia, he was educated there and in Britain. He graduated as a lawyer from Universidad Javeriana, Bogotá in 1993, after leading the Student Movement that initiated the 1990s wave of constitutional reform throughout Latin America. He obtained his

LLM with Distinction from University College London, and his PhD in Philosophy from the King's College, University of Aberdeen. He is on the editorial boards of *Naked Punch: An Engaged Review of Arts and Theory*; *International Law, Colombian Journal of International Law*; *Universitas, Xavier University Law Review* (Colombia), and *Open Law Journal*, and is on the advisory board of the *Law, Social Justice & Global Development Journal*. He is recognized as one of the most representative voices of contemporary Latin American philosophy and literature.

Dr Simon Howell is a research fellow in the Global Risk Governance programme. He is the Research Director at African Police Civilian Oversight Forum (APCOF). He has a few interests, most of which seem to revolve around drugs, gangs, and violence in South Africa. He holds a PhD in political philosophy from Rhodes University, South Africa.

Dr Kojo Koram is a Lecturer at the School of Law, Birkbeck College, University of London. His teaching and scholarship focus on a critical legal approach, with a particular interest in how law facilitates racial differentiation. He undertook a PhD at the School of Law, Birkbeck College, focusing on the international drug treaties as an instantiation of the continuing legacy of imperialism in international law. Whilst studying for a PhD, he also worked for the UK's centre of expertise in drug law, Release, as a legal adviser. In this role, he advised at several drug and alcohol centre legal outreach projects across London on a variety of frontline, social welfare legal issues.

Dr Dawn Moore is an Associate Professor at Carleton University, in Ottawa, Canada; she researches on critical theory, crime control and punishment. She recently won the SSHRC funding for a new project which builds on her previous work concerning the constitution of criminalized subjectivities, explored through the lens of drug treatment courts. She has an ongoing interest in the 'characters' of criminal justice and how people are made up in order to be governed. She also continues to be interested in questions of political and public engagement. She is following up her previous work with Mike Mopas on public criminology, this time critically exploring recent activist movements around prisoner's rights with an eye to considerations of feminist and anarchist engagement with public criminology. Finally, she is working in collaboration with a number of feminist prison scholars across the country on what we are terming the 'Prison Transparency Project'.

Their focus is on how prisoners experience imprisonment as well as exploring both major and minor human rights abuses within carceral regimes.

Dr Katherine Pettus is the Advocacy Officer for Human Rights and Palliative Care at the US-based International Association for Hospice and Palliative Care (IAHPC). She holds a PhD in Political Theory from Columbia University, New York, and a Masters in Health Policy and Law from the University of California San Diego. Her PhD dissertation appeared as a book, *Felony Disenfranchisement in America*, now in its second edition with SUNY Press, and her Masters thesis studied the interface between international law and access to essential controlled medicines. As the IAHPC's Advocacy Officer, Katherine travels to meetings around the world, advocating for improved access to internationally controlled essential medicines such as morphine, as a component of the right to health. Katherine writes regularly on policy issues for the IAHPC newsletter, the European Association for Palliative Care Blog, and eHospice.

Shaun Shelly is a researcher at the Department of Family Medicine, at the University of Pretoria, South Africa. He is also a Africa & MENA Representative for the International Drug Policy Commission Strategic Sub-Committee.

Elise Wohlbold is a doctoral candidate (ABD) in Law and Legal Studies at Carleton University in Ottawa, Canada. Her research project explores the historical trajectory of trans rights politics in Canada, and how trans activists are using and also rejecting law as a tool to advance claims for equality. She holds an MSc in Gender Studies from the London School of Economics and Political Science (LSE).

Index